Interventions for Reading Problems

The Guilford Practical Intervention in the Schools Series

Kenneth W. Merrell, Founding Editor
T. Chris Riley-Tillman, Series Editor

www.guilford.com/practical

This series presents the most reader-friendly resources available in key areas of evidence-based practice in school settings. Practitioners will find trustworthy guides on effective behavioral, mental health, and academic interventions, and assessment and measurement approaches. Covering all aspects of planning, implementing, and evaluating high-quality services for students, books in the series are carefully crafted for everyday utility. Features include ready-to-use reproducibles, lay-flat binding to facilitate photocopying, appealing visual elements, and an oversized format. Recent titles have Web pages where purchasers can download and print the reproducible materials.

Recent Volumes

Clinical Interviews for Children and Adolescents, Second Edition: Assessment to Intervention
Stephanie H. McConaughy

RTI Team Building: Effective Collaboration and Data-Based Decision Making
Kelly Broxterman and Angela J. Whalen

RTI Applications, Volume 2: Assessment, Analysis, and Decision Making
T. Chris Riley-Tillman, Matthew K. Burns, and Kimberly Gibbons

Daily Behavior Report Cards: An Evidence-Based System of Assessment and Intervention
Robert J. Volpe and Gregory A. Fabiano

Assessing Intelligence in Children and Adolescents: A Practical Guide
John H. Kranzler and Randy G. Floyd

The RTI Approach to Evaluating Learning Disabilities
Joseph F. Kovaleski, Amanda M. VanDerHayden, and Edward S. Shapiro

Resilient Classrooms, Second Edition: Creating Healthy Environments for Learning
Beth Doll, Katherine Brehm, and Steven Zucker

The ABCs of Curriculum-Based Evaluation: A Practical Guide to Effective Decision Making
John L. Hosp, Michelle K. Hosp, Kenneth W. Howell, and Randy Allison

Curriculum-Based Assessment for Instructional Design:
Using Data to Individualize Instruction
Matthew K. Burns and David C. Parker

Dropout Prevention
C. Lee Goss and Kristina J. Andren

Stress Management for Teachers: A Proactive Guide
Keith C. Herman and Wendy M. Reinke

Interventions for Reading Problems, Second Edition:
Designing and Evaluating Effective Strategies
Edward J. Daly III, Sabina Neugebauer, Sandra Chafouleas, and Christopher H. Skinner

Classwide Positive Behavior Interventions and Supports:
A Guide to Proactive Classroom Management
Brandi Simonsen and Diane Myers

Interventions for Reading Problems

Designing and Evaluating Effective Strategies

SECOND EDITION

EDWARD J. DALY III
SABINA NEUGEBAUER
SANDRA CHAFOULEAS
CHRISTOPHER H. SKINNER

THE GUILFORD PRESS
New York   London

Library of Congress Cataloging-in-Publication Data

Daly, Edward J., 1963–
  Interventions for reading problems : designing and evaluating effective strategies / by Edward
    J. Daly, Sabina Neugebauer, Sandra Chafouleas, Christopher H. Skinner. — Second edition.
      pages cm. — (The Guilford practical intervention in the schools series)
  Includes bibliographical references and index.
    ISBN 978-1-4625-1927-9 (pbk. : alk. paper)
  1. Reading—Remedial teaching. I. Title.
LB1050.5.D28 2015
372.43—dc23
                                                                                    2014046263

To our teachers and mentors,
who proved to us that modeling is the best form of teaching

Brian K. Martens,
Joseph C. Witt, and Dave Barnett

—EJD

Catherine Snow, Paola Uccelli,
and Sandra Chafouleas

—SN

Brian K. Martens
and Scott W. Brown

—SC

Edward S. Shapiro,
F. Edward Lentz Jr.,
and Robert J. Suppa

—CHS

About the Authors

Edward J. Daly III, PhD, is Professor of Educational Psychology at the University of Nebraska–Lincoln. He worked for several years as a school psychologist and has been training school psychologists in consultation and academic and behavioral intervention since 1995. His research focuses on developing functional assessment methods for academic performance problems. He has coauthored or edited several books and numerous chapters and journal articles on this topic. Dr. Daly served as editor of the *Journal of School Psychology* and associate editor of both *School Psychology Review* and *School Psychology Quarterly*. He also has served on a number of editorial boards for journals, including the *Journal of Applied Behavior Analysis* and the *Journal of Behavioral Education*. Dr. Daly is a Fellow of Division 16 (School Psychology) of the American Psychological Association (APA). He is also a Board Certified Behavior Analyst (Doctoral).

Sabina Neugebauer, EdD, is Assistant Professor of Reading in the School of Education at Loyola University Chicago. Her research focuses on the language and literacy development of linguistically diverse students from childhood through adolescence. Dr. Neugebauer's work aims to identify linguistic and affective factors that influence students' reading comprehension for the purpose of improving the literacy outcomes of students in traditionally underserved schools. Dr. Neugebauer has conducted experimental evaluations of vocabulary interventions with bilingual students and struggling readers as well as longitudinal studies on adolescents' motivation to read. She has published in journals including *The Reading Teacher, Reading Psychology, Learning and Individual Differences,* and the *Journal of School Psychology.* Dr. Neugebauer has also taught and collaborated with teachers across multiple settings, including elementary and middle school classrooms, in the United States and abroad.

Sandra Chafouleas, PhD, is Dean for Research and Professor of School Psychology in the Neag School of Education at the University of Connecticut. Prior to becoming a university trainer, she worked as a school psychologist and school administrator in a variety of settings for children with behavior disorders. Dr. Chafouleas's primary area of research relates to school-based behavioral issues, and she has served and is serving as Project Director on related projects funded by the Institute of Education Sciences, U.S. Department of Education. The author of over 100 refereed articles, book chapters, and books, she is a Fellow of both the American Psychological Association and the Association for Psychological Science and an invited member of the Society for the Study of School Psychology. Her commitment to graduate education is reflected in her receiving the UConn Alumni Association Award for Excellence in Graduate Teaching.

Christopher H. Skinner, PhD, is Professor and Coordinator of School Psychology Programs at the University of Tennessee. His research focuses on enhancing educational outcomes for students with or at risk for disabilities. Working with professional educators, Dr. Skinner and his students develop, evaluate, and disseminate contextually valid intervention procedures. His current efforts focus on conducting comparative effectiveness studies that allow researchers and educators to identify instructional and remedial procedures that enhance learning rates. He is a recipient of the Lightner Witmer Award, Senior Scientist Award from APA Division 16 as well as the Fred S. Keller Behavioral Education Award from APA Division 25 (Behavior Analysis).

Contents

7. Vocabulary   124

8. Reading Comprehension   151

CHAPTER 1

Introduction and Overview

Just think for a moment about what you are doing right now and about how often throughout the day (*each* and *every* day) you rely on the very skill you are applying to this text. For those of us fortunate enough to learn this vital skill, we do it so often we barely think about how it impacts our lives. The Greek philosopher Aristotle stated that we don't need to know we have a brain to think. Likewise, a proficient reader doesn't need to know, or be conscious of, the processes that allow reading to happen. Some of you may even be "multitasking" right now—which only proves our point. More likely, someone else thought about and planned relevant reading experiences for us so that it would become automatic. It is almost inconceivable to us now that at one point in our lives we were completely unaware that everything in our environment from apples and oranges (objects) to running and standing in awe (actions) to justice and beauty (principles) could be represented and expressed on a page through a common set of symbols. But, if we dwell on this thought for a minute, it should boggle our minds that the mere juxtaposition of this finite set of symbols in various combinations produces a meaningful representation of reality, or at least an expression of someone's perception of it. We surely take for granted the many complex experiences that had to be planned for us to become facile readers. Table 1.1 highlights some of the most critical accomplishments necessary to make reading a useful activity for learning and enjoyment. Staggering numbers of students have difficulty with reading. According to the most recent report by the National Center for Education Statistics (NCES, 2013), 65% of fourth-grade students are reading below the "proficient" level, that is, these students were unable to "integrate and interpret texts and apply their understanding of the text to draw conclusions and make evaluations" (p. 6). Furthermore, students who fall behind early on will continue to struggle because reading demands in schools increase over time. Currently, only 8% of 15-year-olds in the United States score at proficient levels on international

TABLE 1.1. Reading Encompasses a Wide Variety of Skills

- The skills and knowledge to understand how speech sounds are related to print
- The ability to decode or decipher unfamiliar words
- The ability to read fluidly and quickly
- Sufficient background information and vocabulary to foster understanding
- The development of strategies to extract the meaning of the text
- Motivation to read

Note. From U.S. Department of Education (1999).

assessments, with the average reading scores of U.S. students falling below 19 other participating countries (*http://nces.ed.gov/surveys/pisa/pisa2012*). Reading proficiency levels are even lower for students in underresourced urban schools, and there are large discrepancies between students from diverse linguistic and cultural backgrounds and native English speakers. English learners (ELs) are functioning at about five grade levels below their white and Asian peers (NCES, 2011). Reading is obviously foundational to most other subjects that students study in school and to most activities after graduation. Reading problems can have an extremely adverse effect on quality of life, limiting educational and employment opportunities, as well as access to a variety of enjoyable activities.

Unfortunately, schools generally have not been sufficiently organized to meet the needs of students who have reading problems or students who came to school ill prepared to learn to read. Only 25% of preservice teachers report that their training program provided a strong focus on the early components of reading (NCES, 2011). Preservice teachers take, on average, 1.3 courses in reading instruction in university training programs (National Research Council, 1998). Those with expertise in assessment and consultation are often called upon to help in cases where children are having difficulty learning to read. In some instances, however, these professionals may be even less prepared to resolve reading difficulties than the teachers and administrators who turn to them. This book takes the perspective of the consultant who is working with others to solve a problem, regardless of whether it is an individual child problem (e.g., a fourth grader referred for reading problems) or a systemwide problem (e.g., a large number of students with low reading levels in a school). That said, we hope that this book will be useful to teachers too. Reflective teachers consult with themselves (hopefully, not aloud!) and often engage in problem solving by themselves or with colleagues.

The purpose of this book is to provide a comprehensive but concise overview of how to improve reading performance for children who are having difficulty learning to read. The book has a procedural or "how-to" focus and describes how to assess and intervene with reading problems and evaluate outcomes of interventions. It addresses the full range of reading problems, from early literacy, when students are establishing the building blocks for successful reading, to complex comprehension problems that may manifest themselves in content areas such as science or social studies. In addition to addressing assessment and intervention for students who already exhibit reading problems, a portion of the book is devoted to examining reading difficulties from a broader, systems-level perspective. In some school districts, the sheer number of children with reading problems challenges educators to find and implement efficient prevention and remediation strategies. We hope that the up-to-date content for best practices across the spectrum of reading needs and the descriptions of methods for choosing and evaluating interventions will serve you well in your practice. The strategies we offer are scientifically based. More importantly, however, you will be given methods for investigating, yourself, whether those scientifically based strategies are working for your students—the real essence of science-based practice. You might be confident that a proven method will work, but you won't really know until you try it out with the student(s). This process is one of verifying an already scientifically valid method for a particular student or group of students. You might think of it as a type of mini-scientific experiment with the student(s) with whom you are working.

CHARACTERISTICS OF THE APPROACH TAKEN IN THIS BOOK

It all starts with getting the wrong answer. A parent is reviewing letters with her child, for example, and he says *b* for *p*. A teacher points to the word *cat* and the student says *cab*. A teacher notices that the student didn't answer the independent seatwork questions correctly. There's a problem. Maybe the child simply didn't understand. The parent says, "Let's try again. What is this letter?" If the child gets it right the second time around, the adult moves on and may not think about it any further. However, if the child gets it wrong the second time, the parent or teacher corrects the child ("No. That's a *p*. Can you say *p*?") and makes a mental note. If it happens often enough—if the child eventually gives one wrong answer too many—the adult will realize that there is a problem. On the other hand, as long as the child is giving the right answer, there is no need to infer a problem. Indeed, our natural tendency is to assume the opposite. We come to believe that he or she "knows" or "has learned," and we are satisfied with the child's performance as long as the answers are correct.

The point of departure for the task at hand is when the child gives one-too-many wrong answers. Therefore, this book is not intended to focus primarily on reading instruction (although designing reading interventions requires knowing something about effective reading instruction) or structuring curricula (although designing reading interventions often requires modifications to curricular materials and how instruction is delivered). Rather, it is all about problem solving when one or more students are not giving the right answers during the course of typical instruction in the curriculum. The regular curriculum (and all the other experiences in and out of school) may be fine for the majority of students. The focus here is on those students who are perceived by teachers, parents, or others as having a problem.

The approach taken in this book is outlined in Table 1.2. First, we evaluate a child's ability to read by having him or her read and not by giving complicated tests to make sophisticated diagnoses. In other words, we advocate for assessing student performance directly by using typical curricular tasks. Not only has this proven to be the best method for addressing reading problems, but it also increases clarity of communication with stakeholders. We aren't talking about concepts that only the most sophisticated measurement person

TABLE 1.2. Characteristics of the Approach Taken to Reading Intervention

1. Student performance is assessed directly by measuring performance in typical curricular tasks.

2. Intervention targets student performance in important curricular tasks.

3. The intervention is focused on the components of instruction and the procedures necessary to improve ongoing instruction.

4. Observable and measurable improvement in student learning, over time, is the criterion for successful intervention.

can understand. With a complete and adequate explanation, most constituents (parents, teachers, and others) can understand the importance of reading assessment measures such as correctly read words per minute and errors per minute (methods explained in later chapters). In fact, when assessment data are plotted on a graph, our constituents can decide *for themselves* whether the outcomes were positive or not. They no longer need to rely on the expert to interpret results for them. Instead, *they* are empowered to address their children's or students' needs better (Erchul & Martens, 2010). The overall outcome is likely to be more positive for the children.

Furthermore, because the focus of our attention is on how well the child reads in the classroom or home context, the goal of intervention is to assist the child to read and react appropriately to the content in ways that teachers and parents expect (e.g., through answering comprehension questions). If an intervention is successful, the child is now answering correctly (thereby reversing the trajectory of wrong answers that led the teacher or parent to perceive a problem in the first place). This approach to intervention is a direct one, in which assistance to the learner facilitates frequent, correct answers. Viewed in this way, the goal of reading intervention is deceptively simple: We strive to do what it takes to help students "get it right" when the teacher or parent wants an answer. In Chapter 2, we discuss a learning model—the instructional hierarchy—that helps you to understand how to achieve this goal. The instructional hierarchy model explains why the interventions work and when a particular intervention strategy is appropriate; the model therefore serves as the overarching framework for the intervention process.

Intervention involves primarily having the student read a lot and using methods that facilitate correct answers. Because we have defined the task as a problem-solving one, we emphasize the *components* of instruction more than general reading curricula or instruction from start to finish. Our assumption is that some type of reading instruction is being delivered but is not helping students to get the right answers. As noted earlier, it is the preponderance of wrong answers that leads to the realization of a problem. We don't expect, however, that you are in a position to radically alter the curriculum that is being presented to the student. Consultants rarely are in this position when they are taking a case-centered approach to intervention. We are not referring to, or even addressing, curriculum consultants who may be called in to help a school district evaluate various reading curricula. Instead, it may be the special educator, the school psychologist, or the external consultant who is called upon to conduct assessments and provide recommendations for one or more children. In this case, the best approach is to analyze the components of instruction (and instructional tasks) to determine what is missing so that the evaluator can assist teachers in making current instruction more effective. Therefore, in most cases teachers won't be expected to stop and start all over again. Interventions that target adjustments and modifications to ongoing classroom routines and instruction will probably be more successful than interventions that involve changing everything the teacher is currently doing. A major task of diagnosing the learner is diagnosing the instruction the learner is receiving (Engelmann, Granzin, & Severson, 1979). As this book outlines the components of instruction that facilitate better reading, specific attention is paid to the procedures that should be followed to improve student reading. When possible, we have included step-by-step protocols for a number of different types of interventions.

To illustrate this approach, we turn to a published study that targeted remediation of severe reading problems related to accuracy and fluency with a very intense intervention. In an effort to remediate severe reading problems, Torgesen et al. (2001) provided instruction to 60 students with severe reading problems on a one-to-one basis two times a week for 50 minutes per session over a period of 8–9 weeks. The instructional intervention was explicit and systematic. Activities targeting accuracy and fluency skill building in phonemic awareness and individual word reading and writing were delivered using one of two approaches: auditory discrimination or phonics. Following accuracy and fluency building, generalization training (i.e., practice applying the skills in the classroom) occurred once per week for an additional 8 weeks. Student progress on multiple outcome measures was tracked for 2 years. Results suggested that both programs were equally effective in producing substantial improvement over the long term. In fact, over half of the students demonstrated accelerated reading growth to an extent that allowed them to fall within the normal range. This finding is amazing, given the severity of the deficits exhibited by the students prior to receiving the intervention. Thus, overall results suggested that the specific instructional activities were not as important as the inclusion of components of instruction that systematically built accuracy and fluency and then taught students to generalize newly learned skills to classroom curricular tasks. In this study, these principles included explicit instruction involving direct teaching and modeling along with multiple opportunities to practice and receive feedback.

Although the participants in this study were older children who already exhibited significant reading problems and the interventions were more intensive than is instruction typically available in the school setting, implications can be drawn regarding effective reading instruction for all students. Torgesen et al. (2001) suggested that two factors were important in producing substantial growth over the long term: the right level of intensity and teacher skill. In other words, the teacher must have the skill to assess an individual student's instructional needs, choose instructional strategies targeting those needs, and then monitor the effects of instruction. Students with reading problems require explicit and systematic instruction that is matched to their skill level. Effective instruction provides ample opportunity for guided practice with new concepts and cues students when to use skills in classroom activities. The conclusion? There is probably more than one way to go about teaching basic reading skills, but certain factors, such as explicit and systematic instruction and progress monitoring (among others), are minimally necessary to get the job done.

Professionals have an ethical and a legal responsibility to be accountable for student outcomes, lest students be deprived of their right to a *free and appropriate education* (Jacob, Decker, & Hartshorne, 2011). This responsibility means that we must evaluate whether students are learning. Otherwise, we can't call what's being done *instruction*. It amounts to nothing more than presenting the curriculum. The best way to measure learning is to systematically examine student progress over time. If a referred student is behind others, he or she needs to catch up and attain at least the minimal skills necessary to be successful in other parts of the curriculum. Not only is *rate of learning over time* the single best indicator of improvement, it also tells educators the degree to which students are catching up with their classmates. For these reasons, *observable and measurable improvement in student learning over time* is *the* criterion for successful intervention and constitutes the core principle of science-based practice. In order to accelerate student performance, interventions (and not just students) are evaluated and modified based on assessments over time.

A BRIEF OVERVIEW OF THE SECOND EDITION

The content of the book has been significantly updated due to the changing landscape of education since the first edition of this book: the students we serve are changing, schools have been making systemic changes to address reading problems, there is a greater appreciation of the importance of traditionally neglected areas for intervention (e.g., vocabulary), and the tools have gotten better. Therefore, we updated the content of the book to better achieve the principal objective of this book as established in the first edition: to create a context for consulting and conducting reading interventions. Knowing procedures for improving reading will only get you so far if you don't understand the developmental process of acquiring reading and what effective teaching looks like. Also, you need to understand the dynamics of how to facilitate reading interventions if you are not the one actually carrying out the intervention. Each of these issues is discussed in Chapter 2. Since the first edition, schools have embraced response to intervention (RTI) as a framework for creating a continuum of interventions for students of all abilities. Thus, a chapter on multi-tiered interventions was added to guide you in structuring and assessing intervention effects within an RTI model (Chapter 3).

The field is coming to a greater understanding of the diverse needs of students requiring intervention, especially in the area of linguistic diversity. As such, a chapter was added discussing intervention with diverse learners (Chapter 4). Principles and guidelines for optimizing interventions are described in this chapter. The next four chapters (Chapters 5, 6, 7, and 8) address the four broad areas identified by the research literature as comprising the process of reading development: "alphabetics," oral reading fluency, vocabulary, and comprehension, respectively. The chapter on vocabulary is new. We hope you grow as excited as we are about the innovative interventions that are emerging in this area. The other chapters (Chapters 5, 6, and 8) all have updated content in the areas of assessment and intervention. Each chapter begins with a brief rationale for why the skills associated with that domain are critical to becoming a competent reader. Each chapter also gives specific information about assessment and intervention methods. As noted earlier, protocols that outline procedural steps and tables with relevant information about which decisions to make are provided, when needed. Chapter 9, the final chapter, explains various methods for demonstrating results. This step is especially important if you are trying to justify the value of a reading program in the eyes of professionals, authorities, and other constituents. This chapter goes beyond describing individual results and shows how to demonstrate effectiveness (or, if you are less successful, areas where change is needed) across students. This step may be the most important part of the process for evaluating the integrity of your intervention model, if you plan to do more than just a single intervention. New graphing and data-analysis tools that have appeared on the scene since the last edition are addressed so that you can conduct program evaluation with state-of-the-art methods.

In summary, this book provides a full-service guide to directly assessing, consulting about, and developing reading interventions when there is classroom instruction of some type already in place. Simple and effective instructional strategies for the target areas of alphabetics, fluency, vocabulary, and comprehension are included. Finally, a model for evaluation of effectiveness across cases is included to help you demonstrate accountability for your services. It is our hope that you will find this information useful in your daily efforts to help children become successful readers.

CHAPTER 2

Where Do You Start as a Consultant?

Although your eyes are probably riveted to the child referred for reading problems, we invite you to change your focus momentarily to understand more broadly why the child is having a problem with reading tasks in the first place. Diagnosing the child with tests will not be very fruitful if you fail to consider the impact of the classroom and instruction on the student's performance. Engelmann et al. (1979) put it bluntly when they pointed out that "the only way to draw conclusions about deficiencies involves first determining the degree to which the learner's performance is controlled by instruction" (p. 362). It is critical, therefore, to first diagnose the instruction the child is receiving. You need not take your eyes off the child, however. We suggest instead a broader visual field, which means that you may need to step back. Within this broader field, your focus will shift periodically from the child to other factors and back to the child. The child should *never* leave your field of vision entirely.

This chapter addresses effective reading instruction by focusing on critical attributes of effective reading instruction for students who are at risk of or currently experiencing reading failure. It differs from the rest of the book in that it describes what could or should be happening *before* a referral. In the following chapters, we emphasize procedures, techniques, and decision steps for intervening once the problem has been detected and one or more students have been referred. The information presented in this chapter, however, is critical to the goals of the latter chapters. As a consultant, you need a template for effective instruction in order to understand the child's problem. This template should guide you in filtering out what is helping the referred student to learn, what is potentially harmful to this learning, and what is missing instructionally. We begin by discussing the "targets" for reading across the curriculum: various skills in "alphabetics," reading fluency, and comprehension. The targets are the skills children need to master to become proficient readers. These targets serve as prerequisites for more complex skills. (Teachers should organize their instruction around one or more of these targets at any given time.) The delivery of effective instruction is then described, with special emphasis on how instruction should be adapted to the student's level of proficiency. Our goal is to give you a framework for identifying the components of effective reading instruction.

Next we address factors that are likely to impact your ability to effect change as a consultant within the overall organizational school system: the organizational capacity of the school to accept intervention. Failure to acknowledge the school's organizational capacity or incapacity for change may doom the whole enterprise. Finally, the chapter ends with a brief overview of resources available on the Internet. These resources can assist you with the assessment and intervention activities described in the remainder of the book. Consider this chapter as a point of departure for understanding why the child with a reading problem is not progressing successfully and for identifying resources that may be helpful to you in developing reading interventions. The latter chapters on individualized assessment and intervention for early literacy, reading fluency, and reading comprehension have more of a "how-to" focus.

READING TARGETS
ACROSS THE CONTINUUM OF READING PROFICIENCY

For students to learn, the teacher must effectively coordinate what is taught, how students are managed during instructional time, and how instruction is delivered in the classroom. Although the process is complex, learning is likely to occur if the student consistently and frequently produces correct responses to reading material in carefully chosen and sequenced instructional activities. How students *respond* is a key element in designing instruction. Consensus has been achieved in the field of reading research regarding the *types of responses* teachers should be teaching. The most prominent example of this consensus can be found in the National Reading Panel (NRP, 2000) report. Following a congressional mandate, the NRP reported a synthesis and evaluation of research on reading instruction. The entire report is organized around *targets* (our term) for instruction. These targets, which include alphabetics, reading fluency, and reading comprehension, have emerged from many years of research reports and other reviews, including but not limited to the report of the National Research Council (NRC, 1998) and the seminal review and summary of Marilyn Adams (1990). Before we explore how teachers manage instruction, we examine each distinct area of reading. Keep in mind that, whereas specific intervention procedures are covered in later chapters, the goal of this chapter is to give you a general understanding of what and how teachers should be teaching so that you can function as a more informed consultant.

Alphabetics refers to the student's ability to manipulate sounds in words ("phonemic awareness") and the acquisition and use of letter–sound correspondences in reading and spelling (phonics; NRP, 2000). Instruction in phonemic awareness and phonics, the two areas that represent the broader category of alphabetics, helps students to achieve proficiency with these skills. The manipulation of sounds in words requires the ability to isolate sounds in words, delete sounds from words, break words into individual sounds, match sounds, categorize sounds, and blend sounds—all skills that are predictive of reading acquisition (NRP, 2000). Furthermore, sounds must be linked to letters, the objective of phonics instruction. Different approaches to phonics instruction vary in the degree to which they make the correspondences between letters, sounds, and spelling patterns explicit for students. These correspondences, however, are not useful to students if they are unable to blend sounds together to decode or break them apart to write words (NRP, 2000). Students need to master both phonemic awareness and phonics. When instruction is successful in teaching these skills, students are able to decode words accurately, which (as the NRP report points out) facilitates comprehension.

Reading fluency refers to accurate, fluid decoding and word recognition. To achieve fluency, a student must read at the appropriate speed. The NRP report (2000) describes fluency as "one of several critical factors for reading comprehension" (p. 7) and characterizes the frequent neglect of reading fluency instruction as "unfortunate" (p. 7). Reading fluency is a prerequisite to independent comprehension of text. Anyone who has listened to a child laboriously decode words or text at a rate of one word per 3 seconds (which amounts to a rate of 20 words per minute) understands what it does to the child's ability to understand what he or she is reading. Reading fluency has gained a lot of credibility as a target for assessment and instruction (Chard, Vaughn, & Tyler, 2002; Fuchs, Fuchs, Hosp, & Jenkins, 2001; Kame'enui & Simmons, 2001), thanks to a perceived need for direct and sensitive measures of student performance. Indeed, reading fluency is the single-best indicator of reading proficiency for younger students (Shinn, Good, Knutson, Tilly, & Collins, 1992).

Defined as the "essence of reading" by the NRP, the report describes *reading comprehension* as a complex cognitive activity that involves intentional problem-solving thinking processes. The panel states: "The data suggest that text comprehension is enhanced when readers actively relate the ideas represented in print to their own knowledge and experiences and construct mental representations in memory" (2000, p. 11). The very complexity of text comprehension requires the teacher to use a combination of instructional techniques to teach effectively. Table 2.1 contains specific instructional strategies recommended by

TABLE 2.1. Instructional Strategies Identified by the NRP (2000) Report for Each Instructional Target

Reading targets	Necessary prerequisite skills	Instruction
Alphabetics		Phonemic awareness and phonics instruction
Reading fluency	Ability to segment and blend words in sounds	Guided, repeated oral reading
Comprehension	Fluent decoding and word recognition	Vocabulary instruction; comprehension monitoring; cooperative learning; use of graphic and semantic organizers (including story maps); question answering and immediate feedback; student-generated questions; use of story structure to help recall of story content; summarization

the report for each of the three areas. Although alphabetics and reading fluency are prerequisites to independent text comprehension, the report recommends integration across all four areas—alphabetics, fluency, vocabulary, and comprehension—to create a complete reading program. However, a classroom that neglects the prerequisites and emphasizes a more complex skill (e.g., reading passages aloud) when students are not adept at prior skills (e.g., blending and segmenting sounds) is not meeting the students' needs and (1) makes the learning task more difficult than necessary and (2) slows down the students' progress. As an aside, these circumstances may make the conditions particularly ripe for misbehavior, which is often motivated by a need to escape difficult task demands.

QUALITIES AND CHARACTERISTICS OF EFFECTIVE READING INSTRUCTION

In the spirit of creating a template for effective instruction, we examine the critical attributes of effective instruction from the perspective of the child who is at risk for, or already experiencing, reading failure. Consistent with effective instructional practices with these students (Lane, Gresham, & O'Shaughnessy, 2002), the approach outlined here involves more explicit forms of teaching. By *explicit* we mean clearer identification of skills and "hands-on" direct instruction that lead the student to mastery (Howell & Kelly, 2002). First, let's imagine that you are walking into the classroom while reading instruction is ongoing. Of course, you have to stay for a while or make several visits to get a complete perspective of how the teacher is instructing. What do you see? Are students working on tasks that are important and helping them to become better readers? Are the lessons and the teacher's interactions with students helping them to read better?

The Instructional Hierarchy

We begin the analysis with the needs of the student. To be effective, instruction must be aligned with each student's level of proficiency. The instructional hierarchy (Haring, Lovitt, Eaton, & Hansen, 1978) is a simple model that has proven useful for understanding why, and under which conditions, instructional procedures are effective (Daly, Lentz, & Boyer, 1996). The basis of this model is a learning hierarchy through which the student progresses as he or she learns a new skill (see Figure 2.1). First, students acquire new responses. At the *acquisition* stage, the new responses are not in the students' repertoire. Therefore, teacher efforts must be directed toward increasing accurate responses and decreasing inaccurate responses. Assuming that students are progressing as expected—that is, they are accurate most of the time and have few errors—the next level of proficiency to achieve is that of fluency. At the *fluency* stage, students respond both accurately and quickly. Fluency is especially critical for reading because readers must quickly and effortlessly identify sequences of letters as words. At this point, teaching strategies should differ from instruction designed to promote acquisition. As we noted earlier, a breakdown in fluency translates into a breakdown in comprehension. Fluency is a necessary but not sufficient condition for overall read-

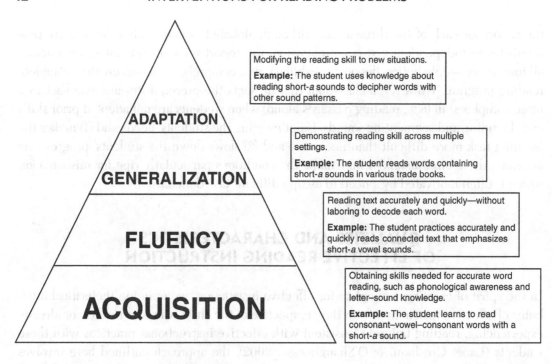

FIGURE 2.1. The instructional hierarchy.

ing competence. Fluency, as discussed here, is not just oral reading fluency. Students should display fluency in all of the critical targets—alphabetics, phonics, and comprehension—as well as oral reading.

Fluency is not the end goal. The student must be able to generalize the newly fluent skills to new texts, across time, and to more complex skills. The teacher engages in other instructional activities to promote *generalization*. We hesitate to characterize generalization as a next step in a hierarchy for fear that we lead you to believe that the teacher must wait until the student is both accurate and fluent before teaching generalization. Although the strategies that promote generalization differ from those used to promote accuracy and fluency, these strategies should be used throughout the whole instructional process. For example, if the teacher is using flashcards to teach students to read words that appear with high frequency in text (e.g., *the, for, there*), the teacher also should be teaching students to read those words in connected text. Fluency with flashcards does not guarantee that students will be able to read the words when they appear in stories; the teacher must explicitly have students read these words in text if he or she wants students to generalize the new recognition to connected text. Therefore, whether the teacher is aligning instruction to facilitate skill acquisition or fluency, he or she should always emphasize generalization by teaching students to use newly acquired reading skills across words with lots of examples, different texts, across time, and in comprehension activities. Strategies that teachers can use to promote proficiency at each level of the learning hierarchy are listed in Table 2.2. When you are evaluating a child in a classroom context, ask yourself whether the student is at the acquisition or the fluency stage. If there are many incorrect responses, he or she is probably

TABLE 2.2. The Instructional Hierarchy: Aligning Instructional Practices with Student Levels of Proficiency

Proficiency level	Characteristic performance	Instructional strategies
Acquisition	Student working on accurate answers	Demonstration/modeling; prompting correct answers; error correction; feedback for every response
Fluency	Student answers are accurate but slow	Practice; incentives for speed; feedback after multiple student responses (e.g., whole worksheet completed)
Generalization	Student working on accurate and fluent performance	Practice and feedback across instructional items (e.g., reading many long-vowel words); practicing the skill across similar types of instructional items (e.g., reading long-*a* and long-*e* words); explicitly teaching the student when, and when not, to use the skill and assigning practice (e.g., reading long-*a* words and short-*a* words); using the skill to perform other skills successfully (e.g., reading long-vowel words in phrases and paragraphs)

just acquiring the skill. If there are many correct answers but each takes a long time or if decoding the words takes a long time, then you know that the student needs to work on fluency. This model represents one way to determine whether student proficiency and teaching methods are appropriately aligned. Instructional procedures that are misaligned with the student's level of proficiency (e.g., independent practice is assigned when the student is not accurate) will not improve, and will probably hinder, student learning.

Prerequisite Skills

If the student is just acquiring a new skill, an even more basic question that you should be asking is whether the student has the prerequisite skills necessary to learn the newly targeted skill (Howell & Nolet, 2000; Wolery, Bailey, & Sugai, 1988). Prerequisite skills are any skills that are necessary before a more complex skill can be learned. Indeed, a student's prior knowledge is the best predictor of how much he or she will learn during a lesson (Howell & Nolet, 2000). If prerequisite skills have not been learned, the teacher will either need to teach an easier version of the skill (e.g., teaching just short-*a* vowels rather than teaching all the short vowels together) or an easier skill altogether (e.g., teaching segmenting and blending skills before phonics; Wolery et al., 1988).

Teaching Materials and Difficulty Levels

Examining the instructional materials used to teach students will help you considerably in determining the appropriateness of instruction. We recommend that when you first walk into a classroom (or even before), you carefully examine the materials and instructional activities being used for teaching reading. Asking yourself the right questions will help you to "get a handle" on how well the classroom is meeting students' needs. Table 2.3 out-

TABLE 2.3. What You Need to Do and What You Need to Ask to Understand the Impact of the Classroom on Student Learning

Your "to-do" list . . .	Inquire through asking and observing . . .
• Find out whether the child is at the acquisition or fluency stage with the skill(s) on which he or she is currently working.	Are there frequent incorrect answers? Are answers correct but slow?
• Examine the instructional activities and determine whether there is a match or mismatch between student proficiency level and instructional methods.	Does instruction target the appropriate types of student responses (e.g., segmenting and blending sounds, letter–sound correspondences, reading fluency, comprehension)? Are the instructional procedures (e.g., modeling, practice) appropriate for this level of proficiency? Is the difficulty level appropriate? Are enough examples and instructional items presented and is there a variety of examples and nonexamples? Does the student actually have to use the skill to get the right answer? Is the range and sequence of responses sufficient to guarantee that the student will be able to perform the skill in the future and with similar examples he or she hasn't yet encountered?
• Consider how instruction is sequenced.	Is modeling of new skills followed by guided practice, and then by independent practice? Is there a criterion of some sort (other than the passage of time) for deciding when the student has learned the new skill and that it is time to move to the next target? Is the teacher actively promoting the generalization of newly acquired skills to other texts, across time, and to improve comprehension?
• Check to see how skills are being monitored.	Is there adequate feedback or assessment information that tells the teacher what to do next, based on how the student is currently doing?

lines where you should direct your attention and the key questions you should ask. The difficulty level of instructional tasks reflects whether the student is appropriately placed in the curriculum. Is the student mostly accurate in his or her responses? If not, he or she should be. Gickling and Rosenfield (1995) recommend that students' accuracy during reading instruction should be between 93 and 97%. They also recommend that accuracy should be 70–85% for practice exercises. When student accuracy is not up to these levels during reading instruction (including reading aloud and guided practice), task difficulty level is probably too high; tasks need to be regulated so that students can achieve more success (Gickling & Rosenfield, 1995). When task difficulty level is appropriate, other problems are forestalled. For example, when the student is able to do most of the work accurately, he or she does not have the time to misbehave in the classroom. For these reasons, we recommend that you consider which skill is being targeted for instruction and whether or not the activities are at an appropriate instructional level for students.

may be why math behaviors escalate in some students

Other Qualities of Teaching Materials

When examining the instructional materials and activities, it is not sufficient to note whether the students are working on alphabetics, phonics, fluency, or comprehension tasks with a high degree of accuracy. The quality of the instructional activities also impacts student performance, and the selection and sequencing of examples and instructional items affects the rate of learning (Kinder & Carnine, 1991). While teaching a new skill, the instructional materials used should present a wide variety of examples and applications that differ from one another as much as possible, while still exemplifying the skill being taught. For example, when teaching students how to read words with *a* as the short vowel, many different words with short *a* should be presented (e.g., *mad, bat, fan*). This variety helps students apply the skill of reading short *a* to future words (i.e., generalization). Students must learn to not overuse particular skills, however. To help students avoid this problem, instructional materials should include nonexamples that *resemble* bona fide examples but differ in the critical attribute that makes them different. For instance, when teaching how to read long-*a* words like *fade*, nonexamples like *fad* should be interspersed during the lesson. As a nonexample, *fad* resembles *fade* in every way except for the critical attribute that distinguishes them (i.e., *e* following the consonant *d*). This step helps students to learn when to use the skill and when not to use the skill.

The final point to look for when you are examining the instructional materials and activities is whether students actually get to practice the skill that is being taught. Although this sounds obvious, it is not; there are many curricular materials that provide additional "hints" or that allow students to get the right answer for the wrong reason (Vargas, 1984). This principle hit home for one of us (EJD) when, while looking over the shoulder of one of his daughters who was doing a homework exercise on writing numbers in 1's and 10's columns, he became aware, through questioning, that she had figured out where to put the numbers without even being able to read the double-digit numbers! Though this example is not directly related to reading, you need not look far for direct examples. When students can fill in the blanks for vocabulary words embedded in definitions based on the number of letters in the word, they are certainly not learning vocabulary words.

The most common source of reading materials is basal reading packages. Basal readers contain texts and instructional activities that guide teachers in reading instruction by providing "instructional manuals . . . with detailed lesson plans and activities for the whole school year, and accompanying reading and lesson materials for students" (NRC, 1998, p. 189). The NRC report demonstrates that because (1) new editions are revised based on market research, (2) revisions occur every 3 to 5 years, and (3) there is a time lag between preferred instructional practices and when they appear in new reading series. Analyses of the content of basal reading packages indicate that there is wide variability in their recommendations for such instructional activities as reading aloud to kindergartners, blending and segmenting activities, teaching sound–symbol relationships, use of text that is decodable according to conventions of phonics, and even writing (Adams, 1990; NRC, 1998). Another problem with basal reading packages is that to handle the diversity of reading skills in classrooms, most basal reading series either present a wide selection of optional activities or give directions to have students choose activities (NRC, 1998). As a result, the teacher receives little explicit guidance in how to teach effectively so that all students can learn. The report's sobering analysis of basal readers is nothing short of scathing:

> Programs that ignore necessary instructional components tacitly delegate the pedagogical support on which their sales are predicated to the intervention of teachers, tutors, or parents. Even when a program does address key instructional components, it may or may not do so with clarity or effect. In this vein, a particular problem is the currently popular publishing strategy of accommodating the range of student interests and teacher predilections by providing activities to please everyone in each lesson. By making it impossible for teachers to pursue all suggestions, the basal programs make it necessary for teachers to ignore some of them. A good basal program should clearly distinguish key from optional activities. (p. 207)

It's obviously not safe to assume that the reading curriculum being used will guide the teacher in knowing how to respond to the referred student's reading problem.

Summarizing with an Example

To summarize the dimensions of effective instruction discussed thus far and to highlight a few others that are also important to the delivery of instruction, we will put all these principles in the context of Mrs. Walker's reading class. Mrs. Walker could be teaching virtually any of the elementary grades. She should be doing the following things, regardless of the grade level. First, Mrs. Walker chooses appropriate tasks and adjusts the difficulty to obtain the optimal ratio of correct answers to incorrect answers. If skills that are prerequisites to what she intends to teach have not been learned, she modifies her lesson plan to teach the prerequisites. When she introduces activities, she explains why the students are working on them, thereby maintaining a cognitive focus in her classroom (Ysseldyke & Christenson, 1993). Additionally, she gives clear instructions for how to complete the task along with a description of incentives for finishing work accurately (e.g., "When you are done with your seatwork assignment, you may have time in the play area").

When she is teaching a new skill, she shows students how to do the skill (providing modeling), and offers opportunities for guided practice with immediate feedback for performance. Mrs. Walker maintains a brisk pace when instructing by presenting instructional material rapidly enough so students don't have time to fool around and are accountable to give answers frequently (Carnine, 1976). Mrs. Walker directly teaches students to discriminate when to use the newly learned skill and when not to use the newly learned skill. To achieve the latter, she carefully sequences items so that there is both variety and nonexamples. In addition, she gives rules for when to use the skill, if appropriate. During guided practice Mrs. Walker has students articulate the rules to be sure they are learning them. Once students have achieved accuracy in the use of the skill, she provides ample practice with feedback about performance to promote fluency. To help students generalize the newly learned skill, Mrs. Walker has them use the skill with many different types of problems and in the context of other skills and "real-world" applications. Under these conditions we expect to see high levels of *active student engagement,* including writing, reading aloud, silent reading, asking and answering academic questions, academic game play, and discussion about the subject matter (Greenwood, Terry, Marquis, & Walker, 1994). Finally, Mrs. Walker moves on in the curriculum only when she sees evidence that the students have actually learned the skill and can use it in meaningful ways.

Of course, Mrs. Walker has a diversity of skills-related needs in her classroom, so she has a lot to manage at one time. Like many teachers, Mrs. Walker uses instructional groupings to meet this diversity of needs. However, decisions about issues such as whether to move students on in the curriculum depend on how well each individual student responds to her teaching (and not just the passage of time). She demonstrates sensitivity to students' needs by altering instruction based on how well they handle the demands placed on them.

Sufficient Time for Learning and Meaningful Active Engagement

Teachers must devote sufficient time to reading instruction (Gettinger, 1995). Better teachers devote more time to instruction (Rosenshine, 1980). Because time is not sufficient in itself, however, students must also be actively engaged in reading (Gettinger, 1995). If 2 hours are scheduled for language arts but the referred student spends only 4 minutes reading during the 2-hour period, then the student is not likely to become a good reader any time soon. You will note that instructional procedures and materials discussed up to this point either prompt the student to respond in some way or provide feedback to the student regarding his or her responses. Classrooms where students are busy but little reading is going on are not making the most of the time available for reading instruction.

Responsive Instruction

Obviously, instruction involves more than just presenting activities from a curriculum or basal reading series in sequence. Yet, it can turn into this kind of rote activity if decisions are based on the passage of time (e.g., the teacher teaches one story per week regardless of how students do with the story) or pressures to move through the curriculum at a certain pace in order to finish before the end of the school year. Problems can occur for other reasons as well. Instruction must be based on what students already know, how proficient they are with current objectives, and how well they are progressing in response to the teacher's efforts. Otherwise, students won't learn. Effective instruction is *responsive* to students, beginning with the skills or lack of skills they bring to the classroom and the progress they are making or not making after instruction has begun. For instruction to be responsive, there must be a feedback loop whereby the teacher gets solid and reliable feedback about whether the student has truly learned what was taught. The student's behavior should signal to the teacher what to do next (Daly & Murdoch, 2000). When there is a lack of good information about what the student knows, has learned, and is learning, a better monitoring system or feedback loop is needed, and instruction should be realigned with the student's needs. Therefore, checking out how the teacher monitors students is a necessary step. If there is no systematic assessment of student progress going on, putting a system in place is an important first step. A teacher who uses the results to make decisions about what to teach next is responsive to his or her students' needs.

As you take this approach, you may hear objections that teachers don't and can't provide instruction for an individual student. True. However, teachers *do and must* (1) make instructional decisions for each and every student in the classroom, and (2) deliver instruction to every child in the classroom. The decision to put five children in a small reading group for instruction represents individual decisions for each one of those children (i.e., five decisions). We are certainly not advocating individual instruction for all children. We are, however, advocating instruction that is *responsive to every student's needs*. Otherwise, it's not instruction; it's just presenting curriculum materials. Some students will probably still learn with a standard approach to delivering the curriculum. The student(s) you are worried about, on the other hand, probably won't! The goal is to make the right instructional decisions for *every* child in the classroom. The diversity of student skills that is typical of classrooms requires teachers to do different things for different students, regardless of whether or not they group them for some activities. A variety of assessment strategies that are sensitive to student growth are described in the following chapters. Using these methods will help teachers put in place the kind of feedback loop needed to be sensitive to students' instructional needs.

IDENTIFYING THE ENTRY POINT
FOR INTERVENTION EFFORTS

All this knowledge about effective instruction and how to facilitate effective interventions for reading problems is useless if the organizational systems of the classroom, school, and school district do not have the capacity for change. If some teachers or schools have been unwilling to change to meet the instructional needs of students, educational reforms like No Child Left Behind (NCLB) and the new academic expectations created by the Common Core State Standards (CCSS) may provide just the right motivating conditions necessary to make them more willing to change. NCLB emphasizes school accountability and empirically proven practices and promises to apply consequences when students don't improve. That said, it would be naïve to assume that federal legislation or the CCSS are sufficient to get unmotivated schools "in gear" and working on the problem. You will not be an effective consultant if you are unable to assess the ability of the organization to change and modify its procedures and adjust your services accordingly. In a broader sense, your consulting responsibilities bring you into contact with at least one organizational system (e.g., a school), which, like an individual human being, has its own needs and limitations (Skrtic, 1991). It would be unwise to forge ahead with an intervention and ignore the organizational structure, needs, and limitations of the school system. The most salient factors that will affect (positively or adversely) the likelihood of developing a successful intervention include (1) the frequency of reading problems in the classroom, school, and school district; (2) available resources for intervention; and (3) whether intervention is truly an organizational priority

**TABLE 2.4. Stumbling Blocks
to Effective Consultation**

1. Too much effort for too little yield
2. Unsound instructional environment
3. Conflicting organizational priorities
4. Unwillingness to cooperate
5. The right questions are not being asked

for the classroom, school, and district. We have identified potential stumbling blocks that may affect a school's capacity for change; Table 2.4 lists reasons why consultants may be ineffective in their attempts to help schools intervene with reading problems.

Too Much Effort for Too Little Yield

In many cases, designing individualized interventions for each and every child who is having a reading problem may be an overwhelming task. The first question that you must ask yourself is whether the referred child is one of only a few cases or whether this child is representative of the problems of many children in the system (i.e., classroom, school, or school district). In other words, is this a low-rate problem or a high-rate problem? If it is a high-rate problem, individualized assessments and interventions will be costly and time consuming—and not the most effective approach. In this case, a more efficient and defensible approach is to adopt a validated reading program and apply it to the school or the district. Proven strategies such as Direct Instruction and Success for All, which are instructional methods that replace typical basal reading approaches, are likely to improve the instruction that the students are receiving and reduce the need for expensive diagnostic procedures that must be administered to students who are failing, or at risk for failing, thereby making it more cost effective overall (Adelman, 1982). You can obtain more information about Direct Instruction by visiting the website of the National Institute for Direct Instruction at *www.nifdi.org*. Information about Success for All can be found at *www.successforall.org*. The school or district is likely to produce better effects by investing in a program that has been proven to be effective, and reserving time and resource-consuming diagnostic practices for the children who do not improve when the newly adopted instructional program is in place. This is precisely what NCLB prescribes.

If the incidence of reading problems in the school is not widespread, then we suggest the individual kind of analysis described throughout the rest of the book. A more careful examination of the individual circumstances of the reading problem will reveal the mismatch between the child's instructional needs and how classroom instruction is arranged and delivered. Fortunately, the assessment methods described in the latter chapters are simple and time efficient, making them appropriate for group administration in most circumstances. The assessor can evaluate all the children in a classroom or a representative sample in a school building in far less time than it takes to conduct an eligibility determination assessment for a single child. By looking for all students who could benefit from intervention, you can quickly gauge whether an individualized or a group intervention is warranted.

Unsound Instructional Environment

In a poorly managed classroom, newly devised intervention procedures will quickly become a burden to the teacher. Unfortunately, many teachers are ill prepared to teach reading. As noted in Chapter 1, the average number of courses on reading instruction taken by teachers is only 1.3 (NRC, 1998). Effective reading instruction involves more than simply following the activities outlined in a basal reader. Although inservice teacher education can generally improve student achievement (NRP, 2000), the fact that so little money is allocated by districts for this purpose, combined with the variable quality of the teacher inservice education that is provided (NRC, 1998), reduces the chances of the inservice model truly improving teacher performance. Our intention is not to disparage teachers' abilities but to give a realistic perspective on how ill prepared some teachers might be to teach reading effectively.

When classroom instruction is not well managed, you are faced with a dilemma. Pursuing a child-focused, individualized reading intervention may help the child and "fill in the gaps" where current reading instruction is not doing the job. However, if the teacher has difficulty managing instruction in the first place, will he or she be able to manage an additional intervention on top of what is being done ineffectively? If, on the other hand, you work with the teacher to facilitate a more general intervention to improve the overall planning and delivery of reading instruction, improvements in the class structure and delivery of instruction for the whole class may or may not pay off for the individually referred child. In other words, if you can get the teacher to use higher-quality materials, improve the clarity of directions and instruction, and improve guided practice and feedback for the class as a whole, this may still not be enough for the individual child about whom you are consulting.

Given that there are advantages and disadvantages to both tactics, we feel that the best approach in this situation is to help the teacher improve the overall instruction in the classroom. If the teacher is able to change instruction but the target child does not improve, the fact that the teacher successfully implemented a new instructional program should increase your confidence that he or she can make other changes successfully as well. You should then work to develop a more individualized intervention to meet that child's needs. Furthermore, other children will benefit from the improved instruction.

Conflicting Organizational Priorities

Schools' priorities may actually hamper intervention efforts. This problem can manifest itself in several forms. District-adopted curricular materials may not be the most effective materials for teaching reading. Districts may be wooed into adopting a new or revised reading program that reflects the most popular educational trend but doesn't provide sufficient guidance in effective instruction to teachers. Very few basal reading programs actually structure lessons carefully enough to allow students to truly master the material (Adams, 1990; NRC, 1998).

Desire to change is not enough. Tangible support must be put behind that desire. Schools might recognize a need for intervention, but administrative support may be weak. If, for example, administrators are not willing to provide teachers with support so that they have time to consult and problem solve or receive adequate training, teachers won't become more effective. Tangible support must also be directed in the right way. Education tends to be fad oriented. Giving teachers release time so that they can go to inservice training on the latest reading instruction method won't help anyone if that method is not backed by good scientific research. Schools need to increase their standards for what constitutes an effective intervention. Indeed, NCLB mandates it.

Unwillingness to Cooperate

Schools or teachers may be unwilling to cooperate with efforts to design effective reading interventions. In that case, you will spare all involved a lot of tension and headaches if you help the school or teacher understand that *your* ability to help is severely limited when there is a lack of a shared desire to make the plan work. It is necessary to understand that there may be other rewards accruing to teachers who refuse to cooperate. For instance, if referral for evaluation has generally led to students being identified as learning disabled and removed (at least partially) from the classroom, then you are asking the teacher to do more work by engaging in a consultation process that will involve classroom modifications, when the alternative (i.e., removal from the classroom) involves less work and responsibility. Even very effective teachers will probably feel some relief when a student is identified as learning disabled, because the label at least partially absolves the teacher from responsibility, and it means that someone else will be taking charge of the child's instruction.

The Right Questions Are Not Being Asked

The problem of not asking the right questions is related to the prior problem of uncooperativeness. Unfortunately, schools have set up a categorical system for identifying problems that describes them as occurring *within* the child. School psychologists and other educators spend a significant amount of time trying to diagnose what's wrong with *the child*. The focus is on asking, "How do we diagnose whether the child has a problem and what kind of problem is it?" A more productive approach is to ask (1) why there is a problem in this particular classroom, (2) what we can do about it (based on the results), and (3) how we can show whether modifications improved reading performance or not. An effective consultant frames the critical questions in terms of the interaction between a learner and his or her environment and then gathers information to identify the locus of the mismatch. When designing an intervention, the effective consultant should be asking:

- "Who will be doing the intervention?"
- "How do we know that this person is adequately trained?"

- "How do we know that the person is, in fact, doing the intervention correctly?"
- "How do we show whether it is effective or not?"

The remainder of this book deals with how to frame the problem-solving process within these question frameworks and, more importantly, how to go about answering them.

INTERNET RESOURCES

We have identified a number of resources on the Internet that can support your intervention efforts and supplement the model (with materials and intervention ideas) that is presented in this book. The following websites give information about effective instruction, identifying effective reading interventions, or gathering materials for monitoring student outcomes.

Aimsweb

Aimsweb touts itself as "the leading assessment and RTI solution in school today." It offers a large number of products and services related to reading assessments, the results of which can be evaluated online. The online service even prompts instructional decisions when sufficient data have been gathered. These materials and services, available for a fee, will allow you to do many of the things that are discussed in the following chapters. The Aimsweb website address is *www.aimsweb.com*.

Dynamic Indicators of Basic Early Literacy Skills (DIBELS)

DIBELS is a set of methods and materials for assessing early literacy, fluency, and comprehension skills. Developed by researchers at the University of Oregon, DIBELS has become popular nationally with school districts that are trying to live up to the requirements of the NCLB. The website contains free assessment materials as well as assessment and scoring rules that can be downloaded. A large national database is available to users who wish to compare their students' performance with other students' scores. Through the DIBELS data system, quarterly reports for students, classes, schools, and districts can be generated for a small fee. The website even has video clips demonstrating proper administration methods. There are many links to other useful literacy sites. The website address is *http://dibels.uoregon.edu*.

Headsprout

Headsprout is a reading instruction program in which lessons are taught on the Internet for kindergarten to fifth grade. It is heavily based on explicit teaching of phonics. The designers of this program have been using fluency-based instruction very effectively for a number of years (especially for students with high-incidence disabilities, such as learning disabilities and attention-deficit/hyperactivity disorder). Check it out at *http://headsprout.com*.

Intervention Central

This website contains many resources for creating a wide variety of curriculum-based measurement materials (including a manual for how to use curriculum-based measurement and various readability formulas for determining the difficulty level of reading passages), intervention strategies, and information for improving the functioning of school-based intervention teams. Curriculum-based measurement is a popular and valid fluency assessment method that is covered in detail in the following chapters. You can find it at *www.interventioncentral.org*.

National Center on Intensive Intervention (NCII)

The self-stated mission of the NCII is "to build district and school capacity to support implementation of data-based individualization in reading, mathematics, and behavior for students with severe and persistent learning and/or behavioral needs." The website provides resources for training and expert consultation, as well as evaluations of commercially available assessment and intervention tools and technical assistance for implementation support. You can find the website at *www.intensiveintervention.org*.

National Center on Progress Monitoring

This website contains an extensive library of articles, presentations, and links to other resources on monitoring student performance and instructional decision making. It contains information for individual classroom-, building-, local-, and even state-level monitoring. You can find it at *www.studentprogress.org*.

National Reading Panel

The NRP report gives a comprehensive overview of empirical reading research across the full spectrum of reading skills. You can use the information to identify empirically validated intervention strategies. You can find the report at *www.nichd.nih.gov/publications/pubs/nrp/pages/smallbook.aspx*.

CHAPTER 3

Multi-Tiered Reading Interventions

with Tanya Ihlo

THE ORIGINS OF RESPONSE TO INTERVENTION
AS A MULTI-TIERED INTERVENTION MODEL

The advent of response to intervention (RTI) in the last decade of the previous millennium and the first decade of the new millennium as a systems-level service delivery model represented a major paradigmatic shift in the way children's academic problems were viewed, which had a significant impact on how instruction was designed and delivered. Prior to RTI, the psychometrically unsound practice of identifying students as having learning disabilities on the basis of a significant and severe discrepancy between an IQ score and a norm-referenced achievement test score was common practice. This means of identifying students assumed that the students' difficulty learning to read was due to a psychological processing deficit of some type that resided within the child. Testing was conducted to identify students who suffered psychological processing deficiencies for special education (i.e., categorical) services. Unfortunately, these testing results said nothing about what needed to be done to teach referred students. So once a student was identified as having a learning disability, an educator had to then collect other data to assess the student's instructional needs. RTI turned educators' attention from within-child psychological processes (that could not be measured reliably and had no value in identifying effective treatments) to directly and repeatedly measuring the skills students needed and adapting instruction to meet those needs. In reality, the practice of repeatedly measuring students' performance on vital skills over time constitutes more of a test of the instruction than of the student. RTI acknowledges

Tanya Ihlo, PhD, is Project Manager in the Nebraska Center for Children, Youth, Families, and Schools at the University of Nebraska–Lincoln.

that there is a continuum of student needs, with some students requiring more explicit and intense instruction than others. A well-designed RTI model provides a fluid continuum of instructional intensity (usually across tiers, discussed below) in which students can be flexibly placed and removed according to how they progress in learning academic skills. This approach is very different from the severe-discrepancy approach, which sought to place students categorically based on the assumption of a psychological processing deficit. By design, it is intended to meet the needs of *all* students within a flexible system and not just preoccupy educators (usually school psychologists following up on referrals from teachers) with finding students with disabilities. This chapter provides a brief introduction to RTI to help you situate reading interventions in this popular multi-tiered intervention approach. You can go into more depth on this topic by referring to Burns, Riley-Tillman, and VanDer-Heyden (2012) and Fuchs, Fuchs, and Vaughn (2008).

A watershed moment for RTI was the publication of the President's Commission on Excellence in Special Education report (2002). This Commission was charged with reporting on needed changes to federal special education law. A thorough investigation of the research and expert testimony on learning disabilities identification practices revealed that the practice was error prone, denied services to students who were very much in need of them, did not assess the skills most in need of improvement, and had no validity for prescribing effective treatment. Indeed, the report made a number of scathing comments about the severe-discrepancy approach, pointing to the glaring inadequacies that had been previously articulated in the extant research across diverse fields (e.g., special education, school psychology, psychometrics). The document appears to have created a unifying voice for practitioners and researchers who were dissatisfied with then current practices. Positively, the report recommended an approach based on measuring a student's responsiveness to instruction over time and adjusting instruction according to student progress, most notably increasing the intensity or type of instruction when a student did not make adequate academic gains. This recommendation is the heart and soul of RTI. The subsequent reauthorization of federal special education law—the Individuals with Disabilities Education Improvement Act (IDEIA) of 2004—allowed schools to begin to use a method for determining students' responsiveness to instruction (and therefore needed level of instructional intensity) as a basis for learning disability classification. The idea caught on like wildfire, even though this was not a mandated change in practice. Many school districts either had high-quality intervention-based services in place or were eager to make the change, and many schools initiated an RTI process because they saw it as merely a matter of time before it became a mandate.

The idea of testing students' responsiveness to instruction as a basis for identifying need was largely an extension of a problem-solving approach that grew out of the popular behavioral consultation model (Bergan & Kratochwill, 1990; Kratochwill & Bergan, 1990). Behavioral consultation in turn drew its practices of repeated measures over time, use of single-case experimental design elements (e.g., having two phases—baseline and intervention—for evaluation), and iteratively evaluating the results of interventions of increasing intensity from the field of applied behavior analysis. Many school districts in the 1980s and 1990s had "prereferral intervention teams" whose practices were more or less based on the behavioral consultation model. At their best, prereferral intervention teams engaged in data-based problem solving for students referred for academic and behavior problems in schools in an attempt to stave off a referral for psychoeducational evaluation. RTI essentially represented an extension and formalization of this problem-solving process. What differed was that the results could now be used for determining students' eligibility for special education services as a student who is learning disabled, creating greater continuity in the assessment database that would be generated for classification decisions.

RTI quickly came to be viewed as more than just special education reform. RTI adherents saw the potential for prevention of future learning problems, with the explicit goal of reducing the number of children being classified while improving their instructional opportunities. This new focus brought about a need for systemic change that created better coordination and integration of instruction and support services, and efficient resource allocation with existing resources (because no additional funds were being provided to school districts). Recent work in the development of mental health prevention models (e.g., Adelman & Taylor, 1998, 1999) and comprehensive behavioral intervention models like positive behavior support (PBS; Lewis & Sugai, 1999) at the time RTI was getting off the ground influenced the emerging models for RTI. Mental health services were conceptualized along a continuum from broad-based intervention efforts (e.g., public health and safety programs) applied to a population (e.g., a community) to intense services for the most extreme cases (e.g., emergency/crisis treatment for a small number of individuals; Adelman & Taylor, 1998). In the same vein, RTI models were structured to include multiple tiers that had interventions of different intensity at each tier. Influenced perhaps by PBS, the three-tier model became the most common one for RTI. Reschly and Bergstrom (2009) point out that tiers are differentiated according to (1) the intensity of instruction and (2) the frequency of measurement. Both intensity of instruction and frequency of measurement increase as a child moves from Tier 1 to Tier 2 to Tier 3.

HOW MULTI-TIERED INTERVENTIONS ARE STRUCTURED IN RESPONSE TO INTERVENTION

Although RTI was created to examine student responsiveness to instruction, RTI also calls for responsiveness on the part of the teacher and other school personnel—data-based responsiveness to student progress and instructional adjustments that are aligned with the results. Thus, to be effective RTI must be designed as a responsive system to be implemented throughout the whole school building. But what does it look like organizationally? The Institute of Education Sciences (IES), the research branch of the U.S. Department of Education, formed a panel of experts to review the research on RTI and create recommendations for schools. Those recommendations were published in 2009. The panel made five recommendations for practice, presented in Table 3.1. According to these recommendations, the critical elements of RTI are screening, differentiated instruction, progress monitoring, and increasing intensity of instruction. Routine screening (recommendation 1) at multiple time points during the school year provides information about students' progress.

TABLE 3.1. IES Panel Recommendations for RTI

1. Screen all students for potential reading problems at the beginning of the year and again in the middle of the year. Regularly monitor the progress of students who are at elevated risk for developing reading disabilities.

2. Provide differentiated reading instruction for all students based on assessments of students' current reading levels (Tier 1).

3. Provide intensive, systematic instruction on up to three foundational reading skills in small groups to students who score below the benchmark on universal screening. Typically these groups meet between three and five times a week for 20–40 minutes (Tier 2).

4. Monitor the progress of Tier 2 students at least once a month. Use these data to determine whether students still require intervention. For those still making insufficient progress, schoolwide teams should design a Tier 3 intervention plan.

5. Provide intensive instruction daily that promotes the development of various components of reading proficiency to students who show minimal progress after reasonable time in Tier 2 small-group instruction (Tier 3).

Most schools doing RTI routinely screen their students (three or four times a year) using curriculum-based measurement oral reading fluency and, for kindergarten and first-grade students, other early literacy measures (e.g., letter naming, letter sounds, phoneme segmentation). For those students who have or are at risk for reading disabilities, more frequent progress monitoring should be used. Screening and progress monitoring results are the feedback mechanisms for examining how well students are responding to instruction; they allow educators to be responsive to students' needs.

Differentiated reading instruction (recommendation 2, Table 3.1) means that instruction is adapted to students' level of need. In many cases, differentiated instruction will happen in the classroom in the core reading program. In other cases, differentiation will occur through the multi-tiered intervention process, with some students simply receiving regular classroom instruction in the core reading curriculum and some students receiving supplemental interventions in addition to core reading instruction. Schools generally organize differentiated instruction through multiple tiers after differentiated instruction in the classroom has not produced expected improvements. Although there are no formal mandates for using a three-tier model and some school districts actually use four-tier or five-tier models, we will describe the three-tier model because it's the most common model used. Tier 1 refers to the "core" reading instruction that all students receive. Schools generally devote between 90 and 120 minutes to core reading instruction (Linan-Thompson & Vaughn, 2010). A good core reading program will lower the incidence of reading problems. A poor core reading program will increase the number of students who need remediation. For this reason, the process of evaluating the core reading curriculum as a part of the RTI program will be discussed in the next section. Students who do not meet proficiency benchmarks are selected for more intense intervention at Tier 2. These students continue to receive core reading instruction, but also receive supplemental instruction (usually about 30 minutes a day, four or five times a week) in small groups with more frequent monitoring (e.g., once weekly). The close monitoring allows educators to quickly determine whether the student in a Tier 2 intervention is progressing or not. For efficiency purposes and because there are a number of good commercial supplemental reading instruction materials, Tier 2 interventions are usually delivered using a "standard treatment protocol intervention" (Batsche et al., 2006), meaning that the same instruction is delivered to all the students at Tier 2. What differentiates the Tier 2 intervention is that it increases students' practice and feedback in target skills (Linan-Thompson & Vaughn, 2010). The IES panel recommended (3) that at least three foundational reading skills be addressed, and that instruction be carried out in small groups. Again, progress monitoring data should be gathered for these students (recommendation 4). Students who do not progress adequately with Tier 2 intervention should receive specially designed instruction at Tier 3 (recommendation 5). Tier 3 intervention may occur before, during, and after an evaluation for special education eligibility. All of the progress monitoring data up to this point can be used as a part of a full and comprehensive evaluation for special education eligibility if needed (but cannot be used as the sole source of data).

Although the use of standard treatment protocols at Tier 2 may appear to contradict the individualized problem-solving process out of which RTI grew in the first place, the contradiction is more apparent than real. First, the decision to place a student in Tier 2 based on screening or progress monitoring data is a form of data-based problem solving. A good Tier 2 intervention will address many students' difficulties. Standard treatment protocols are developed to ensure that sound instructional principles are applied to all the relevant skills that students need to master. Second, the use of a standard treatment protocol should not supplant the type of ongoing problem solving and adjustments that some students will surely need (Daly, Martens, Barnett, Witt, & Olson, 2007). Some students may need minor adjustments like a little more practice or a more intense form of error correction. Minor adjustments do not call for a more intrusive intervention like placement in a more restrictive tier, and problem solving and differentiated instruction can go a long way to ensure that a student is receiving the instruction he or she needs within a given tier before moving the student to a more restrictive tier. Movement across tiers should be fluid, based on screening and progress monitoring results. Ideally, students at upper tiers will successfully move back to lower tiers. However, a student can move in and out of a tier multiple times.

This overview of RTI would be woefully incomplete if we failed to address two other critical elements to RTI. First, the *real* starting point for RTI is to evaluate your reading curriculum and, if it is inadequate, systematically strengthen it or choose a better one. As noted earlier, prevention of reading problems through a strong core curriculum is necessary for an effective intervention plan. The following section describes how to evaluate your reading curriculum for scientific support, elements of strong reading instruction, and how well it is working for your students. Second, the final section explains how to make modifications *within* tiers in an RTI program. Although flexibility is a hallmark of multi-tiered intervention models, educators should make every effort to maximize student growth at each tier by making instruction at that tier as strong as possible. To this end, we examine ways to improve instruction within the current reading program.

EVALUATING AND SELECTING A STRONG CORE CURRICULUM

Although this is a book about intervention, preventing problems before they occur may be one of the most important steps you can take toward intervention. Interventions themselves are unnatural intrusions in an existing system. They require additional resources and effort on the part of an already busy staff. If the problem can be stopped before it occurs, the system will function more smoothly. Prevention is cost effective. A strong core reading curriculum and effective regular education instructional practices will reduce the number of students who need intervention. Furthermore, Tier 2 and Tier 3 interventions are not intended to supplant regular classroom instruction. Rather, they are designed to supplement it. Therefore, selecting a solid curriculum is important to your intervention efforts. The core curriculum is an integral part of any RTI system. A good reading curriculum is one that *has been shown* (through rigorous empirical research) to be effective and *can be shown* (through your own data) to be effective with your students. There are three parts to evaluating and selecting a reading curriculum. First, you should examine the scientific evidence supporting its validity. This step will narrow down the candidates of potential curricula. Second, you should inspect each potential curriculum for critical elements of effective instruction. Not all reading curricula are equal. Some excellent guides to scrutinizing the planning, materials, and instructional routines of curricula will be described to help you with this process. Third, you can use RTI progress monitoring and benchmarking data to evaluate the effectiveness of the curriculum with *your* students. This is the most valuable source of evidence for the effectiveness of the curriculum: Are your students making adequate progress and are you seeing reductions in students' risk status? Finally, because there is no perfect curriculum, we present some common problems with core curricula and how they often need to be strengthened. Each topic will be discussed in turn.

Looking for Research-Based Curricula

In this age of accountability, all educational practices are expected to (1) be based on scientific research and (2) produce meaningful, measurable outcomes. This includes schoolwide reforms, assessments, instruction, interventions, and even the curriculum. This standard is especially important for the curriculum because of its broad effects: it is administered to virtually every student in the school. You should therefore be able to find solid scientific research supporting the curriculum, or at least the components of the curriculum (e.g., curricular sequences, instructional practices). The President's Commission on Excellence in Special Education report (2002) strongly emphasized the need for scientifically based research. NCLB also established scientifically based research as the standard for educational practice and defined it in the following way:

> Scientifically based research (as defined in the *ESEA*): (a) Means research that involves the application of rigorous, systematic, and objective procedures to obtain reliable and valid knowledge relevant to education activities and programs; and (b) Includes research that (1) Employs systematic, empirical methods that draw on observation or experiment; (2) Involves rigorous

data analyses that are adequate to test the stated hypotheses and justify the general conclusions drawn; (3) Relies on measurements or observational methods that provide reliable and valid data across evaluators and observers, across multiple measurements and observations, and across studies by the same or different investigators; (4) Is evaluated using experimental or quasi-experimental designs in which individuals, entities, programs, or activities are assigned to different conditions and with appropriate controls to evaluate the effects of the condition of interest, with a preference for random-assignment experiments, or other designs to the extent that those designs contain within-condition or across-condition controls; (5) Ensures that experimental studies are presented in sufficient detail and clarity to allow for replication or, at a minimum, offer the opportunity to build systematically on their findings; and (6) Has been accepted by a peer-reviewed journal or approved by a panel of independent experts through a comparably rigorous, objective, and scientific review. [34 CFR 300.35] [20 U.S.C. 1411(e)(2)(C) (xi)] [sec. 9101(37) of the *ESEA*]

Unfortunately, this lofty standard is more easily described than realized. Standards for scientific evidence are rather general in nature and interpreters of research have to apply them to particular research studies (e.g., Did this curriculum outperform another curriculum?) for which it might not be readily apparent whether a standard is met or not. Scientific standards are not easy to quantify. There are not hard-and-fast rules about the number and quality of studies that need to be conducted to present a very convincing case. In addition, there are no regulating agencies for determining quality, and decisions about which curriculum to choose are under local control. A diversity of methodologies, samples, procedures, and experimental rigor may make it difficult to compare studies. And, finally, consumers' level of expertise with research methodology and statistical analyses may make it difficult for them to discern the good from the bad and the ugly.

A simple way to start this complex task is to begin by looking primarily at published research in "peer-reviewed" journals. Journals that publish peer-reviewed papers have submitted the paper to a rigorous review process by scholars in the field prior to publication. Beware of studies that are reported secondhand or that are reported in non-peer-reviewed publications. For example, a curriculum publisher may refer to research studies attesting to the validity of its curriculum in its promotional materials. These studies often lack important elements of experimental control. Go directly to the study itself to see if it satisfies your requirements for good evidence. We recommend that you use search engines like Google Scholar and PsychINFO to obtain independent reports of studies of any curricula that you are considering.

Studies differ in rigor according to the kinds of designs used by the researchers. For example, experimental studies directly manipulate variables (e.g., applying an experimental treatment/program to one group while not applying it to another group), whereas correlational studies just measure how different conditions covary (e.g., whether class size correlates with disruptive behavior). One cannot establish causation based on a correlational study because another variable might be responsible for changes in the measured variables. Of the experimental designs, the randomized control trial study is the gold standard. It contains one or more control groups and uses randomization to assign participants to conditions. Studies that contain control groups and a direct manipulation of variables but do not use random assignment are quasi-experimental designs. In these studies, there may be group differences between conditions that can account for the results.

The next step is to examine the details and findings of the studies. To help you with this, the IES developed guidelines for evaluating the scientific rigor of studies and reported them in a document titled "Identifying and Implementing Educational Practices Supported by Rigorous Evidence: A User Friendly Guide" (available at *www2.ed.gov/rschstat/ research/pubs/rigorousevid/index.html*). Table 3.2 contains 10 questions from the guide that can be used to evaluate whether an intervention (or curriculum in this case) is backed by "strong" evidence of effectiveness. "Yes" responses for all questions except item 2 and the second question for item 5 (for which "No" responses are expected) are expected for a study to contain strong evidence of effectiveness. These questions establish a high standard for evidence. It's possible and perhaps even likely that you will not find any studies that meet all the criteria. However, meeting the criteria is more of a question of degree than attaining an absolute standard, especially for an area for which there is so little empirical research. In other words, the studies that meet the most standards should be given the heaviest weight in your deliberations. The IES guide has useful checklists that can be used by school personnel to evaluate studies of the curricula under consideration. The IES guide describes two levels of evidence: "strong" and "possible" evidence of effectiveness. Of course, selecting a curriculum is a task for a group of people and not a single individual. Therefore, the checklists can be used as a point of departure for discussion of the scientific merits of the studies that the curriculum committee is considering. The guides can help to frame the discussions about the most important factors that should be considered, helping the commit-

---

TABLE 3.2. IES Guidelines for Evaluating Whether an Intervention Is Backed by "Strong" Evidence of Effectiveness

1. Does the study clearly describe (1) the intervention, (2) how the intervention differed from what the control group received, and (3) the logic of how the intervention is supposed to affect outcomes?

2. Is there any indication that the random assignment process was compromised?

3. Does the study provide data showing that there was no systematic difference between the intervention and control groups before the intervention?

4. Does the study use outcome measures that have been shown to be reliable and valid?

5. Is the subject attrition small? Are there differences in attrition between the intervention and control groups?

6. Does the study report outcomes even for members of the intervention group who did not complete the study?

7. Does the study obtain long-term outcome data to show that intervention effects were sustained over time?

8. In the report of the results, does the study report the size of the effect and the statistical tests showing the effect is unlikely to be due to chance?

9. Are any observed differences between subgroups (e.g., Hispanic students vs. Caucasian students) treated with caution?

10. Does the study report the intervention's effect on all the outcomes that the study measured, and not just those for which positive effects were obtained?

tee to steer away from the potentially harmful influences of personal biases and marketing techniques. They outline a multistep process for determining just how well supported the intervention is, taking into consideration the kind of designs used in the study (e.g., randomized control trial, comparison-group). We recommend that this analysis of the research be done by a school-based team of individuals who have a stake in the reading curriculum. The exercise will be most informative and should prompt rich discussion about just what the team is looking for in a curriculum.

Unfortunately, you are likely to discover that there are very few actual scientifically rigorous studies of curricula per se. And of those that have been conducted, very few of them will meet the standards of the randomized control trial. So, although research on the curriculum or curricula you are considering is the first thing you should do, you should also look for another type of study as well. Most publishers will claim that their curriculum contains research-based elements, things like content sequencing and instructional practices that align with scientific evidence. Twyman and Sota (2008) describe these kinds of curricula as "research informed" because they were designed with best practices and the most recent research in mind. In this case, you compare the curriculum with the existing research on instructional practices. The curriculum that is most aligned with the current state of the art is presumed to be the strongest curriculum. Twyman and Sota warn, however, that curricula that are research informed have not necessarily been extensively field tested and examined in controlled research. Therefore, although it's a good thing when a curriculum is research informed, the research is still only meeting a lower standard of evidence than we would generally prefer. Be careful about growing overly enthusiastic about the curriculum, and wait until you see how (and if) it impacts your students before coming to any definitive conclusions about it. Finally, we recommend that you consult the What Works Clearinghouse (*http://ies.ed.gov/ncee/wwc*) for reviews of curricula. Most of the reviews are for programs and interventions, but they do contain reviews of some curricula.

Using Screening Data to Evaluate Your Core Reading Curriculum

Screening and benchmarking have become common practices. Many elementary schools regularly gather basic skill fluency data (e.g., oral reading fluency) for all of their students at regular intervals as a part of their RTI model. Yet, they do not use the data for decision-making purposes. It's akin to getting an MRI (magnetic resonance imaging; screening an entire building or district can be almost as scary!) without bothering to interpret the results to determine whether medical intervention is warranted. Other schools are good at using their screening data to identify students in need of intervention and placing them at different instructional levels, but fail to exploit this rich database even further. Screening data can also be used to determine the overall educational health of the school population. By analyzing the data at a more global level (described below), they will help you to diagnose the effectiveness of your core curriculum and the regular classroom instruction. A strong core that is well delivered minimizes the number of students needing more intense intervention. For practical purposes, those expectations have been operationalized within the three-tier model in terms of percentages of students at each level. A commonly accepted standard for the distribution of students' needs is that at least 80% of students meet expected levels of achievement, that no more than 15% of them are at the strategic (i.e., Tier 2) level, and that no more than 5% of them are at the intensive (i.e., Tier 3) level (Batsche et al., 2006). If more than 20% of students need supplemental interventions, meeting all those students' needs adequately is going to be very taxing on the system. Obviously, some schools have students with more intense social and behavioral needs, and they will discover that their numbers are quite discrepant from these guidelines. However, educators should focus on factors over which they have control, and the guidelines can be used to diagnose the strength and effectiveness of the curriculum they are using and intervene if necessary. This broader and more general guideline (i.e., 80% at Tier 1, 15% at Tier 2, and 5% at Tier 3) can be broken down into four diagnostic questions you should ask of your screening data. Those questions appear in Table 3.3. If the answer to one or more of these questions is yes, there may be a problem with the core curriculum and/or how it is being delivered in the classroom.

When screening data are compiled to make decisions about students' placement in tiers (i.e., who will receive only Tier 1 instruction and who will receive intervention in Tiers 2 and 3?), individual results are compared with benchmarks. The most common method is to use DIBELS (*https://dibels.uoregon.edu*) or Aimsweb (*www.aimsweb.com*) benchmarks (described in more detail in Chapter 6). Each student's results are compared with an expected level of performance at a particular time of year (i.e., fall, winter, or spring). Students fall at either the benchmark (Tier 1), strategic (Tier 2), or intensive (Tier 3) levels. Coding each student's results accordingly will allow you to calculate and analyze the overall percentages of students needing instruction at the different tiers. Displaying the aggregated results for the school population as a bar chart makes the response to question 1 clear. For example, the oral reading fluency results for the entire second grade in an elementary school are displayed in Figure 3.1 (top) as a column (cone) chart. The expected distribution of students across tiers appears to the left ("Expected"), and the actual distribution of second-grade students meeting benchmark criteria appears to the right ("Second Grade"). You can see that (1) fewer than 80% of students meet the benchmark criterion for Tier 1, (2) 7% of the students fall at the strategic level, and (3) a disproportionately large percentage of students (22%) fall at the intensive level. In this example, 80% of students do not meet expectations with Tier 1 instruction alone, meaning that the answer to question 1 is "yes" (Table 3.3).

TABLE 3.3. Strengthening Core Instruction: Questions to Ask of Your Screening Data

[handwritten margin note: #1 if yes to any of these may be a problem w/ core curric.]

1. Do your data show that fewer than 80% of students meet your expectations with Tier 1 instruction alone?

2. When student data are disaggregated by language status (English learners), free-and-reduced-lunch status, special education status, and gender status, are there substantial achievement differences among groups of students?

3. Do more than 20% of students require Tier 2 or Tier 3 intervention?

4. Of those students meeting expectations at the beginning of the year, are fewer than 95% of them continuing to meet expectations by the middle of the year? How about by the end of the year?

The data were further coded and disaggregated by student characteristics (EL status, free-and-reduced-lunch status, special education status, and gender). The results are displayed at the bottom of Figure 3.1. The first cone is the expected distribution of scores (i.e., 80% meeting the benchmark level, 15% at the strategic level, and 5% at the intensive level). The other cones present the results for pairwise comparisons (non-English language learners [Non-EL] vs. English learners [EL], non-free-and-reduced-lunch vs. free-and-reduced-lunch [F/R] students, Non-special education [Non-SPED] vs. special education [SPED] students, and gender—male vs. female). Results readily reveal differences among all student groupings, answering question 2 in Table 3.3 in the affirmative. Furthermore, it is clear from both data displays that more than 20% of students do require Tier 2 or Tier 3 intervention, also yielding an affirmative answer to question 3.

The fourth question in Table 3.3 addresses the rate of progress over the year for the students who achieved benchmark status in the fall screening. If these students who are receiving Tier 1 instruction only are not progressing adequately, it provides evidence that the core curriculum (and/or the way it is being delivered) is not doing its job. More and more students are being placed in Tier 2 or Tier 3 interventions as the year progresses. The question is, where do these students fall in the middle of the year, and where do they fall at the end of the year? An example of the results for an entire second grade appear in Figure 3.2. In this case, by the middle of the year, 9% of these students were placed in Tier 2 interventions and by the end of the year, 11% were in Tier 2, and 2% were in Tier 3 interventions. There appears to be a slight decline over the course of the year in the students who are making expected progress with just Tier 1 instruction. This information, along with the previous results, suggests that this elementary school should examine its core curriculum for reading. In this example, only results for second grade were presented. Normally, a school would do this analysis for all of its grades (e.g., kindergarten through fifth grade for a typical elementary school). Getting more out of your screening data in this way gives you good snapshots of how your school population is doing and serves as excellent feedback on the quality of the core curriculum.

Common Problems with Core Curricula

There is no perfect curriculum. However, some curricula are definitely better than others. Your experience with a curriculum and the results it produces in your students will tell you whether you made a wise choice or not. Even with a solid curriculum, adjustments will probably need to be made. Our experience working with school districts and helping them review and evaluate curricula has led us to make some observations about common problems with core curricula. The list that appears in Table 3.4 is not an exhaustive one. But it will give you an idea of the things you should be looking out for. For example, as important as phonemic awareness instruction is, we have noticed that some curricula spend too much time on these skills, both within instructional sessions and over the entire curricular sequence. Phonemic awareness skills should be finely honed. However, brief instructional activities that zero in on critical skills with laser-like penetration are usually sufficient. Once students master these skills, they should progress to phonics instruction, which will require them to integrate these skills into word reading.

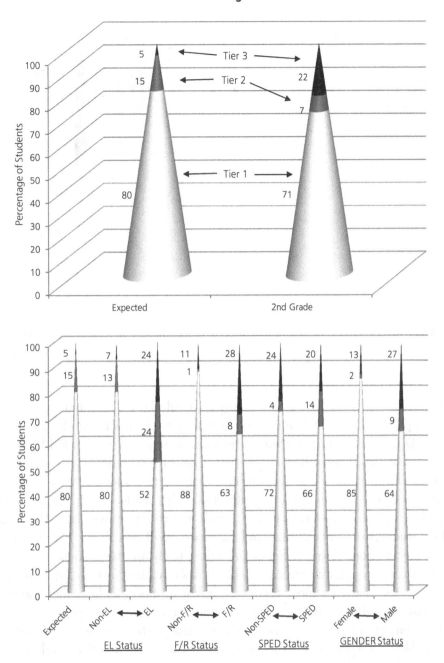

FIGURE 3.1. Expected versus actual results for school screening data.

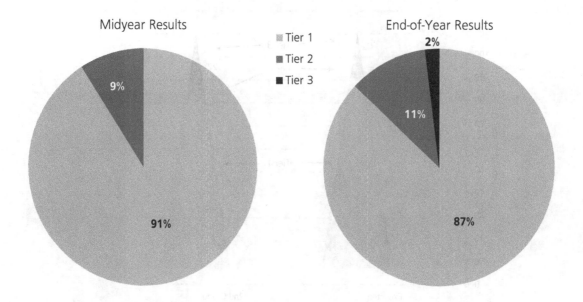

FIGURE 3.2. Percentages of students at all three tiers for midyear and end-of-year school screenings.

In the area of phonics instruction, many curricula lack a research-based scope and sequence for phonics skills to be taught. An exemplary model of a research-based scope and sequence is Direct Instruction (Carnine, Silbert, Kame'enui, & Tarver, 2010). To be effective, phonics instruction must be very explicit. Explicit instruction makes it highly likely that students will give correct answers when prompted to respond and leave no room for making incorrect associations. Phonics instruction helps the learner to apply fine-grained distinctions between written letters to form words. It is a very analytic task. If instruction is not explicit, students will get confused and the process will slow down. Phonics instruction should also have a strong error correction procedure to ensure that students do not practice errors more than they practice correct responses when reading text. In addition, some curricula frankly label activities incorrectly, calling, for instance, a phonemic awareness task a phonics task. We caution you not to assume that curriculum developers are always right about what their activities are intended to achieve. Analyze the lessons for yourself. Another common problem with phonics instruction is a lack of sufficient practice. Students generally need a lot of practice before phonics skills will allow the kind of fluid reading necessary to achieve reading fluency. Look also at the curriculum to examine how and if it teaches students to analyze and decode multisyllabic words. Finally, many curricula use too many rare words while not including sufficient word repetitions within texts, high-frequency words, and words with predictable phonetic patterns (Hiebert, 2005; Hiebert & Fisher, 2005).

Until recently, oral reading fluency was an overlooked part of the curriculum. Fortunately, some influential expert panel reports (National Reading Panel, 2000; Snow, Burns, & Griffin, 1998) have influenced the field and eventually publishers to give a greater role to reading fluency instruction. Fluency is the bridge between foundational reading skills and the higher-order reading skills like comprehension and vocabulary. Without fluent reading,

TABLE 3.4. Common Problems with Core Curricula

Phonemic awareness

- Too much time allocated per instructional session.
- Taught for too long.

Phonics

- Lack a research-based scope and sequence.
- Not explicit enough.
- Insufficient correction procedures.
- Mislabel activities (e.g., a PA activity labeled as a phonics activity).
- Lack sufficient practice.
- Lack strategies for multi-syllabic word reading.
- Fail to attend to the length of the words and repetitions in decodable readers.

Fluency

- Texts for fluency practice not appropriate.
- Incorrect application of "repeated readings."
- Often include activities which are not research based (e.g., Readers' Theater).
- Insufficient opportunities for students to hear fluent reading.

Vocabulary

- Selected words may not be the words your students need.
- Lack explicit instruction.
- Lack student-friendly definitions.
- Insufficient examples and nonexamples.
- Lack sufficient practice.

Comprehension

- Include too many strategies and skills or use different terms for similar strategies.
- Lack explicit instruction in use of strategies.
- Insufficient background information to build prior knowledge.
- Confuse products with process.
- Text doesn't match skill being instructed.
- Text difficulty level too high for student for independent comprehension.

students cannot focus on the meaning because they are laboring over decoding words. To be maximally effective, reading fluency instruction should be conducted in texts of appropriate difficulty level, should incorporate repeated readings of the same passage, and provide models (i.e., examples of fluent reading) when students' fluency levels are low (Chard et al., 2002). Unfortunately, a number of curricula fall short in these areas by including texts that are too difficult or too easy, incorrectly using the method of repeated readings, including activities that lack research support, and fail to provide sufficient modeling by fluent readers.

Vocabulary instruction has been around for a long time. But it is only recently that educators have begun to take it seriously. Traditional vocabulary exercises often lack the critical components of instruction that have emerged in the research. First and foremost, you should analyze the words being taught to be sure that they are the actual words students will need to be successful in your curriculum. Using a tiered approach to selecting vocabulary words can be helpful. Beck, McKeown, and Kucan (2013) suggest a method for categorizing words as Tier 1 words, basic words that most students will pick up easily without explicit instruction (e.g., *table, chair, happy*); Tier 2 words, medium- to high-frequency unfamiliar words that will be useful to students because they will likely encounter them in the future across a variety of contexts (e.g., *enormous, excited, awful*); and Tier 3 words, rare words that are often limited to a specific domain (e.g., *tundra, cataclysm*) to help with selection of appropriate words to teach explicitly. Tier 2 words are then selected for explicit vocabulary instruction during reading because they will be the most useful to students over time. The teacher should provide explicit instruction in vocabulary that includes the use of definitions that are friendly to students and the use of examples and nonexamples of the words that are relevant to the students. Vocabulary instruction cannot just rely on seatwork exercises such as looking words up in the dictionary. Finally, there should be sufficient practice to ensure that students actually learn what the words mean (and not just finish the exercise).

Comprehension is obviously the goal of reading instruction and incorporates all of the other components of reading while placing additional demands on the learner, making it the most complex skill to teach. It is unfortunate when comprehension instruction confuses students (as a result of complexity) rather than clarifies for students. We have noticed several ways in which reading curricula can really muddle things for students. First, they often teach too many strategies in a superficial way rather than focusing on a smaller but clearer and more functional set of strategies. Sometimes, reading curricula use different terms for similar strategies. Reading comprehension is yet another area where strategy use is often not explicitly taught. Furthermore, for reading comprehension to occur (and therefore for instruction to be effective), context is everything. Meaningful understanding only occurs within a context for the information that is provided by the text. In part, students must draw on prior knowledge to understand the context of the passage to be read. When students lack that prior knowledge, the curriculum should provide sufficient background knowledge prior to having the student read the text. Our observation has been that many curricula do not do a good job of this. Teachers should systematically check students' prior knowledge and, when lacking, should build prior knowledge to help the student interact meaningfully with the text. Be on the lookout for these types of problems with your reading curriculum, and correct them once they are identified. A strong curriculum does not just consist of textbooks and lessons. It is refined over time to make sure it is having the greatest impact on the local student population. Curriculum issues relate to Tier 1 reading instruction in the general curriculum. The rest of the book focuses on appropriate reading strategies for Tier 2 and Tier 3 interventions. However, it is important to discuss important considerations in making adjustments across tiers in an RTI model.

MAKING ADJUSTMENTS WITHIN TIERS

The continuum of services created by RTI is a significant step toward resolving many of the problems associated with a strictly categorical approach to meeting students' needs. Besides overcoming the psychometric problems created by categorical classification described earlier in this chapter, RTI allows for more fluid movement between tiers and provides interventions of increasing intensity before long-lasting decisions with significant consequences (e.g., being classified as learning disabled) are applied to the child. Students can move up and down through the tiers as progress monitoring data reflect their responsiveness to instruction and supplemental interventions.

Students with significant difficulties whose profile does not match categorical classification requirements can still receive services. This fluidity between tiers is a great advantage of RTI. Nonetheless, keeping students at and within lower tiers insofar as it is possible and meeting their needs with the least amount of intervention necessary are desirable goals. The system can be strained if students' placements in tiers are being frequently changed and if too many students are being placed in the higher tiers. Tiers 2 and 3 are costly and resource-intensive levels of educational support. Therefore, schools should be making every effort to keep students at the lowest tier necessary to meet their needs (and therefore not moving higher if at all possible). RTI is an organized problem-solving model that is administratively efficient. But problem solving should not be limited to placement across tiers. RTI is certainly not intended to absolve teachers and other instructional support personnel from the responsibility of doing problem solving within the classroom or within the intervention group.

There are a number of things that can be done to intensify or individualize instruction within a tier. These strategies should be tried and evaluated before students are moved to a higher tier. Kupzyk, Daly, Ihlo, and Young (2012) describe five areas to investigate for strengthening instruction for the student who is not making adequate progress within a classroom and/or within an intervention group. They are listed in Table 3.5. First, to check the skills targeted for instruction (recommendation 1, Table 3.5), one should examine the sequence of skills being taught. Instruction should follow a logical and empirically supported progression of skills: newly learned skills should rely on previously instructed skills and the newly learned skills themselves will need to be used in the subsequent skills in the sequence. This step requires you to check to see if there is an explicitly articulated skill sequence with more basic and foundational skills (e.g., teaching sound blending) being taught before more complex skills (e.g., phonics). Direct Instruction (Carnine et al., 2010) is an excellent example of a curriculum with a carefully delineated skill sequence. Before instruction is delivered in a skill, the teacher should check to see if the student has the prerequisite skills needed to be successful. For example, if a student has not mastered basic phonics skills, he or she is going to have difficulty mastering oral reading fluency skills. Teachers should do assessments of skills before placing students in the curriculum sequence to ensure appropriate difficulty level. A student may be experiencing problems if the correct sequence of skills is not being taught or if he or she is being instructed in the wrong place in the sequence, and corrections need to be made.

TABLE 3.5. Modifying Instruction within Tiers

1. Check the skills targeted for instruction.
2. Check for guided practice.
3. Check for independent practice.
4. Check implementation fidelity.
5. Check the motivating conditions.

Note. Based on Kupzyk, Daly, Ihlo, and Young (2012).

The manner in which new skills are introduced and taught is critical to whether the student will master it or not. Instruction should be designed to promote a lot of responding on the part of the student. However, because the student has a skill deficit, the teacher must be highly interactive, set the student up to respond correctly (and not practice mistakes), and be responsive to the student's current level of competency with the skill. Interactive teaching calls for initial guided practice (recommendation 2, Table 3.5). To deliver guided practice, the teacher should use explicit instructions for how to respond, modeling of correct responding, supervised practice with immediate feedback, error correction, and adjustments to the amount of independent practice as students' skills grow stronger (Kupzyk et al., 2012). If independent practice is assigned too soon, students will respond with errors and will take more time to respond than necessary. Therefore, poor student progress may occur as a result of a lack of sufficient guided practice before independent practice is assigned. If the error rate is high and/or students are taking a long time to complete assignments, there is a good chance that guided practice is not being used well.

All too often, students spend insufficient time learning new skills and the next skill or a more difficult assignment is introduced prematurely. Unfortunately, many curricula and intervention programs fail to provide sufficient practice opportunities (Chard et al., 2002). Independent practice builds fluency, which makes it easier for students to maintain and generalize skill use later (Binder, 1996). Independent practice is appropriate (and necessary!) when student responding is accurate. Therefore, when errors are low to nonexistent, it's time to have the student practice the skill repeatedly. Although this step is so basic and fundamental to learning, it is sorely neglected in schools. Edmonds and Briggs (2003) found that only 3% of instructional time was devoted to fluency building in first-grade reading instruction. Without a high fluency level, subsequent skills and tasks in the curriculum will be more difficult to learn than they should be. You should explicitly examine whether independent practice is being used (recommendation 3, Table 3.5). Fortunately, because the student's error rate is low, he or she can practice under a wide variety of circumstances. Peers, parents, paraprofessionals, or other support staff can help with practice sessions. One simple strategy is to offer students a reward for meeting a predetermined criterion following practice and let the student practice on his or her own. If the reward is appealing enough, the student will probably be motivated to practice more. Rewards do not have to be complicated or elaborate. Simple school-based activities like computer time, free time, being the line leader, visiting a preferred person in the building (e.g., the gym teacher or the principal), and taking the attendance card to the office can be very motivating for students. Poor student progress may be an indicator of insufficient practice. Before increasing practice time, however, check the student's skill level to be sure that the assignments are at the appropriate difficulty level.

As noted earlier in the chapter, the results of student assessments are as much a test of the instruction as they are of the student. In other words, a lack of progress tells us more about the effectiveness of the instruction than about any qualities of the student. The previous items dealt with the content of instruction and how it was delivered. Another question is whether the instruction is being delivered correctly. The requirement for an explicit skill sequence described earlier (recommendation 1, Table 3.5) implies that there is a plan for

Module 1
Letter D.

when skills are introduced (*what* is being taught). Equally important is the need for clear and systematic instructional delivery (*how* it is being taught; recommendations 2 and 3, Table 3.5). If the plan for *what* and *how* seems adequate, you should examine whether instruction and/or intervention is being delivered as planned (recommendation 4, Table 3.5). Is explicit instruction being delivered correctly? Is it delivered frequently enough? A written plan for instruction and/or intervention steps will make it easier to answer this question. An independent observer (e.g., support personnel, a teaching coach) can directly observe instruction to see whether the proper steps are being followed. Having the teacher keep a log of lessons and students' work products (i.e., assignments) can also help you track the frequency of instructional sessions. This information is as important as any other aspect of instruction when you are problem solving. For a student making poor progress, one cannot conclude that an instructional plan is ineffective if there is no evidence that it was done correctly and as consistently as planned. Unfortunately, the research evidence strongly suggests that without regular monitoring and performance feedback, intervention plans are rarely followed correctly (Noell, 2008). Some may feel that this step is invasive. After all, isn't the teacher responsible for doing his or her job? Why should someone else be checking his or her work? The purpose of this step, however, is not to evaluate the teacher, but to give the teacher support to meet the instructional needs of a student who is struggling. A good consultant will want to see how things are going in the classroom and evaluate the impact of instruction. Shortly after classroom observations, the observer should discuss which steps of the plan were followed and which ones were not followed, and problem solve with the teacher as difficulties arise. Plans are usually developed in meetings far removed from the instructional context. When the teacher is implementing the instructional plan, there will often be things that were overlooked during the planning session or unexpected changes to the routine may have occurred. It is very important to communicate to the teacher that the support personnel are standing by the teacher to help him or her give the plan the best shot possible.

By its very nature, education involves presenting a continuous series of difficult tasks to a learner who has a limited skills repertoire. All of us can think of learning experiences that were difficult and sometimes even exasperating. Carefully designed instruction can alleviate a lot of the difficulty and set the student up for success by sequencing tasks and providing sufficient guided practice before independent practice. However, instruction will not be effective if the appropriate motivating conditions are not created. Many students are rewarded with work completion by receiving . . . more work! When the task is difficult in the first place, getting to do more of the same work for completing one's work is hardly motivating. Problem behaviors begin to emerge. Students discover that they can get teacher attention or peer attention, or even get out of work by being sent, for example, to the principal's office for acting up during instructional time. Effective use of positive consequences for task engagement and work completion will strengthen academic skills and reduce problem behavior. Therefore, we strongly encourage you to examine whether the teacher is creating the necessary motivating conditions (recommendation 5, Table 3.5). Many of the assumptions we make about what motivates students (e.g., they should want to do it, they are motivated by good grades, they are motivated by the same things that motivate other children) are incorrect when it comes to students who are having difficulty. Motivational strategies are easy to investigate and easy to deliver, and they make instructional time much more efficient, because a motivated student is going to get his or her work done (assuming it's of appropriate difficulty level) more quickly. To examine motivational strategies, check out what happens before students work on assignments. Are the students told why they are doing the task? Are the students told what will happen when they complete their work? In other words, does the teacher offer positive consequences for completing their work? During and after instruction, check to see whether the teacher praises completion and effort. Following assignment completion, does the teacher deliver positive consequences? Rewards for work completion need not be expensive or difficult to implement. A brief break, access to a preferred activity (e.g., 10 minutes of computer time), or even a privilege (e.g., being the line leader, taking the attendance card to the principal) contingent on completing assignments might be sufficient. It's important to keep in mind that the work is more difficult for the student you are concerned about than for the typical student. Therefore, giving the student a motivational boost may be necessary.

CONCLUSIONS

Multi-tiered intervention models are very appealing and now very popular because of the flexible continuum of services they afford educators seeking to meet the needs of all students. However, a rush to establish Tier 2 and Tier 3 intervention programs may cause educators to neglect the critical importance of beginning the whole process with a close examination of the core curriculum at Tier 1. This chapter examined why it is so critical to ensure good instruction and a good curriculum at Tier 1 and described methods for evaluating the core curriculum. It starts with a careful review of the research for the core curriculum being used (or under consideration for adoption) and a systematic analysis of screening data aggregated over all the students in the school. The chapter also described common problems in core curricula that arise and what you can do to address them. Finally, the issue of making adjustments within tiers was addressed to help you maximize success within each tier.

Differentiated instruction to meet the academic needs of a diverse student body is at the heart of RTI. It is important to note, however, that differentiating instruction does not simply refer to moving students across tiers. Differentiated instruction should be occurring within *all* tiers, most especially Tier 1. This is where the interventions that appear throughout the rest of this book come in. They can be used to make modifications at Tier 1, Tier 2, or Tier 3. Their use at Tier 1 may forestall the need to move a student to a higher tier. At Tiers 2 and 3, they can be used to strengthen existing treatment packages or even design them. The interventions in the following chapters can be flexibly combined to meet the individual needs of students, the whole purpose of multi-tiered intervention models.

CHAPTER 4

Diverse Learners

Today's classrooms include increasing numbers of children from linguistically and culturally diverse backgrounds. According to the NCES school-age children (i.e., children between the ages of 5 and 17) who spoke a language other than English at home increased from 4.7 to 11.2 million between 1980 and 2009—10–21% of the population in this age range (Aud et al., 2011). Teachers are faced with providing appropriate and effective instruction for a population of students who must meet the same developmental literacy milestones as their English-speaking peers, in addition to learning the language. This additional challenge has historically posed a problem for educators in differentiating between language differences and reading difficulty early in language and literacy development.

A multi-tiered approach to instruction provides an opportunity to avoid the potential misidentification of ELs (e.g., struggling reader or struggling language learner) and instead equips educators with rich and explicit instructional techniques in the context of a responsive pedagogical model (IDEIA, 2004). A growing body of research on responsive evidence-based approaches to pedagogy demonstrates that high-quality instruction for English speakers is also effective for ELs, particularly in the context of a unified system of instruction that builds in additional supports (Fien et al., 2011). In order to best support the literacy learning of these students, in this instructional framework, an understanding of the language and literacy characteristics of this heterogeneous group of learners and how these differences can inform the research-based practices chosen and implemented is necessary. This chapter begins by discussing who these learners are and proceeds by reviewing how to best address their instructional needs and increase their existing assets in a multi-tiered framework. Furthermore, this chapter also addresses research-based assessments for these learners—a crucial aspect of instructional decision making for learners who may be experiencing growth across multiple areas (e.g., content as well as language and literacy proficiency).

WHO ARE ENGLISH LEARNERS?

There are many terms to describe students who come to school with varied levels of proficiency in English; knowing what the different terms communicate about a students' level of exposure to English has important implications for the code-based language skills and reading strategies that may be most relevant for those learners. Students who come from homes where a language other than English is spoken are referred to as *language-minority* (LM) students (e.g., August & Hakuta, 1997; Short & Fitzsimmons, 2007). Many of these students may be bilingual in English and their home language, some may be more proficient in their home language than English as well as vice versa, and in some cases the knowledge and/or vocabulary in each of these languages may be distinct with English being the language of academic vocabulary. Over 460 languages are spoken by LM students; three out of four speak Spanish, with the Spanish speakers continuing to be the largest growing group (Crawford, 2004; Francis, Rivera, Lesaux, Kieffer, & Rivera, 2006). Table 4.1 lists the most commonly spoken home languages.

Language minorities, or *English learners* (a term used in several more recent reports), are broad terms that do not stipulate a particular proficiency level. By contrast, the term *limited English proficient* (LEP) is used by the federal government to identify LM students whose English ability prevents them from participating independently in instruction. This same group of learners (i.e., LEP students) is often labeled *English language learners* (ELLs) or *English learners* (ELs), terms that encompass the same population but highlight their accomplishments as opposed to their deficiencies.

However, understanding the literacy strengths and weaknesses of ELs (e.g., students ranging from high proficiency to low proficiency in English) is complex. The designation EL

TABLE 4.1. Most Commonly Spoken Home Languages of ELs

Language	Student count
Spanish	3,618,000
Vietnamese	92,000
Chinese	77,000
Arabic	65,000
Hmong	43,000
Korean	43,000
Tagalog	39,000
Haitian	37,000
Russian	34,000
Somali	26,000

Note. Student counts are rounded to the nearest thousand. Data from U.S. Department of Education, Office of Elementary and Secondary Education (2011).

may reflect students' performance on a language proficiency assessment, achievement test, criterion-based assessment, home language questionnaire, teacher observations, portfolio, and more, in combination or alone; the mode of assessment is dependent on the state, school district, or school. As such, students with very different language and literacy abilities may be listed under this same category depending on which criteria are used to determine their language status. These students' language and literacy skills may be qualitatively different based on when they arrived in the United States, how much schooling they received in their first language, and how many reading materials were available in their home environment. Despite these differences there are several fundamental aspects of second-language development that are crucial for teachers of students of ELs to know.

In the chapters that follow we address how these understandings should inform instruction with specific literacy-related skills. These aspects of language learning are easily integrated into a multi-tiered instructional model, where instruction can be tailored to students with a variety of literacy needs. In the next section we address research-based guidelines and practices for English language that incorporate these understandings and can address potential reading challenges experienced by this group.

EVIDENCE-BASED GUIDELINES AND PRACTICES FOR ENGLISH LEARNERS

In this section we review some basic evidence-based guidelines for reading instruction for ELs and discuss some specific instructional strategies that are in line with these guidelines and provide hands-on recommendations for tailoring instruction to ELs. The content of this book is intended to go beyond a discussion of central tenets of EL instruction and instead conceptualize EL-specific practices as part of a systematic framework for prevention and improvement. This is particularly useful for ELs, as their multiple languages, diverse instructional settings (i.e., potentially a mix of experiences in the United States and their sending country), and educational trajectories are less charted. The lack of clarity on the linguistic and academic development of these youth make a more responsive system for determining appropriate and useful instruction central to their educational success.

Specific research-based practices that demonstrate this approach and have strong evidence to support their effectiveness are delineated by the What Works Clearinghouse's practice guide for elementary ELs (Gersten et al., 2007). The practice guide provides five recommendations for effective literacy and English language instruction targeted for ELs. They include:

1. Conduct formative assessments for ELs measuring phonological processing and letter knowledge, as well as word and text reading.
2. Provide intensive small-group interventions for those students determined to be at risk using direct explicit instruction in the five core reading elements (phonological awareness, phonics, reading fluency, vocabulary, and reading comprehension).

3. Provide teacher-structured, peer-assisted learning in heterogeneous ability group-ings for approximately 90 minutes a week, practicing and extending material already taught in class.
4. Include high-quality vocabulary instruction throughout the day with both a focus on in-depth instruction of content words as well as the meanings of common words, phrases, and expressions that are still unfamiliar to learners.
5. Teach academic language starting in the primary grades using supplementary mate-rials to the core curricula when needed.

Each of these recommendations was determined based on experimental studies that met the What Works Clearinghouse's stringent and rigorous standards as well as expert opinion on EL practices.

Formative Assessment

The first recommendation regarding formative assessment is fundamental to the success of a multi-tiered framework, which invariably includes screenings and progress monitoring measures. Such assessments are crucial for all learners but are particularly informative in the case of ELs, for whom the benchmarks for their reading trajectory are still under debate and who are at greater risk of falling academically behind as a result of their generally smaller vocabulary (on average) than their monolingual peers (Short & Fitzsimmons, 2007); with less access to classroom vocabulary these learners are prevented from fully benefit-ing from the curriculum. Furthermore, the focus on early formative assessments for these students is crucial to their scholastic success in that ELs are more likely to attend schools in high-poverty areas (Gándara, Rumberger, Maxwell-Jolly, & Callahan, 2003; Parrish et al., 2006; Rumberger & Anguiano, 2004), increasing the likelihood that their performance may reflect inadequate instruction as opposed to language difference or disability, with each situation requiring a different pedagogical remedy. Assessments with ELs should be used to inform instructional decision making for students who require additional support and to monitor their reading development and progress. Screening and progress monitoring measures allow educators to determine if students are indeed responding to the classroom instruction or whether they require more individualized intervention. Phonological aware-ness assessments including sound blending, segmenting phonemes, and rhyming; knowl-edge of the alphabetic principle with regard to letter-naming speed and accuracy; and oral reading fluency have all been hailed by the American Psychological Association as valid screening measures (American Educational Research Association, 1999).

Beyond just screening, oral reading fluency measures have also been used to monitor progress over time for ELs. An example of an oral reading fluency measure is an assessment that requires students to read aloud a never-before-seen, grade-appropriate passage with the number of words read correctly scored (Kaminski & Good, 1996). Several studies sup-port the use of oral reading fluency measures to be sensitive and useful for progress moni-toring and accurate in helping to identify students who are at greater risk of reading failure. Research by Vaughn, Linan-Thompson, and Hickman (2003) supports the use of oral reading fluency measures with ELs as a useful means of determining RTI. They found that an increase in reading one additional word per week was a useful benchmark for indicating responsiveness to instruction and for decisions regarding the appropriateness of exiting a program. However, given that EL students may grow at different rates based on instruction or stage of language development, responsiveness should not be assessed at one time point but should be looked at in the larger context across multiple time points (Al Otaiba et al., 2009).

We now address some practices that educators can use in a multi-tiered framework, once students in need of support have been identified. A more lengthy discussion about the challenges of assessing ELs is addressed at the conclusion of this chapter.

Small-Group Interventions

Once learners who require additional support have been identified there are a variety of evidence-based practices that have been found to improve the reading performance of these learners. Different classroom grouping configurations can enhance exposure to oral language and scaffold more in-depth learning. One example is homogeneous ability groups. Multiple studies have concluded that small-group reading interventions in homogeneous groups of ELs at risk of reading difficulty can help improve ELs' reading performance (Denton, Anthony, Parker, & Hasbrouck, 2004; Gersten et al., 2007; Vaughn, Cirino, et al., 2006; Vaughn, Linan-Thompson, et al., 2006). Small groups of three to six students provide an opportunity for educators to use explicit and in-depth language instruction across the five core reading elements (e.g., phonological awareness, phonics, reading fluency, vocabulary, and comprehension). A major feature of small-group reading interventions is that they include rich and explicit language scaffolding, exposure, and opportunities for student expansions (Vaughn, Cirino, et al., 2006). Indeed, it is particularly important with ELs to provide a wealth of language models and opportunities for expanding on their own language expression.

Several high-quality randomized control trials (August & Siegel, 2006; Gersten et al., 2007) have identified four overarching principles that characterize small-group interventions that are effective with ELs:

1. Multiple opportunities for students to respond to questions.
2. Multiple opportunities for student practice reading both words and sentences.
3. Clear feedback from teacher when student makes errors.
4. Explicit instruction in all areas of reading, including explicit comprehension, instruction, and explicit vocabulary instruction with sufficient coverage of five areas: phonological awareness, phonics, reading fluency, vocabulary, and comprehension.

Heterogeneous Ability Groupings

A different approach to grouping beyond homogeneous student configurations is dividing students into heterogeneous pairs. Peer-assisted learning for students who exhibit different levels of English proficiency and academic skill can be a useful activity for improving ELs' reading comprehension (Saenz, Fuchs, & Fuchs, 2005). In pairs students can review materials presented by the teacher, providing more opportunities to expand on ideas more in-depth in a low-risk situation (e.g., with a peer, not the whole class) in a social context. While occuring in pairs, it is important that these activities be scaffolded by the teacher, explicitly instructing students in how to organize their discussion. In a meta-analysis conducted by Gersten and his colleagues (2007) the median amount of time dedicated to peer-assisted learning strategies was 90 minutes a week. An example of a program that pairs students of different strengths and weaknesses, including both ELs and monolinguals, is the Peer-Assisted Learning Strategies (PALS) program (Fuchs et al., 2001; Fuchs, Fuchs, Mathes, & Simmons, 1997). This program uses peer-mediated instruction, which involves having the students work in pairs or small groups to provide tutoring to one another in three reading strategies: retelling (i.e., sequencing information), paragraph shrinking (i.e., generating main idea statements), and prediction relay (i.e., generating and evaluating predictions). In addition to being trained in each of the reading strategies, students are taught to correct their partner's reading errors, award points for correct responses, and provide consistent encouragement and feedback. PAL tutoring sessions usually last approximately 35 minutes and are conducted three to four times a week.

High-Quality Vocabulary Instruction

Evidence-based vocabulary instruction is important for all learners, monolingual and ELs alike. However, an explicit evidence-based approach to vocabulary instruction for ELs is vital, as English proficiency is the largest predictor of academic success for ELs (Suarez-Orozco, Suarez-Orozco, & Todorova, 2008). Indeed, providing these students with in-depth discussion of content vocabulary using various supports including pictures, manipulatives, and/or hands-on activities has been shown to be particularly effective, providing multi-model cues for learning (August & Shanahan, 2006). While curriculum vocabulary is sufficient for monolingual students, ELs may need additional support beyond prescribed curricular vocabulary, including explicit instruction for common words and expressions that are unfamiliar to ELs. Previewing vocabulary before the lesson (e.g., reviewing content words before the lesson and providing a list of these words and their definitions) and using semantic maps to help students make connections between words or drawing on their existing knowledge can be particularly useful for content vocabulary development and make activities more authentic. For example, discussing the word *prejudice* as it relates to the civil rights movement is made easier when students can draw from their own understandings of discrimination and being judged, connecting their existing knowledge base to curricular content and new vocabulary.

Academic Language and the Use of Supplementary Materials

It is important when instructing ELs to distinguish between their knowledge of basic interpersonal communication skills (BICS—the language of the playground) and their cognitive academic language proficiency (CALP—academic language; Cummins, 1984, 2000). BICS is language that is conversational and social in nature. Thus, it is language that is highly contextualized. Students can use nonverbal and verbal clues to understand the meaning of their interlocutor's oral communication through gesture, facial expressions, intonation, and other contextual features of the conversation (Cummins, 1984). The amount and type of contextual clues may vary with BICS. For example, when a student is talking one-on-one with a teacher, the student can see the teacher's movements and gestures toward objects, which is easier to understand than a less contextualized interchange such as a telephone call. In this case, the student can rely only on voice cues and prior knowledge of the conversation's topic or purpose to understand the interlocutor's meaning. By contrast, CALP is largely decontextualized, that is, nonverbal cues are predominantly absent, and the language used is more abstract and dense with regard to both concepts and amount of adjectives and nouns (Nagy & Townsend, 2012). Scholastic text would be an example of CALP. CALP may also vary in its level of decontextualized information. An academic text would be more decontextualized than a science experiment in which a teacher can demonstrate what to pour through gestures. Nonetheless, one of the significant features of CALP is that the message is more decontextualized and abstract than for BICS interchanges. Given these differences it is only logical that BICS is usually learned first, followed by CALP (Cummins, 1984).

To demonstrate the divergent language features of BICS and CALP we describe the case of Katie, a second grader who moved to the United States from Mexico when she was 2 years old. Katie's parents speak Spanish at home, but her older brother, Julio, is also learning English in school. Katie is almost fully proficient in using BICS. For example, one Monday morning Katie is able to communicate to her teacher that she has encountered a spider in the classroom. Katie might report the spider to her teacher by saying, "That spider was scary. Yuck, it really got me scared. And, I am afraid it might still be in the classroom!" Katie has successfully communicated the problem, but her language to do so is repetitive (i.e., "afraid," "scary"), uses informal language (i.e., "Yuck!"), and assumes a level of contextual knowledge (i.e., that the spider is no longer visible but was seen moments before). These are all characteristics of normal social speech. In contrast to Katie's BICS used to communicate her seeing a spider in the classroom, her teacher's language to discuss their unit on spiders is very different and uses CALP. For example, Katie's teacher Ms. Evans might explain, "The brown widow is suspected to have originally come from Africa. However, it was first described in South America, but we aren't sure where it originated. The web of these tropical creatures is not very orderly." Ms. Evans's use of CALP demonstrates how academic language includes more varied word choices (i.e., *black widow*, and *tropical creatures*), is decontextualized in that it does not depend on context clues (i.e., discusses an object that is not present), uses more complex transitions (i.e., *however* and *but*) and more sophisticated vocabulary (i.e., *originated*). Whereas Katie may be able to understand the social language exchanged with her peers and in face-to-face social conversations with teachers or specialists, she may still struggle with the more complex language demands of CALP.

Each of these levels of language mastery needs to be explicitly taught in school, as both forms are often decontextualized in that the social or physical context may not provide sufficient information for the student to understand adequately (Snow, 1994). However, BICS can often be learned on the playground or in other social contexts (e.g., with Katie's brother) whereas ELs may have fewer opportunities to be exposed to CALP beyond school contexts. Repeated, modeled, and intensive exposure to language is crucial for ELs' language development. Thus, daily academic English instruction (i.e., CALP) in the core curriculum is central to developing their academic skills. A recent meta-analysis demonstrated that a block a day of academic English instruction was particularly beneficial to the language and literacy development of ELs (Gersten et al., 2007).

Many of the recommendations and practices described are also important for English-only students, and benefit these students in the same way. A multi-tiered framework lends itself to modifications and adjustments, which in many cases may still be warranted for these learners; quality research-based pedagogy is always important, but the distinct characteristics of this group still require additional differentiated instruction and supports that may not be necessary for the typically developing child for whom English is the native language. Some examples of minor adjustments that may be particularly relevant for ELs include focusing on sounds not found in the first language when teaching auditory discrimination skills; providing students with home-language synonyms or cognates (words that resemble each other in form and meaning—e.g., *anxiedad* in Spanish and *anxiety* in English) when teaching English vocabulary words; and integrating explicit and deliberate English language development, such as highlighting sentence connectives (e.g., *however, therefore, as a result*) and anaphoric references with reading objectives. Another example, mentioned previously, is explicitly teaching common words not included in the core reading program. Differentiated instruction on these commons words might include giving students a list of words to have handy during the lesson and previewing these words before the lessons so students can reference the list during the core reading program time with existing knowledge about the words (Fisher, Frey, & Rothenberg, 2011).

Another useful strategy for instructing ELs is the use of sentence frames that can be used in Tier 1 and Tier 2 instruction, with varying levels of support and scaffolding across these two interventions. For example, a frame in social studies might be "These are dissimilar/similar because _____" to help support ELs' familiarity with English syntax and grammar rules that may interfere with their understanding the content being presented. It also provides a scaffolded opportunity for them to demonstrate what they know without cognitively taxing language barriers (Echevarria & Vogt, 2011). Furthermore, the language trajectory of these students is less well documented, meaning that progress monitoring of this group of learners should be more frequent than their monolingual counterparts. Even in Tier 1 instruction these students should be assessed more than three times a year (Collier, 2010).

HOW TO APPROPRIATELY ASSESS ENGLISH LEARNERS

Assessment is a crucial aspect of a multi-tiered framework; however, understanding if assessments are reliable and valid for ELs is an area of concern for many educators. When trying to determine which assessment to use and how to understand their implications for instruction we encourage you to be cautious in the conclusions that can be drawn from commonly used assessments.

Many commonly used English language assessments focus on expressive language skills (expressive vocabulary, oral language fluency, etc). ELs tend to have stronger receptive skills than expressive language-based skills and so these assessments may underestimate the knowledge base of these students. For example, ELs may need more extended time; the added cognitive load of translating from their native language to English may be particularly laborious (August & Hakuta, 1997; Abedi, 2004). These assessments should not be used to make inferences about students' knowledge base more generally as the higher analytic skill of these students will not necessarily be as evident due to the linguistic constraints of the task. English assessments that involve higher-level analytic skills should only be administered if the student has a basic knowledge of English vocabulary. Without a basic knowledge of English vocabulary these students will not be able to showcase their application of background knowledge, inference skills, and comprehension strategies, skills that cannot be enacted if they do not have a sufficient grasp of the language of assessment (Martiniello, 2008).

However, oral language assessments can inform areas in which students may need further instructional support, for example, if they lack background knowledge or academic vocabulary. Assessments exploring multifaceted reading abilities like reading comprehension may assume a level of background knowledge necessary to comprehend the text. For example, an EL may not easily understand a story about "counting sheep" if he or she is unfamiliar with the American middle-class bedtime ritual. These kinds of cultural biases embedded in common assessments pose a challenge for teachers who do not use these assessments to inform instruction but instead use them as benchmarks for student abilities. It is important when analyzing data from these assessments to acknowledge that many commonly used assessments were designed and administered to English-only samples and so the interpretation of standard scores or percentile ranks may not reflect the language and literacy development of second-language learners (Abedi, 2004). Thus, instructors should be cautious about the results of these measures.

One recommendation for avoiding the underestimation of students' language and literacy abilities is to assess students in their native language, if possible, particularly in cases where the student has attended native-language schooling and potentially developed literacy skills in his or her first language. Strong predictors of reading include phonological processing and rapid basic reading; exploring these measures in both languages can be particularly useful as phonemes may differ across languages (this is further reviewed in Chapter 5). The Test of Phonological Processing Spanish (TOPPS; August et al., 2001) and the Auditory Analysis Test (AAT; Quiroga, Lemos-Britton, Mostafapour, Abbott, & Berninger, 2002) were developed to better understand a student's ability to manipulate different phonemes in his or her native language. Understanding whether student phonological errors are a function of a deficit or a lack of familiarity/exposure to English phonemes is useful for subsequent instructional decisions about which skills need to be practiced.

Another potential native-language assessment is the Woodcock–Muñoz Language Survey (Woodcock & Muñoz-Sandoval, 1993, 2001), which not only provides information on students' language proficiency in both Spanish and English but in addition was based in part on work conducted on BICS and CALPS. Unlike the majority of informal assessments used in classrooms that tend to assess BICS, the Woodcock–Muñoz Language Survey specifically assesses students' CALP development in both languages (Rhodes, Ochoa, & Ortiz, 2005). The Picture Vocabulary and Verbal Analogies subscales assess verbal CALP and the Letter–Word Identification and Dictation subscales asses CALP reading and writing skills. This assessment provides an opportunity to assess these skills in the native and non-native language for students whose first language is Spanish.

However, native-language assessments are not without challenges of their own. On the one hand students' vocabulary may be distinct in their two languages, making solely a native-language assessment once again an underestimation of their abilities. Furthermore, when vocabulary assessments are translated from English to a child's native language, word frequency may differ across languages. In other words, many vocabulary tests are designed to tap frequently used vocabulary words, but synonyms for most frequently used words in English may not reflect, for example, the most frequently used words in Spanish. In such a case the native-language test would not accurately assess a student's knowledge base since it is likely testing rare words. Just as measures with English-only samples have validity problems with this population, native language assessments may be similarly normed on other native-language populations. For example, an expressive vocabulary assessment for Spanish-speaking students in Spain or Spanish-speaking students in Cuba may not be appropriate for Spanish-speaking students in the United States.

Another means of disaggregating potential language difficulties from language difference beyond testing students in their native language is to compare student performance on listening comprehension measures and reading comprehension measures. Examining, for example, students' scores on the Woodcock Language Proficiency Battery (Woodcock, 1990) in these two subtests or on the Wechsler Individual Achievement Test–III (WIAT-III; Wechsler, 2009) will help educators identify whether these students are struggling solely with decoding problems or if language is the bigger problem. In some cases, students may be having difficulty understanding the vocabulary of the text and thus be unable to understand the ideas and content of a reading passage (Geva, 2000; Lesaux & Geva, 2006).

DETERMINING AREAS FOR GROWTH

It is essential that assessments be used for the purpose of better understanding students' strengths and weaknesses, and that these tests should reflect knowledge of language and literacy benchmarks for ELs. A prerequisite to implementing evidence-based practices for English-only students as well as ELs is the use of formative assessments for understanding students' language and literacy strengths and weaknesses. Particularly relevant for ELs in the early grades are formative assessments of students' phonological awareness, alphabet knowledge, and basic phonics rules, which can shed light on the kinds of instruction that will support these learners—areas that predict later reading performance (Baker & Good, 1995; Lesaux & Siegel, 2003; Wiley & Deno, 2005).

These early screening measures are an important means of informing instruction, but they do not indicate which students will respond to instruction and which students will struggle with reading. These assessments can help provide next steps for targeting areas for explicit instruction. Indeed, many measures of syntax, listening comprehension, and oral vocabulary fail to predict who will learn to read and who will not (Bialystok & Herman, 1999; Geva, Yaghoub-Zadeh, & Schuster, 2000; Limbos & Geva, 2001). Yet, although these oral measures can be used to identify areas of needed instruction, they do not necessarily indicate disability or predict long-term difficulty. Educators should continue to monitor the progress of these students multiple times a year throughout the early years to better understand how students are responding to explicit instruction in areas of weakness.

Useful screening and progress monitoring tools that target ELs specifically were created by World-Class Instructional Design and Assessment (WIDA, 2011; *www.wida.us/index.aspx*). WIDA, a consortium of 27 states in the United States, designed a set of PreK through 12th-grade language proficiency standards that address English language and content-area achievement and concordant assessments that match these proficiency standards. Screening assessments like the WIDA-ACCESS Placement Test (W-APT) are used to ascertain the proficiency of incoming students likely to be designated as ELs. This assessment provides educators with useful information for identification and placement decisions, placing students on a language development continuum (entering, beginning, developing, expanding, bridging, and finally reaching) across language domains (listening, speaking, reading, and writing) based on WIDA's English language proficiency standards. Additionally, Assessing Comprehension and Communication in English State-to-State (ACCESS) for English Language Learners is another assessment created by WIDA that addresses academic English language proficiency standards across the five content domains (Social and Instructional Language, English Language Arts, Math, Science, and Social Studies) in four language domains (listening, speaking, reading, and writing), which can help provide information regarding appropriate language supports needed and student progress. We highlight WIDA tools because they are EL-specific and focus on the dual challenge for ELs of learning language and content simultaneously and the strong focus on academic language—the language of school being an important indicator of EL proficiency necessary for school success. Academic language is reviewed in more detail in Chapter 7, but it is important to mention here, as the decontextualized language characteristic of text is especially challenging for ELs to understand. Furthermore, the distinction between conversational and academic English is crucial for accurate assessment of these students (Cummins, 1984, 1991), which will also be addressed in Chapter 7.

CONCLUSIONS

In this chapter we have addressed the specific challenges facing ELs and the general instructional practices and techniques that are especially useful for this population of learners. We elaborate on quality instruction for these learners because misconceptions about second-language learning frequently held by educators may prevent them from delivering high-quality instruction for ELs. Commonly held (but erroneous) beliefs about appropriate "phases" of language development may harm students more than help them. For example, many teachers promote the use of simplified language as a means of supporting ELs' academic language development and allow ELs a "silent period" that is believed to be a natural phase in language learning. In reality, what these students really need is explicit instruction using academic language (Schleppegrell, 2004; Snow & Uccelli, 2009). High academic language standards and expectations are essential to the academic success of these students. Furthermore, the practices discussed regarding the use of small student groupings (both homogeneous and heterogeneous ability groups) emphasize the importance of active and frequent teacher-scaffolded language production (Anthony, 2008; Swain, 2005). This is in contrast to the idea that a "silent period" is necessary before true proficiency will develop. Instead, language learners should be encouraged to speak and speak often across the proficiency continuum. Last, while research abounds on the time necessary for students to acquire language, the length of time is contingent upon the kinds of instructional supports provided and the amount of explicit instruction received. Regular use of the research-based practices described in this chapter will promote more rapid language acquisition and better content learning.

CHAPTER 5

Early Literacy

Early literacy skills are defined as those reading skills typically learned during the primary grades, and which form the building blocks of reading success. Generally, the foundational reading skills are defined as including *phonological awareness, phonics, vocabulary, fluency,* and *comprehension.* As discussed in this chapter, the primary grades offer a critical period for skill acquisition and fluency building across all of these foundations, with mastery expected in areas of *phonological awareness* and *phonics* specifically. Although it is important to acknowledge that all of these foundational skills influence and reinforce one another to support skilled reading, this chapter is primarily focused on assessment and instruction relevant to code-based skills (i.e., phonemic awareness, letter–sound correspondences) given the importance of these skills as necessary prerequisites to fluent reading. In addition, although there is overlap both within and across chapters, separate chapters have been specifically dedicated to coverage of skills related to meaning making (i.e., vocabulary and comprehension).

A substantial literature base has emphasized the importance of establishing early literacy skills in order to become a successful fluent reader (see Adams, 1990; NRP, 2000), and the lack of these skills distinguishing poor from good readers. Failure to obtain early literacy skills can create a domino effect that decreases the likelihood of achieving grade-level reading skill. In addition, deficits in early literacy skills persist, meaning that they can be found in older children and adults who are poor readers (Fletcher, Lyon, Fuchs, & Barnes, 2007; Pratt & Brady, 1988). As a result of increased knowledge about both the importance of and characteristics of quality instruction related to early literacy skill acquisition, information and related materials have proliferated in the literature. In this chapter, we bring a synthesis of that information in a concise yet comprehensive format that addresses issues relevant to both content (*what to teach*) and delivery (*how to teach*) for all students.

Throughout this book, we emphasize the relevance of a multi-tiered approach to instruction to support students with diverse language and literacy needs. A critical aspect of this instructional framework is quality of core instruction in these early literacy skills in the classroom. To determine which students are failing to meet adequate progress, the core instructional context must also include effective instruction, prevention, and intervention. Subsequent tiers are intended to provide more intensive support to students who are struggling to meet curricular benchmarks, not to compensate for instructional deficiencies at the level of the whole classroom (Tier 1). Tier 1 instruction provides students with explicit instruction that is adequately differentiated for learners with diverse needs, and includes early intervention practices. If effective, it can minimize or reduce the number of students requiring Tier 2 supports (*www.rti4success.org*). For reading, the primary grades (K–2) form a critical period for prevention and early intervention efforts. Core classroom instruction should include quality instruction on foundational reading skills, coupled with careful monitoring regarding the progress of each student toward expected benchmarks. Further, subsequent decision making based on these formative assessments should lead to implementation of additional supports for those not meeting appropriate benchmarks. In this chapter, we explore early literacy skills and provide information on research-based practices and assessments that target early literacy skills as well as provide guidelines for how to intensify instruction for students who need additional supports.

WHAT IS EARLY LITERACY?

Definition

One of the first tasks to understanding the selection and monitoring of early literacy interventions is to define the term. *Early literacy* typically refers to the set of "basic" skills that are foundational to fluent reading. Researchers have examined skills such as letter knowledge; phonological awareness; concepts of print; and naming of letters, colors, and objects to determine acquisition rates and prediction of later achievement (e.g., Blachman, 1994; Daly, Wright, Kelly, & Martens, 1997; Walsh, Price, & Gillingham, 1988). Early literacy, however, should not be confused with *emergent literacy*, which refers to a broader concept of literacy that begins before formal instruction and leads to awareness and knowledge of print that includes attitudes, skills, and knowledge sets that are precursors of reading and writing (Gunn, Simmons, & Kame'enui, 1995). Definitions and examples of the skills and knowledge associated with emergent literacy can be found in Table 5.1.

As mentioned earlier, foundational reading skills include code-based skills as well as meaning-making skills; both contribute to successful reading comprehension. All of these skills support reading but receive different instructional emphases across the grades. In Figure 5.1 we list foundational reading skills that are necessary for a "healthy diet" of literacy across the grades, and also highlight when certain skills should receive greater emphasis based on curricular benchmarks.

TABLE 5.1. Skills and Knowledge Associated with Emergent Literacy

Area	Definition	Examples
Awareness of print	Knowledge of the conventions, purposes, and uses of print	Print, not pictures, tell the story or provide a message Writing creates a story
Relationship of print to speech	Understanding the physical, situational, and structural differences between oral and written language	Distinguishing oral conversation from a "real" news item Oral language expresses and explores, whereas written prompts comparison and analysis Speech is more informal than writing
Comprehension of text structures	Knowledge about grammar and organization of stories	Recognizing opening and closing phrases such as "once upon a time"
Phonological awareness	Sensitivity to the sounds in oral language	Early skills include rhyming, alliteration, and sentence segmentation
Letter knowledge	Knowledge of the alphabet and related sounds	Exposure to and "games" with alphabet books, blocks, shapes

Note. Based on Gunn, Simmons, and Kame'enui (1995; adapted from VanKleeck, 1990).

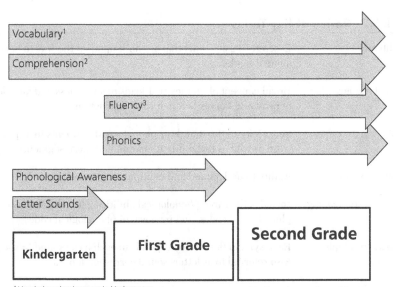

¹ Vocabulary development in kindergarten
² Listening comprehension in kindergarten
³ Fluency with high-frequency words transitions to fluency with connected text by second half of first grade

FIGURE 5.1. Foundational reading components across the primary grades. Based on Gersten et al. (2008).

This chapter focuses primarily on the skills of phonological awareness, letter sounds, and phonics. A brief description of each skill covered in this chapter appears in Table 5.2. These skills are more discrete in that they require a finite amount of knowledge to achieve mastery (e.g., there are only 26 letters in the alphabet and more than 40 phonemes). This is in contrast, for example, to vocabulary for which the number of words one can learn is not a discrete number, and may be learned over the course of a lifetime. The skill set necessary for comprehending text is also expansive. For example, a strong reader may extract and construct meaning from a newly out fiction book with ease, but when forced to read the *Wall Street Journal*, even this highly skilled reader may struggle with the new jargon and different genre features of such a text. These two less discrete skills are addressed in subsequent chapters. Here, we discuss the skills that are necessary for recognizing the words on the page, before addressing how we make meaning of what a text says.

These discrete early literacy skills are those that children are expected to master during the first few years of formal schooling. Providing explicit instruction in phonological awareness, letter sounds, and phonics has produced impressive results across multiple dimensions (e.g., grades, ages, classrooms; NRP, 2000). These skills can be defined in observable and measurable terms, are responsive to instruction, and, as noted earlier, serve as the foundation for later reading skills, making them common targets for assessment and instruction. A review of our current understanding of these critical early literacy skills that are the focus of this chapter—*phonological awareness, letter sounds,* and *phonics*—is presented next.

TABLE 5.2. Review of Key Terms

Early literacy	Discrete "basic" skills that are built upon on the way to becoming a fluent reader
Emergent literacy	Broad concept of literacy that leads to awareness and knowledge of print and begins before formal instruction
Phonological awareness	Sensitivity to the sounds or phonological segments in a spoken word as well as the ability to manipulate those segments
Phonemic awareness	Ability to understand and manipulate phonemes
Phonological processing	Includes the three phonological abilities: phonological awareness, phonological codes, and retrieval of phonological codes
Alphabetic principle	Each symbol (letter) corresponds to each basic sound in speech. Also referred to as letter–sound correspondences
Letter-naming fluency	Accurate and rapid naming of letters
Fluency	Decoding text with automaticity
Vocabulary	Knowing the meaning of words
Comprehension	Ability to extract and construct meaning from text

Phonological Awareness and Phonemic Awareness

What Are They?

Phonological awareness refers to a sensitivity to the sounds or phonological segments in a spoken word as well as the ability to manipulate those segments. It is important to remember that phonological awareness is a form of sensitivity to oral language that manifests itself in the absence of written language. It encompasses a broad range of skills that can be hierarchically arranged by difficulty and includes sound manipulations at the word, syllable, and phoneme level. For example, beginning phonological awareness may include skill with rhyming or identifying similar word beginnings or endings. Later phonological awareness requires greater, or more explicit, manipulation of sounds. This is when the term *phonemic*, rather than *phonological awareness*, is applicable, because phonemic awareness is an understanding and direct manipulation of individual sounds. These sounds are called *phonemes*. Phonemes represent the smallest distinctive units in the sound system of a language and vary across different languages. Examples of phonemic awareness include segmenting (breaking a word into each sound), blending (putting sounds together to form a word), and deleting sounds, which are skills requiring a higher level of *phonological awareness*. Often, the term *phonological awareness* is used interchangeably with phonemic awareness, however, these terms are different, with phonemic awareness being a specific form of phonological awareness, that is, phonemic awareness is a particular type of understanding of sound units that is focused explicitly on phonemes. Figure 5.2 provides examples of different phonological awareness activities at different levels, the word and syllable level as well as the phoneme level (i.e., skills that require phonemic awareness).

Word Level	Syllable Level	Phoneme Level
• Sound and word discrimination • Example: Which word does not belong with the others? *cat, mat, bat,* **fan** • Rhyming • Example: What words can rhyme with *mat*? (*bat, sat, fat, hat*)	• Syllable splitting • Example: *napkin* has two syllables—*nap* and *kin*	• Blending • Example: I'm going to say some sounds and you guess the word. • Segmenting • Example: Tell me the sounds you hear in the word *man*. • Deletion • Example: Tell me what *pat* sounds like without the /p/. • Substitution • Example: Say *top* but change the /t/ to a /p/ sound.

FIGURE 5.2. Core instruction in phonemic awareness: Example activities across target unit.

An example of skill progression in phonological awareness is presented in Table 5.3. It is important to add a brief note that phonological awareness is only one of the skills within a framework of *phonological processing* abilities. Phonological processing includes at least three areas: phonological awareness, phonological coding, and retrieval of phonological codes (Torgesen, Wagner, & Rashotte, 1994; see Figure 5.3). *Phonological coding* refers to the ability to hold phonological information in working memory; it is often assessed with memory span tasks (i.e., repeating nonmeaningful sequences of verbal items). *Retrieval of phonological codes*, or rate of access to phonological information, is typically measured by rapid naming tasks (letters, digits, colors, objects). Several studies suggest the unique contribution of all of these phonological processing abilities to aspects of later reading (Fletcher et al., 2007; Wagner & Torgeson, 1987).

Although it has been suggested that all of the phonological processing skills may be important in explaining differences in responsiveness to intervention, the degree to which each ability is amenable to change is uncertain. Some phonological processing abilities may be fairly stable core cognitive processes; however, we do know that automaticity of phonological awareness is a pivotal correlate to basic reading and beyond (Fletcher et al., 2007; Lyon, 1995). Phonological awareness is one of the best predictors of reading difficulty in kindergarten and first grade, and it can be taught. As Blachman (1994) pointed out, simply because some students respond more to instructional efforts does not negate the need for intervention; rather, it implies that different levels or types of intervention may be needed for different students. Thus, although more intensive intervention may be required, research

TABLE 5.3. Hierarchy of Phonological Awareness Skills: Possible Activities and Examples

Rhyme	Providing	"Tell me another word that rhymes with *bat*."
	Categorizing	"Which word does not rhyme with *bat—cat, big,* or *sat*?"
	Judging	"Do *bat* and *cat* rhyme?"
Alliteration	Providing	"What is the first sound in *bat*?"
	Categorizing	"Which word has the same first sound as *bat—big, sat,* or *pet*?"
	Judging	"Do *bat* and *big* have the same first sound?"
Blending	One or two sounds	"What word does /p/-/at/ make?"
	Entire word	"What word does /p/-/a/-/t/ make?"
Segmentation	Count	"How many sounds do you hear in the word *sit*?"
	Tap	"Tap your finger for each sound in the word *sit*."
	Name	"Tell me the sounds you hear in *sit*."
Manipulation	Deletion	"If you take away the /s/ in *sit*, what is left?"
	Substitution	"Change the /n/ sound in *net* to /b/. What is the new word?"
	Reversal	"Reverse the sounds in *net*. What is the new word?"

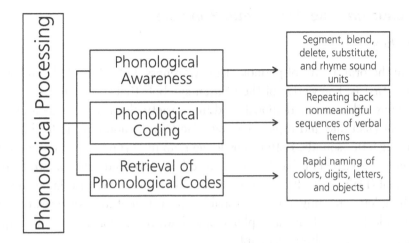

FIGURE 5.3. Components and examples of phonological processing. Based on *www.reading. uoregon.edu/big_ideas/pa/pa_sequence.php*.

studies have shown the efforts focused on intensive, explicit, and systematic delivery can be successful (Fletcher et al., 2007).

When Is Phonological Awareness Typically Acquired?

Rudimentary phonological awareness skills can be evident in preschool children as young as 2 or 3 years old. For example, studies have found that children as young as 3 years possess some awareness of rhymes (McLean, Bryant, & Bradley, 1987) and sentence or syllable segmentation (Fox & Routh, l975). More advanced phonemic awareness typically becomes evident during the first few years of formal school and is generally well established by second grade. A number of researchers have suggested that the greatest increases in phonological awareness occur between kindergarten and first grade, with mastery typically established by the end of first grade (Chafouleas, Lewandowski, Smith, & Blachman, 1997; Fox & Routh, 1975; Liberman, Shankweiler, Fischer, & Carter, 1974; Smith, Simmons, & Kame'enui, 1998).

Our general understanding of the relationship between phonological awareness and reading is that some beginning phonological awareness is needed to facilitate reading. Once reading begins to be established, a reciprocal relationship emerges: each promotes the other (Shaywitz, 2003; Smith et al., 1998). Given that reading success seems to hinge, in part, on having intact phonemic awareness, the early elementary years certainly present a sensitive period for instruction and skill acquisition. In fact, although phonological awareness can be developed in students after this period, "reading" time lost during that period is difficult to compensate for. Older students have to work harder to catch up, and missed reading time during those early years may make reading a more laborious task in the long run for them (Snow et al., 1998).

Letter Sounds and the Alphabetic Principle

What Are They?

In contrast to the oral nature of phonological awareness, letter knowledge refers to orthographic skill—that is, knowledge of the written symbols that represent the sounds in language. This knowledge can be demonstrated in a variety of ways, from accurate naming of letters to fluent (accurate and rapid) naming of letters. In addition, letter knowledge can refer to learning letter sounds. Letter knowledge is an important early literacy skill. Letter-naming fluency, in particular, has been found to be a good indicator or predictor of reading achievement (Daly et al., 1997; Kaminski & Good, 1996). We also know, however, that simply teaching letter naming alone is probably not sufficient to ensure reading success. A combination of letter knowledge and phonological awareness forms the core requirements of understanding the alphabetic principle.

When Is It Typically Acquired?

The acquisition of alphabet knowledge typically involves a gradual accumulation of letter knowledge from 3 to 7 years of age (Worden & Boettcher, 1990). In addition, research has suggested that the speed with which letters are named, not only the naming of them, is important (e.g., Blachman, 1994; Walsh et al., 1988). For example, findings have suggested that rapid naming of letters and words can differentiate good and poor readers, with weaker readers demonstrating slower naming speeds. This finding seems logical in that, when learning most skills, a student first works on performing accurately and then moves to performing both accurately and quickly.

Phonics

Phonics instruction is intended to foster and support students' understanding of the alphabetic principle. Phonics is the ability to match sounds with letters, that is, to match phonemes to graphemes (the written representation of a sound). Importantly, phonics should not be confused with phonemic awareness. The former deals with the correspondence between the sound and the written representation, and the latter addresses the hearing and manipulation of sounds separate from any written representation. Importantly, phonics would have little applicability without phonemic awareness, which helps students to understand that words are broken up into meaningful sound units. Knowledge of phonics helps students to understand predictive relationships between letters and sounds, and recognize familiar words. This sound–symbol relationship is a prerequisite skill that facilitates decoding of words (Juel, 1991). In Figure 5.4, we present a visual representation of the progression of skill difficulty in moving from letter–sound relationships to reading words. Special considerations must be made for ELs (see the box on page 63).

In this chapter, we have reviewed the concepts of phonological awareness and letter–sound relationships to provide the reader with an understanding of how these code-based skills can influence reading development. These skills are the foundation for being able to decode words and thus a prerequisite of fluent reading. Once students are able to decode words, meaning-making skills are central to helping students extract and construct meaning from text. In subsequent chapters, we address the central role of vocabulary and comprehension skills to reading comprehension and how these skills work together to support fluent and persistent reading in the face of challenging curricular texts. However, we want to emphasize again that teaching vocabulary and comprehension skills in conjunction with these code-based skills is central to engaging emerging readers, supporting successful reading, and helping students understand that the goal of reading is understanding the text.

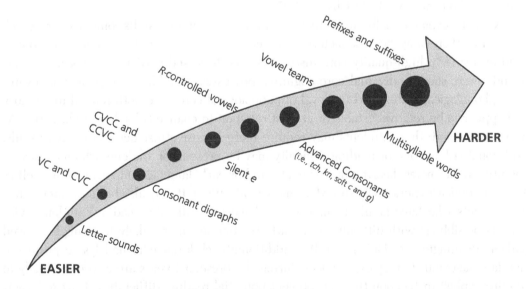

FIGURE 5.4. A continuum of difficulty for teaching letter sounds and simple regular words. Based on *www.reading.uoregon.edu/big_ideas/pa/pa_sequence.php*.

WHY IS IT DIFFICULT FOR SOME STUDENTS TO ESTABLISH PROFICIENT EARLY LITERACY SKILLS?

There are two primary reasons why students struggle to obtain early literacy skills: (1) lack of adequate exposure to quality instruction, and (2) individual risk factors that suggest the need for more intensive early literacy instruction.

First, students may have difficulty obtaining early literacy skills because they have not had exposure to enough instruction and/or appropriate core instruction that is explicit and systematic. Early literacy skills, particularly phonemic awareness, can be difficult to achieve without explicit, systematic instruction. Even for a typically achieving child, it is challenging to think of words as individual sounds. The phoneme is an abstract unit of speech. In addition, phonemes are coarticulated—that is, they sound like one unit—making it even more difficult to differentiate discrete sounds. In fact, there are 44 different phonemes within the English language. The lack of a one-to-one correspondence between the letters that appear on a page and the sounds they make when articulated as phonemes creates ambiguities for the learner. For example, *shirt*, a five-letter word, has only four phonemes because the /sh/ is one phoneme (i.e., sound). Similarly, *cow*, a three-letter word, has only two phonemes due to the /ow/ combination. Furthermore, difficulty in understanding phonemes can vary by the type and number of sounds (Chafouleas, VanAuken, & Dunham, 2001; McBride-Chang, 1995) and even the type of task, as discussed earlier. For example, it has generally been found that sounds that can be held (i.e., *continuant* sounds, such as /s/) are easier to grasp than sounds that cannot (i.e., *stop* sounds, such as /t/). In addition, the fewer the sounds, the better. Generally two- or three-phoneme words are easier to grasp than four-phoneme words, and memory difficulties can arise with words containing more than four phonemes (McBride-Chang, 1995).

A second explanation for difficulty in obtaining early literacy skills comes from research suggesting there may be risk factors that necessitate differential instruction beyond a solid exposure to high-quality core instruction. As discussed earlier, one risk factor may include more stable individual core cognitive processes. In addition to phonemic awareness, phonological coding and retrieval of phonological codes are both related to memory and appear to be relatively stable or at least resistant to change (Fletcher et al., 2007). As previously noted, these students may require more intensive instruction to master skills. Additional risk factors for reading difficulty may be present for students who have severe cognitive deficiencies, hearing impairments, and/or early language impairment, as well as attention-deficit/hyperactivity disorder (Snow et al., 1998). It may also be important to target students who have family members who have had difficulty reading. Students with parents or siblings with difficulty with early reading are more likely to struggle as well (Gilger, Pennington, & DeFries, 1991). Additionally, children who had less exposure to rich language and literacy experiences during the preschool years are also more likely to require explicit instruction that can prevent potential reading difficulties (Hart & Risley, 1995). In sum, diagnostic assessments to identify directions for intervention targets and intensity of services can be more fully informed through full consideration of the child and his or her context.

RECOMMENDATIONS FOR EARLY LITERACY INSTRUCTION IN A MULTI-TIERED FRAMEWORK

It is important to think about quality early literacy as involving two central instructional components: appropriate *content* (what to teach) and *delivery* (how to teach). Within a multi-tiered framework, these instructional components are interrelated and may influence each other. For example, the amount of time spent on a skill set may reflect the number of target skill areas that are needed to support a given child or a group of children. When planning instruction, it helps to consider the components as distinct and to make sure evidence-based guidelines are followed for both. We begin by discussing the *content* of core early literacy interventions based on the early literacy components we have just reviewed.

Key Features of Good Content Instruction (What to Teach) in Early Literacy

Quality literacy instruction should include *multiple literacy skills*, not just focus on one skill. Early literacy training studies have repeatedly suggested that high-quality instruction that integrates core early literacy skills by targeting varied areas of early literacy instruction (e.g., letter–sound, phonological awareness) as well as multiple skills within the different components of early reading (e.g., word, syllable, and phonemic levels) produce the largest, most enduring effects. For example, a 7-week intervention implemented by Ball and Blachman (1991) found that a group receiving instruction only in letter–sound correspondences made fewer gains in areas of early reading, spelling, and segmentation than a group that received a combination of phoneme segmentation and letter–sound correspondence training.

Perhaps the most essential characteristic of good early literacy intervention is that it includes an *explicit approach* to instruction, in which sounds of letters are taught in isolation and then blended to form words. The initial focus is on mastering a few letter–sound correspondences so that words can then be read by putting those sounds together. In contrast, an *implicit approach* focuses on identification of letter sounds within the context of the whole word (Stein, Johnson, & Gutlohn, 1999). Using an implicit approach, context and picture cues are often used to read an unfamiliar word. For example, a teacher provides a clue to the word *bat* by showing students a picture of a bat. In contrast, an explicit approach to code-based skills might have students first practice saying the sound /b/, /a/, and then have students practice the sound /t/. The teacher would review words that start with /a/, like *apple*, and words that start with /b/ and /t/, like *bad, baby, ten*, and *take*, respectively. Finally, students would be asked to say aloud the sounds for /b/, /a/, and /t/ and be asked to blend /b/, /a/, and /t/ for the word *bat*. In addition to an explicit approach to instruction, a number of other characteristics are associated with good early literacy instruction. A list of these characteristics is presented in Table 5.4, which is based on work compiled by Stahl, Duffy-Hester, and Stahl (1998). Although all are important, specific attention should be paid to the idea that instruction should be interesting and stimulating. As stated earlier, explicit instruction for short periods may be all that is needed for most students, with the specific activities tailored to their needs.

TABLE 5.4. Principles of Good Early Literacy Instruction

Good early literacy instruction in code-based skills should . . .
 Develop the alphabetic principle.
 Develop phonological awareness.
 Provide a thorough grounding in the letters.
 Not be boring.
 Provide sufficient practice in reading words.
 Lead to automatic word recognition.

Note. Based on Stahl, Duffy-Hester, and Stahl (1998).

Early literacy can be developed most beneficially through *early, systematic, and direct teacher instruction* in the specific skills of phonological awareness and letter knowledge. This instruction should be focused at a level that allows for high rates of successful student performance. To maximize success, the requirements of a task can be structured in various ways to match the student's skill level. Some options for modifying phonological awareness tasks are highlighted in Table 5.5. For example, a segmentation task could involve segmenting part of a word (easier) or segmenting the entire word (harder). In terms of teaching letter knowledge, the overall goal is to develop automatic recognition. Both Adams (1990) and Stahl et al. (1998) recommend teaching names and sounds because (1) acquisition of letter names is a good predictor of further skills, and (2) knowing names and sounds helps children talk about letters. Thus, it is important to recognize that the level of complexity varies both across and within early literacy tasks. Although the ultimate goal is to give students the ability to produce responses at the phonemic level, initial instruction may focus on phoneme identification prior to teaching phoneme production.

TABLE 5.5. General Considerations When Teaching Phonological Awareness

	Easier example	Harder example
Complexity varies within activities.	Does *sat* rhyme with *cat*?	What rhymes with *sat*?
Awareness at the syllable level is easier than the phonemic level.	/s/ -at	/s/-/a/-/t/
Continuant phonemes are easier than noncontinuant.	/s/- /a/-/t/ ⟶	/p/-/a/-/t/ →
Initial consonants are easier than final consonants.	sat-/s/	sat-/t/
Manipulatives (disks) can be helpful when demonstrating phonemes.	Show me the sounds in *sat* by moving one disk while you say each sound.	Say each sound in *sat*.
Fewer phonemes are easier than more.	*sat*—three phonemes /s/-/a/-/t/	*Saturn*—five phonemes /s/-/a/-/t/-/ur/-/n/

Note. Based on Catts (1995).

An example of an intervention protocol (adapted from a study by Daly, Chafouleas, Persampieri, Bonfiglio, & Lafleur, 2004) for building accuracy with blending and segmentation skills, is presented in Figure 5.5. This protocol can be modified to address fluency building and/or motivation by including, for example, a reward component for correctly read words, or through timing and tracking speed of item completion as a part of an assessment that could be done either at the beginning or end of the instructional session. We would emphasize that it is not essential to use a prepackaged program in adhering to the tenets of an explicit, systematic, and direct approach to early literacy instruction. Utilization of the general principles of good early literacy instruction, such as those presented in the chapter, coupled with good assessment and decision making, form the basis for successful acquisition of early literacy skills. That said, we do acknowledge that prepackaged programs can be very efficient, and high-quality programs do exist. Although not intended to be exhaustive or to suggest endorsement of one over another, we provide some examples in Appendix 5.1 at the end of the chapter. In addition, we encourage readers to review the tools charts available on the websites offered through the National Center on Response to Intervention (*www.rti4success.org*) and the National Center on Intensive Intervention (*www.intensiveintervention.org*) for reviews of other possible options.

Knowing *what to teach* and *how to teach* it should be guided by decision rules drawn from knowledge of the curricular goals and objectives as well as an understanding of the literacy demands this will place on the students in a given classroom. We provide a form to help guide this decision-making process in Worksheet 5.1 at the end of the chapter. Asking a set of questions such as where student skills are currently, how they respond to a given lesson presentation, and whether a lesson is tackling the appropriate skills for a given student are central to responsive instruction. For example, you can teach kindergarten students to increase their basic phonemic awareness skills by having them blend phonemes (e.g., /sss/ /uuu/ /nnn/ is *sun*). You can refer to Worksheet 5.1 to think about whether you have targeted the appropriate objective. Worksheet 5.1 can help you determine whether students are proficient enough in identifying and discriminating phonemes to engage in this activity. After examining the appropriateness of this activity for your students you may find that this activity does not build on their existing knowledge. You might instead focus on clapping out syllables or lead a rhyming activity to extend students' phonological awareness skills before moving on to this more difficult task. Furthermore, given that your students may be at different places in their phonological awareness, using Worksheet 5.1 will help you identify how and in what form you should teach this skill to students.

Also relevant and useful for determining what to teach are the Common Core State Standards (CCSS). The CCSS are a set of standards for what students are expected to learn and are adopted at the state level, with 43 states presently adopting the CCSS (*www.corestandards.org*). These standards were constructed to support student success in college and later careers. Additionally, these standards were created to prepare students to work in a global economy, providing them with knowledge sets that are in line with their international peers. The standards specifically address mathematics and English language arts for K–12 students, and are also applicable for literacy in history/social studies, science, and technical subjects. These standards are relevant and useful for reading instruction because

Component	Corresponding CCSS
Phonemic awareness	RF-2, L-2
Phonics	RF-1, RF-3, L-2
Fluency	RF-4
Vocabulary	RL-4, RF-4, L-1–L-6
Reading comprehension	R-1–R-10, RF-4

they lay out reading skill expectations at each grade level, providing teachers with useful guidelines for establishing what students need to know as well as individual student goals. The CCSS content maps on to the foundational reading skills discussed in this chapter. In the box above, we provide some examples of CCSS that address these various foundational literacy skills. Although not intended to be exhaustive, we provide this list so readers can see how to apply the content of this chapter to the standards listed. We recommend becoming familiar with the standards to help guide class objectives and choose instructional resources. Interested readers should visit the CCSS website (*www.corestandards. org*) to read the language (L), reading foundational (RF), and reading literature (RL) standards that, among other standards, correspond with the target reading components in this chapter for each grade.

Key Features of Good Delivery of Instruction (How to Teach) in Early Literacy

Delivery of early literacy instruction in a multi-tiered framework requires a set of *successive decisions* about appropriate instruction based on student needs. We discuss screening and assessment procedures in more depth later, but a central aspect of a tiered approach and of appropriate delivery of instruction is providing responsive instruction with early screening of all students on these early literacy skills. These assessments can help the teacher better provide students with appropriate Tier 1 teaching using differentiated instruction.

As mentioned in the beginning of this chapter, a tiered framework depends on strong quality core instruction for all students (Tier 1) to prevent an excessive number of students falling below the appropriate benchmarks. Effective core instruction includes *differentiated instruction* for learners across the continuum of early literacy skills in the classroom. Screening data and formative assessments can better help teachers group students into small groups for instruction to target skills more specifically. For example, for students who are struggling with decoding words in a text, the teacher might group these students together

Materials Checklist:

Four flashcards of instructional words (choose words the student is unable to read, but which are decodable and whose letters have predictable and not unusual sounds).

Blank flashcard

Instructions for Administration:

1. Shuffle the instructional cards.
2. Say, "TODAY, WE ARE GOING TO LEARN HOW TO READ SOME WORDS AND THEN PRACTICE BREAKING THEM APART AND PUTTING THEM BACK TOGETHER. DO YOU HAVE ANY QUESTIONS?"
3. Present the **first flashcard**, covering the word with the blank flashcard. Say, "I WILL SHOW YOU SOUNDS IN THE WORD, TELL YOU THE SOUNDS, AND THEN HAVE YOU READ THE SOUNDS."
4. Expose the first phoneme by withdrawing the blank flashcard from it and say, "THE SOUND IS _____." Wait for a student response and say, "GOOD!" [If the student makes an error, say, "NO. THE SOUND IS _____. SAY THE SOUND. GOOD!"]. Repeat this step for all phonemes in the words, successively exposing each phoneme until the student can see the whole word.
5. Say, "LET'S SAY THE SOUNDS TOGETHER AS A WORD. SAY THEM TOGETHER REAL FAST. THE WORD IS _____."
6. Repeat steps 3, 4, and 5 for the **second flashcard**.
7. Repeat steps 3, 4, and 5 for the **third flashcard**.
8. Repeat steps 3, 4, and 5 for the **fourth flashcard**.
9. Shuffle the instructional cards.
10. Say, "NOW, I WANT YOU TO READ THE SOUNDS AND WORDS TO ME. IF YOU ARE NOT SURE OF A SOUND OR WORD, I WILL HELP YOU."
11. Present a flashcard to the student, exposing one phoneme at a time. If the student does not read a phoneme within **3** seconds, say the phoneme for the student and have the student repeat the sound (saying "REPEAT AFTER ME!" if the student does not repeat the sound spontaneously).
12. At the end of the word, say, "SAY THE SOUNDS TOGETHER AS A WORD. SAY THEM TOGETHER REAL FAST."
13. Repeat steps 11 and 12 for the **second flashcard**.
14. Repeat steps 11 and 12 for the **third flashcard**.
15. Repeat steps 11 and 12 for the **fourth flashcard**.
16. Shuffle the instructional cards.
17. Say, "LET'S PRACTICE ONE LAST TIME."
18. Repeat steps 11 and 12 once more for each word.
19. Shuffle the instructional cards and say, "NOW I WILL SHOW YOU THE CARDS AGAIN AND I WANT YOU TO READ THE WHOLE WORD TO ME." (Provide correction and have the student repeat correct responses, if needed.)

FIGURE 5.5. Segmentation and blending lesson.

and provide more intensive phoneme-level instruction while students who are not struggling with the same text may engage in a discussion about text characters and themes in the story. An example appears in Figure 5.6, in which differentiated instruction is included as part of core instruction. Some differentiated instruction practices can look a lot like Tier 2 instruction activities for students who are at risk for literacy difficulties. What is that important is students who need more support receive intensive, systematic, and interactive instruction regardless of the tier (Gersten et al., 2008). For example, a core classroom teacher might provide extra support to the group of students who are having a more difficult time with phoneme blending in a small group. The teacher can provide them with additional opportunities to practice more difficult phoneme combinations, and then give individualized feedback on their responses while other groups of students in the classroom may be focusing on retelling the story read earlier that day to a partner or small group. The small-group blending activities provided by the classroom teacher would likely look a lot like instruction in a Tier 2 small-group session. The goal, regardless of the setting, is to provide students with more intensive and explicit instruction in the area in which they are struggling, no matter if it is in the core classroom or in a Tier 2 small-group setting.

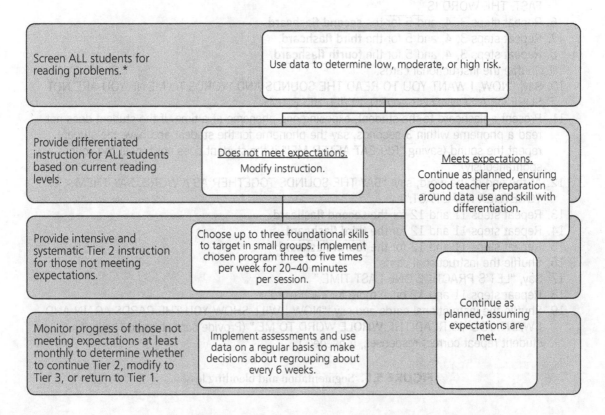

*Recommended screening at beginning of year and then at regularly scheduled intervals (midyear, triannual).

FIGURE 5.6. Flowchart depicting a multi-tiered process for making decisions about reading instruction. Based on Gersten et al. (2008).

Figure 5.6 illustrates how to organize the *lesson time* and *duration* of an intervention across the school year. Perhaps the most astounding finding in literacy training studies is the relatively small amount of training time needed to produce substantial benefits for many students. For example, in the Ball and Blachman (1991) study, students met in small groups for 15–20 minutes, four times per week, for 7 weeks.

Instructional delivery depends on good *screening and data-based decision making*. The flowchart in Figure 5.7 helps guide the selection of appropriate assessment measures and the direction of instructional focus with early literacy skills with an illustration of oral reading fluency. It is important to note that the data on recommended cut points in the flowchart present general guidelines for performance at the end of first grade. The data represent the level of skill generally to be expected by the end of first grade. We caution readers that before evaluating student performance on any early literacy skill and at varying points within and across grade levels, teachers and school psychologists should carefully review publishers' suggested and evaluated norms as a means of comparison for their target population of interest.

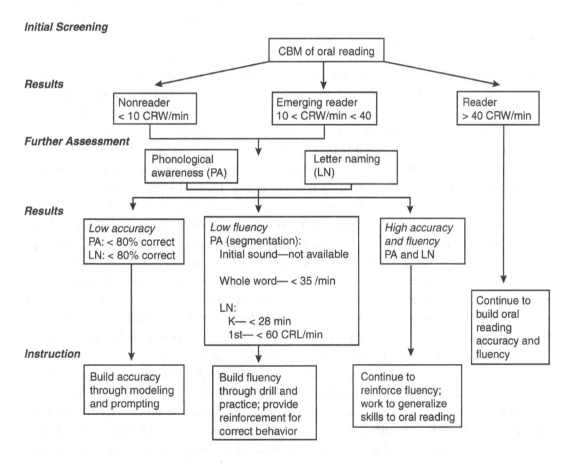

FIGURE 5.7. Flowchart for screening in oral reading fluency at the end of first grade. CRW, correctly read words; CRL, correctly read letters; CBM, curriculum-based measurement.

As noted in the flowchart, the first step in assessment is to determine the student's current level of oral reading skill (i.e., screen for student's level of risk for difficulty) through curriculum-based measurements. In this example, this is done by measuring the number of correctly read words versus errors a student makes in 1 minute while reading a passage taken from curriculum-level materials (described in Chapter 6). Many younger or lower-skilled students may perform poorly on a measure of oral reading skill, meaning that this is not yet an appropriate skill to work on. This initial step establishes baseline information regarding current student level of skill, which can then be useful for evaluating student progress following intervention. As a general guideline, Good and Kaminski (2001) have suggested that by the spring of first grade, established readers should be able to read orally more than 40 words correctly in 1 minute. According to Good and Kaminski's benchmarks, ideally a second-grade student at this same time should read at least 90 correct words per minute. The flowchart indicates that reading between 10 and 40 words correctly per minute is classified as "emerging," whereas reading fewer than 10 is considered "nonreader." Further assessment is recommended for any student falling into these two categories; assessment should focus on the specific early literacy skills of letter-naming fluency and phonological awareness. An example of a letter-naming assessment (Sound Bingo) is presented in Worksheet 5.2 at the end of the chapter. As would be expected, a nonreader probably will need more intensive instruction, whereas an emerging reader may simply need some gaps filled in or additional support. In contrast, an established reader probably already possesses sufficient early literacy skills. Thus, instruction should focus on continuing to build reading accuracy and fluency. When selecting an intervention, a primary goal is to evaluate the current instructional program within the context of the identified needs of the student being assessed. Once the area of weakness has been initially identified and an instructional intervention has been recommended, it is important to repeatedly conduct assessment.

All students' progress should be monitored regularly, with more frequent monitoring for students receiving Tier 2 or small-group instruction. These students should be assessed at least once a month, at least eight times over the school year, and every 6 weeks for the purpose of regrouping these students in or outside of a Tier 2 structure (Gersten et al., 2008). This monthly monitoring will help identify students who may need additional support or intervention. Progress monitoring measures might include letter–sound fluency, oral reading fluency, fluent word recognition and nonword (pseudoword) reading fluency, among others. An example of appropriate assessments for early literacy skills are those provided by the Dynamic Indicators of Basic Early Literacy Skills (DIBELS). DIBELS assessments are used for universal screening and progress monitoring in grades K–6. All measures are standardized, individually administered, validated by research, and quick, as well as efficient for use in classrooms. An example might be the DIBELS Initial Sounds Fluency (ISF) measure, in which students are presented with four different pictures, the examiner names each picture, and then asks the student to point or say the picture that begins with a specific sound said orally by the examiner. For example, the examiner says, "This is *sink, cat, gloves,* and *hat.* Which picture begins with /s/?" The student is also asked to produce the initial sound for the word orally presented by the examiner and which matches the picture. This measure takes approximately 3 minutes to administer and there are 20 forms of the measure so it can be used to monitor a student's progress over time. Thus, teachers and school psychologists alike can monitor over time how long it takes a student to identify and produce the correct sounds per minute and see if this rate improves (*https://dibels.org*).

In addition, it may be appropriate to assess progress in long-term goal areas. For more information about screening, progress monitoring, and intervention tools for early literacy skills we encourage the reader to explore the tool charts on the National Center on Response to Intervention website (*www.rti4success.org*) as well as to examine the assessment and instructional tools provided by the National Center on Intensive Intervention website (*www.intensiveintervention.org*). Although we do not endorse a particular assessment, we do recommend choosing tools that have been evaluated using the standards and review process used by the centers.

Case Example

John is a second-grade student who was described by his teacher as not keeping pace with his peers in reading. When his oral reading fluency was assessed in first-grade reading passages (his instructional level), John correctly read 29 words per minute (see Figure 5.8), placing him in the category of emerging reader. Further assessment of letter naming suggested that John is both accurate (94%) and fluent (72 correctly read letters per minute). Phonemic awareness assessment revealed that John was able to accurately segment the sounds in a word (100% accuracy with the first sound) but did not do so rapidly (fluency of 30 correct segments per minute; Figure 5.8). Thus, the goal was to increase the automaticity of John's phonemic awareness skills so that he is able to segment words with more fluidity

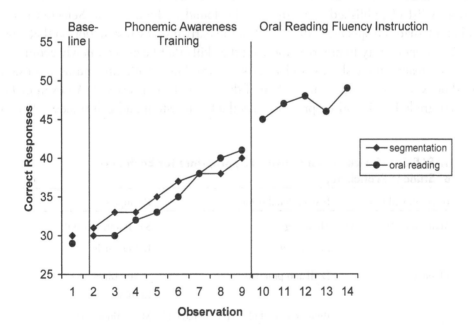

FIGURE 5.8. John: A case example.

without sacrificing accuracy. Instructional recommendations included continued reading practice in controlled text, along with drill and practice and reinforcement for correct performance in phonological awareness. Oral reading and phonological awareness skill (whole-word segmentation) continued to be assessed to monitor his performance. His progress is graphed in Figure 5.8.

Selecting an Intervention Based on Assessment Data

Return for a moment to the flowchart presented in Figure 5.7. This flowchart helps direct you to the area in need of intervention based on the results of the assessment. Instructional intervention should be framed around a clear identification of the student's skill level. For example, if assessment reveals that a student has low phonological awareness accuracy, then instructional goals would include building accuracy through strategies such as modeling and prompting. Enhancing phonological awareness could involve an activity such as Say It and Move It. Table 5.6 outlines the principles of instruction to be applied to each stage along with some specific activity ideas. Digital technologies can be very useful. Programs like Earobics (see Table 5.6) provide students with individualized, explicit instruction on early literacy skills and create individualized reports of student performance to help teachers tailor instruction to students' needs. A good guide for knowing which assessments are most commonly administered for measuring progress during the primary grades is presented in Figure 5.9.

An additional important aspect of selecting an early literacy core program is the selection of appropriate text. Although early literacy instruction can be provided within the use of existing classroom materials, some attention to the selection of reading materials should be given. A list of published programs can be found in Figure 5.10. Selected materials should emphasize the specific skills taught in the early literacy instruction so that students have ample opportunity to practice applying the skills that have been newly acquired. For example, for teaching the short vowel *a*, texts and word lists containing numerous examples of the short vowel *a* should be used. Use of decodable texts is critical. An examination of major first-grade basal reading programs conducted by Stein and colleagues (1999) noted

TABLE 5.6. Instructional Activities Appropriate for Each Level of Student Proficiency

Instructional level	Instructional principles	Examples
Acquisition (accuracy)	Modeling	Say It and Move It
	Prompting	Letter cards
Fluency	Drill and practice	Sound Bingo
		Earobics
	Reinforcement of correct behavior	Mad Minute activities
Generalization		Reading in controlled text

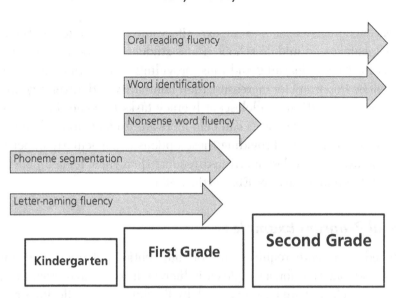

FIGURE 5.9. Recommended reading assessments across the primary grades.

that those programs with a high proportion of decodable text also emphasized an explicit approach to teacher instruction. The bad news is that only one of seven basal student readers (i.e., Open Court's *Collections for Young Scholars*, 1995) contained a sufficient percentage of decodable words (≥ 50%). The implication of this finding is that you may need to spend time sampling various curriculum materials or real texts in order to find appropriate decodable reading materials. For example, Stein et al. suggest taking random selections of text and separating the words into lists of (1) decodable, (2) sight, and (3) nondecodable and noninstructed words. (Specific directions for completing such an analysis can be found in the Curriculum Evaluation Worksheet provided in the Stein et al. article.) Although guidelines for determining appropriate proportions vary depending on intended use, Beck (1997) recommended that text read by students early in first grade should be 70–80% decodable.

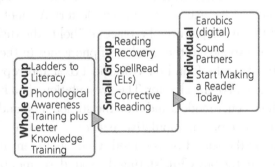

FIGURE 5.10. List of programs for early reading skills. These programs met the What Works Clearinghouse standards and provided results in at least two early literacy skill components, the majority in alphabetic knowledge and fluency.

We would also encourage teachers to use expository and narrative text in their classrooms. In the late elementary and middle school grades students will be increasingly exposed to expository text for content learning and thus, providing them with early experiences with both genres will be important for increasing their familiarity with diverse genres, preparing them for the more sophisticated adolescent literacy tasks to come. Furthermore, providing students with a variety of choices can help motivate students to read *and* keep reading in the face of challenging text. Providing these options is particularly important for boys, students who on average are less motivated readers than their female peers (Marinak & Gambrell, 2010; McKenna, Kear, & Ellsworth, 1995).

Instructional Program Examples

Having outlined some core requirements of intervention selection, we now provide a description of, and materials for, a simple early literacy instructional program. The instructional components selected are based on work by Blachman and colleagues and are clearly described in the seminal study conducted by Ball and Blachman (1991).

Their early literacy instructional program comprises three separate activities that are implemented approximately 15 minutes per day. Instruction is presented in small groups whose composition is determined by instructional skill level. Two of the activities—one emphasizing phonological awareness (Say It and Move It) and the other, letter–sound correspondences—remain consistent across sessions, whereas the third activity reinforces phonological awareness through various fun activities. It is recommended that only a few letters be selected initially for focus, and that words used within activities be sequenced by difficulty, such as beginning with two-phoneme words and then perhaps adding CVC (consonant–vowel–consonant) words. There are no hard-and-fast rules for selection of letters. However, Adams, Foorman, Lundberg, and Beeler (1998) suggest starting with short vowels (*a, e, i, o, u*) and the following consonants: *s, m, d, p, t, n, g, b, r, f, l*, due to their utility for use in monosyllabic words.

Descriptions of each of the three separate activities follow:

1. *Say It and Move It*. In this segmentation activity, the student is taught to represent each sound with a manipulative (e.g., disk, checker, letter). A sheet (can be laminated for durability) is provided that has a picture of a place to "hold" the disks; below it are boxes, the number of which corresponds to the number of phonemes in the presented word (two, three, or four). Directions can be found on Worksheet 5.3a and reproducible examples on Worksheets 5.3b–d at the end of the chapter. The presentation of an item to segment follows a sequence in which the teacher models and then the student responds in the same manner. The student is taught to move one manipulative (e.g., disk) into each box, from left to right, while slowly pronouncing the sound represented. Once a student masters the concept of moving a manipulative into the box while stating the sound, segmenting with two-phoneme words and then three- and four-phoneme words can be introduced.

2. *Letter–sound correspondences*. Teaching letter–sound correspondences includes strategies involving key words and phrases. For example, composing jingles to illustrate

letters (*A*: ants ate apples) is one fun way to reinforce letter–sound correspondences. In addition, games such as bingo can be modified to use sounds and letters (see Sound Bingo, Worksheets 5.2a–c). As a final example, the program outlined in Blachman et al. (2000) describes a game titled Post Office. In this activity, students "mail" letters or pictures into the appropriate pouches. Letters replace the other manipulatives after several letter–sound correspondences are mastered.

3. *Phonological awareness.* The final component of each lesson engages students in another phonological awareness activity, which can vary from lesson to lesson. Examples of other activities include sound blending using puppets, counting the number of phonemes in words, and categorizing them based on common rhymes and sounds. This activity reinforces generalization of learned skills across materials and activities.

Case Example Revisited

Returning to John, our emerging reader (Figure 5.8), we note that he had mastered letter naming but was not yet able to segment whole words fluently. Thus, instructional recommendations included continued reading practice in controlled text along with drill and practice and reinforcement for correct segmenting and blending. Because John is a second-grade student and had demonstrated mastery of letter–sound correspondences, it was decided that a modified Say It and Move It activity would be implemented as the primary phonological awareness intervention. During this activity, the teacher had John manipulate the letters on cards, and the activity was structured as a speed game. That is, John was told to segment as many whole words as he could in 1 minute and to chart his correct segments on a daily basis. Error correction was provided for each mistake, and John received praise and small tangibles (stickers for his chart) for correct performance. John continued to participate in the regular reading curriculum, reading trade books and curriculum materials that appropriately matched his instructional level. Progress monitoring in phonological awareness (whole-word segmentation) and oral reading was continued twice a week; his progress appears in Figure 5.8. Phonological awareness assessment was discontinued once oral reading fluency was established.

CONCLUSIONS

This chapter focused on the important role of early literacy skills as the building blocks of future reading success. Two code-based early literacy skills—phonological awareness and letter knowledge—were highlighted, based on the substantial literature base supporting the critical role these skills play in understanding the alphabetic principle, which is a crucial accomplishment for a student on his or her way to accurate and fluent reading of text. An assessment and intervention framework was presented to guide informed decision making that maximizes progress toward fluent reading. Assessment and intervention materials to implement the decision-making framework were provided and resources for finding and evaluating additional materials were suggested. This chapter was intended to lay out the knowledge sets necessary for early reading, but also to highlight the importance of engaging and explicit teaching, instruction that supports students' knowledge building and their continued interest in reading.

APPENDIX 5.1. ADDITIONAL EARLY LITERACY INTERVENTION PACKAGE RESOURCES

Whole-Class Instruction

Phonemic Awareness in Young Children (Adams, Foorman, Lundberg, & Beeler, 1998).

Brief description: From simple listening games to more advanced exercises in rhyming, alliteration, and segmentation, this best-selling curriculum helps boost young learners' preliteracy skills in just 15–20 minutes a day. This program specifically targets phonemic awareness.

What Works Clearinghouse Reviewed Programs with Effects for at Least Two Early Reading Components

Ladders to Literacy, Preschool Activity Book (Notari-Syverson, O'Connor, & Vadasy, 1998).
Ladders to Literacy, Kindergarten Activity Book (O'Connor, Notari-Syverson, & Vadasy, 1998).

Available from: Brookes Publishing Company, *www.brookespublishing.com*, 800-638-3775.

Brief description: Ladders to Literacy provides classroom teachers with more than 60 culturally sensitive, developmentally appropriate student activities that have been successfully tested for a decade under research and practical conditions alike. Organized into three major sections (Print/Book Awareness Skills, Metalinguistic Awareness Skills, Oral Language Skills), Ladders to Literacy provides the foundation for children to master key elements of the reading process successfully. Of special note are the informal observation guidelines, structured performance samples, and literacy checklist.

Small-Group Instruction

Road to the Code: A Phonological Awareness Program for Young Children (Blachman, Ball, Black, & Tangel, 2000).

Available from: Brookes Publishing Company, *www.brookespublishing.com*, 800-638-3775.

Brief description: For helping kindergartners and first graders who are having difficulty on their early literacy skills, Road to the Code is a successful, 11-week program for teaching phonemic awareness and letter–sound correspondence. Developmentally sequenced, each of the 44, 15- to 20-minute lessons features three activities—Say-It-and-Move-It, Letter Name and Sound Instruction, and Phonological Awareness Practice—that give students repeated opportunities to practice and enhance their beginning reading and spelling abilities. Detailed scripted instructions and reproducible materials—such as Alphabet Picture and Sound Bingo cards—make this program easy for teachers to use.

Phonological Awareness Training for Reading (Torgesen & Bryant, 1994).

Available from: PRO-ED Inc., *www.proedinc.com/customer/productview.aspx?id=838*, 800-897-3202.

Brief description: The Phonological Awareness Training for Reading program is divided into four sets of activities: Warm-Up, Sound Blending, Sound Segmenting, and Reading and Spelling. The warm-up phase includes rhyming activities to help children focus their attention on the sounds in words. Following the warm-up, children begin the formal training program with activities that teach them to blend individual sounds to make words. They then begin the more difficult segmenting activities. In the final phase of instruction, children are taught how to use their phonological awareness skills in reading and spelling. The Phonological Awareness Training for Reading program takes about 12–14 weeks to complete if children are taught in short sessions three or four times a week. The program should be used with at-risk children in kindergarten to help prepare them for reading in first grade or with first- or second-grade children who are having difficulties learning to read.

Lindamood Phoneme Sequencing Program for Reading, Spelling, and Speech (formerly known as Auditory Discrimination in Depth; Lindamood & Lindamood, 1998).

Available from: PRO-ED, Inc., *www.proedaust.com.au/details.cfm?number=313*, 800-897-3202.

Brief description: The Lindamood Phoneme Sequencing Program for Reading, Spelling, and Speech—Fourth Edition (LiPS) is a comprehensive multisensory program that uses explicit, systematic instruction to develop phonological awareness, decoding, spelling, and reading skills. The goal of LiPS is to develop fluent readers and competent spellers. The LiPS program steps are Setting the Climate for Learning, Identifying and Classifying Consonants, Identifying and Classifying Vowels, Tracking Simple Syllables and Words, Basic Spelling and Reading, Learning Sight Words and Expectancies, Tracking Complex Syllables and Words, Multisyllabic Words, and Reading and Writing in Context. To teach sound–letter associations, the LiPS tasks progress from articulatory movement to sound, then to letter. Through guided discovery techniques, students explore the physical movements involved in producing sounds and learn to hear, see, and feel the physical characteristics of sounds. This in-depth knowledge leads to the student's ability to understand how words are constructed and to self-correct—essential skills for independent reading and spelling.

What Works Clearinghouse Reviewed Programs with Effects for at Least Two Early Reading Components

Reading Recovery
www.readingrecovery.org

Brief description: Reading Recovery trains teachers to deliver an early intervention program designed to reduce literacy problems in an education system. Children entering the Reading Recovery program are those from ordinary classes who have the most difficulty in reading and writing after 1 year at school. Since the Reading Recovery program is different for every child, the implementation of a successful program requires thorough teacher training. Using the child's competencies as a starting point, the program advances toward what the child is trying to accomplish. The teaching, therefore, must be individually designed and individually delivered. Using the guidelines in this book, teachers learn how to provide each child with an intensive program of daily instruction that supplements the regular class instruction activities. The goal of Reading Recovery is to help children acquire efficient patterns of learning to enable them to work at the average level of their classmates and to continue to progress satisfactorily in their own school's instructional program.

SpellRead
www.proedinc.com/customer/ProductView.aspx?ID=5364

Brief description: SpellRead is a 1-year, small-group reading intervention program that focuses on phonological automaticity and reading fluency while providing explicit comprehension and vocabulary instruction, as well as opportunities for writing. Using a multisensory approach, students learn to recognize and manipulate the 44 English sounds; practice, apply, and transfer their skills using leveled readers and trade books; and write about their reading. Robust materials help students learn actively and efficiently; age- and grade-appropriate leveled readers and trade books promote the use of new skills. Comprehensive teacher materials help educators effectively implement Phases A, B, and C of the program through explicit instructional strategies. A Web-based Instructor Support System allows educators to monitor progress; compare student, class, and school performance; create reports; and recognize student success with awards and certificates.

Computer Software

The Learning Company
www.broderbund.com

What Works Clearinghouse Reviewed Programs with Effects for at Least Two Early Reading Components

Earobics
www.earobics.com

Brief description: Earobics software provides individualized, explicit instruction in all areas of reading, plus writing. As students engage with the software, the program automatically adjusts based on each student's individual strengths and weaknesses. All instruction builds on the strengths of each learner, and easy-to-read reports help teachers use real-time data to drive tailored instruction. Every response is recorded and available in detailed reports that can be printed or accessed online. Teachers can also customize the program to meet students' learning needs, including selecting directions to be delivered in one of 10 different languages.

Making Decisions about What and How to Teach

Questions to Ask Yourself	Reading Foundational Skill Performance	Decision
1. Have I targeted the right performance objective?	Student meets performance benchmarks in reading skill.	Continue core instruction and periodic screening.
	Student does not quite meet the performance benchmark but is making correct responses.	Continue instruction in this skill objective.
	Student does not meet the performance benchmark after repeated sessions to strengthen the target skill.	Explore whether the student does not have prerequisite skills for the tasks required: a. If yes, alter instruction and look to see if there is change. b. If no, try working on a simpler objective.
2. Should I teach this skill in isolation or in context?	Student has the necessary background knowledge to extract meaning from the context in which the task is happening (e.g., he or she understands that words are made up of letters that have sounds).	Teach letter–sound correspondence using a song about words that start with the letter *a*, and present students with related objects.
	Student does not have sufficient background knowledge.	Teach letter sounds in isolation, establish accuracy, do repetitive drills and integrate the skill in context when the student has achieved a sufficient level of mastery.
3. Should I be focusing on supporting student acquisition or fluency with the skill?	Student provides inaccurate responses. Student is making meaningful errors, but is very slow.	Focus on supporting students in acquiring the skill, providing explicit instruction, modeling, demonstrations, and guided practice with corrective feedback. This phase should involve a lot of teacher support and very little independent work.
	Student is providing accurate responses, with a couple of errors.	Provide drills and focus on automaticity while also ensuring that accuracy is maintained.

(continued)

Based on Howell and Nolet (2000).

Questions to Ask Yourself	Reading Foundational Skill Performance	Decision
4. Am I emphasizing the correct facts, concepts, and strategies?	Incorrect responses reflect inaccurate understanding of basic facts.	Teach factual content through presenting problems and answers (modeling/presenting evidence).
	Incorrect responses reflect a poor understanding of meaning of the task.	Provide examples and non-examples of the conceptual content to help students discriminate conceptual ideas and goals of the task.
	Incorrect responses reflect a misunderstanding of the procedures involved in the tasks.	Talk through each step of the task in a strategic manner to help students understand how to complete the target task.
5. Am I am employing the right instructional activities when I present?	Student is below benchmarks but is making adequate progress.	Continue with the activities you have designed.
	Student is below benchmarks, but has prerequisite skills. Is not making adequate progress, even with appropriate objectives, emphasis, format, and incentives.	Alter the setting, materials used, or delivery of the lesson. For example, you might change your questioning, feedback, pace, explanations, length of lessons, size of the group, lesson sequence, or type of practice.
6. Do I need to make the lesson more interesting? Are students motivated to engage with the lesson?	Student is improving, and is engaged in the lesson and participates without disruptions.	Continue with current lesson presentation.
	Student was previously improving but is now getting worse, and is less engaged in the lesson.	Explain why the task is relevant and important. Begin and end the lesson by explaining how the target skill can be used and allow students to share their opinions and ideas. Consider providing students with self-monitoring activities. Provide students with choice in the activity.
7. Is there more information I need?	You cannot sufficiently answer the six preceding questions.	Keep asking these questions and evaluating!

Directions for Sound Bingo

Materials:

One Sound Bingo card per child
Several bingo chips per child

Directions:

Make copies of the picture and letter squares (Worksheets 5.2b and c). Place these squares into a box or bag. To play, draw one square at a time and show it to the students. If a picture square is drawn, the students should name the picture and give the first sound. Any student who has that picture on his or her cards should place a bingo chip on it. If a letter square is drawn, the student should give the sound of that letter. Any student who has that letter on his or her cards should place a bingo chip on it. The teacher can decide in advance whether the students need to cover a single row or the entire card to get "bingo."

Sound Bingo Card: Letter Squares

S	M	T
D	P	N
G	B	R
C	L	F
H	J	W

Sound Bingo Card: Picture Squares

Directions for Say It and Move It

Materials:

One Say It and Move It worksheet per child
Two to four manipulatives per child (disks, checkers, or letters)

Directions:

Give each child a Say It and Move It worksheet, and the appropriate number of manipulatives. Place the manipulatives on the picture of the treasure chest.

TEACHER: **Watch me and listen. I'm going to say a word.** *[Insert word here.]*

TEACHER: **Now I am going to say it and move it.** Place your fingers on the manipulative and hold out the first sound while you move one manipulative from the treasure chest to the left-most box at the bottom of the sheet. Then, quickly move the second manipulative to the next box while saying the next sound in the word. Repeat until all sounds in the word have been completed.

TEACHER: *[Insert word here.]* Repeat the word while moving your finger from left to right under the manipulatives.

TEACHER: **Now it's your turn. Say** *[insert word here.]* Wait for response.

TEACHER: **Now say it and move it.**

Two-Phoneme Card for Say It and Move It

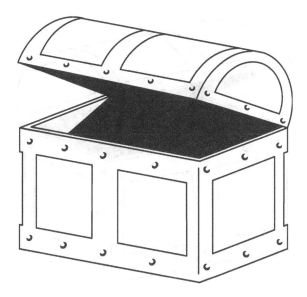

Three-Phoneme Card for Say It and Move It

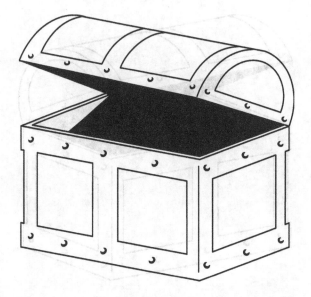

Four-Phoneme Card for Say It and Move It

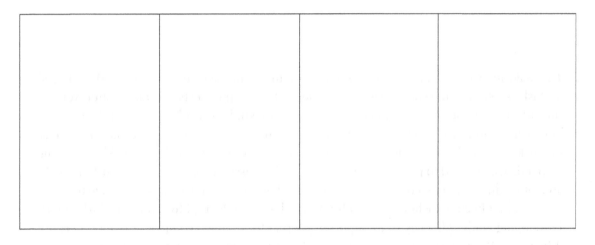

CHAPTER 6

Producing Measurable Increases in Reading Fluency

The majority of educational programs and curricula emphasize accuracy (e.g., 80% correct) on tasks such as homework assignments and end-of-chapter tests. Teachers often rely on this information for decisions about whether to move students further along in the curriculum or not. Although being accurate is important, if a student is to be expected to progress to harder materials and subjects, an equally important criterion is how quickly he or she responds when asked to perform academic tasks. This issue is particularly important in the area of reading, where students learn to read so that they can ultimately read to learn.

Reading fluency includes the ability to read accurately, rapidly, and with little effort. Developing reading fluency is an important step to becoming a competent reader, because it increases the student's capacity to use reading as a helpful tool with more difficult tasks. Alternatively, poor reading fluency is likely to cause poor comprehension and hinder students' motivation to tackle the more complicated tasks of the school curriculum, such as doing research to write a paper. Additionally, fluent readers are more likely to find reading more pleasurable and in many instances may be more likely to choose to read than those who have not developed their reading fluency.

This chapter provides a rationale for targeting oral reading fluency for intervention. Procedures for assessing reading fluency are described, as are strategies designed to enhance it. A variety of empirically validated intervention strategies are described in sufficient detail to get you started. We present each strategy individually, with a rationale for appropriate use, so that you can assemble just the right components to create an intervention tailored to the circumstances of the referral problem. For instance, if you are starting a tutoring program and will be using the intervention with a group of students, a procedurally simpler intervention is probably preferable; you might prioritize a smaller set of strategies. If, however, you are working with a single student who is having severe and persistent difficulties, you probably would want a stronger treatment and would therefore combine more intervention components. The chapter concludes with a description of how these strategies can be embedded in various tutoring and instructional formats, including a description of classwide peer tutoring.

WHY IS FLUENCY IMPORTANT?

Reading fluency can be defined operationally as the number of correctly read words per minute when an individual is asked to read a passage of connected text aloud for 1 minute. We address the details of administration and scoring later. Here we wish to point out that this simple measure has helped to explain a lot of things about the process of reading in general, and about why some readers struggle. Even though there have been differing explanations for why fluency is important, researchers studying reading fluency fully recognize the need for students to develop the ability to read both accurately and rapidly (Daly, O'Connor, & Young, 2014; Skinner, Neddenriep, Bradley-Klug, & Ziemann, 2002). We can readily identify three reasons why you should consider this factor to be a critical and legitimate intervention target (see Table 6.1). Each reason is discussed below.

Fluent Readers Are More Likely to Comprehend

Fluency is a solid indicator of overall reading competence and correlations between reading fluency and reading comprehension are strong (Hintze, Callahan, Matthews, Williams, & Tobin, 2002; Kranzler, Brownell, & Miller, 1998; Marston, 1989; Reschly, Busch, Betts, Deno, & Long, 2009; Shinn et al., 1992). Oral reading fluency is also a good predictor of performance on high-stakes statewide proficiency tests (Hintze & Silberglitt, 2005; McGlinchey & Hixson, 2004). Although not sufficient alone for comprehension, fluency is a necessary condition for adequate independent comprehension.

TABLE 6.1. What the Research Says about Why Reading Fluency Is Important

1. Fluent readers are more likely to comprehend what they are reading.

2. Building fluency is likely to make reading a more rewarding experience and may increase the chances that a student will actually *choose* to read rather than choose to do other things.

3. Building fluency makes reading less effortful and therefore less frustrating for students—factors that also increase the chances that a student might actually choose to read rather than do other things.

There are several ways to look at how fluency affects comprehension. First, the sequence and configuration of letters forming words on the page control your reading when words are correctly read. You can't just make up what you want to read on the page! Interestingly, poor readers tend to overemphasize cues that are not textual (e.g., relying on pictures), to the detriment of their reading, whereas good readers have been shown to attend to virtually every letter on the page (Adams, 1990). When a learner becomes fluent with reading words in texts, the action of reading the word on the page competes more effectively with wrong responses such as making an incorrect guess about a word, waiting for someone to say the word, or looking around. When the reader is fluent, word reading is strong and durable across a variety of texts. As such, correctly reading the word is the most likely response when the word appears in print in the text. This textual control also makes it more likely that the reader will use the previously learned words as a basis for answering comprehension questions when queried by a teacher or parent about what the text is saying. Fluent readers are more likely to generalize to harder tasks such as answering comprehension questions, because their word reading is more strongly connected to the text at the very outset.

An alternate viewpoint is that readers who read accurately but slowly expend a lot of energy (e.g., attention, working memory) attempting to decode words and therefore have a lowered capacity to comprehend while they are reading (LaBerge & Samuels, 1974; Perfetti, 1977; Samuels, 1988). Because the ability to retain information tends to decay over time, it is harder for less fluent readers to relate information presented earlier to material being currently read, especially as they work their way through a long text (Daneman & Carpenter, 1980; Samuels, 1988). Faster readers are more likely to access information presented earlier because the information has had less time to decay.

At one time or another, most of us have experienced problems with accessing information read earlier. For example, imagine Joe, who is lying in his hammock on a nice summer's day, reading a mystery novel for pleasure. While reading he is interrupted when a neighbor's dog unexpectedly arrives and begins barking. Joe, being a good neighbor, marks his place, puts his book down, and spends the next 20 minutes chasing the neighbor's dog. After finally securing the dog and returning it to his neighbor, Joe settles back into his hammock, opens the book to his mark, and begins reading exactly where he left off. Unfortunately, what he is reading makes little sense anymore. Joe does not even know with whom the main character is talking. These comprehension problems are caused by an inability to relate what he is currently reading to what he previously read. Joe remedies this problem by scanning back about four paragraphs and finding where this new person was introduced. As he rereads these paragraphs (getting a running start, so to speak), it comes back to him and the material once again makes sense. Now Joe can comprehend the material he is currently reading because he has accessed material presented earlier. Because he can now understand what he is reading, he once again begins to enjoy reading his novel. In a similar vein, the student who has poor reading fluency will experience interruptions in the flow of the text as he or she tries to decipher what is on the page. Like Joe, this student will have difficulty relating what is being read to what was previously read.

2. *Fluent Readers Are More Likely to Choose to Read*

Those who read accurately but slowly may be less likely to choose to read than those who read fluently (Skinner, 1998). One factor that influences what a person chooses to do is how rewarding the experience is. In general, when faced with a choice between two or more activities, with all other factors held constant, people are more likely to choose to engage in the activity that is most rewarding (Neef, Mace, Shea, & Shade, 1992).

To understand how reward strength is affected by reading speed of fluency consider two students (Fred and Dave) whose data are summarized in Table 6.2. Both Fred and Dave can read and comprehend the same 1,000-word passage that is designed to be funny. Fred reads 100 words per minute and Dave, whose reading fluency is less developed, reads 50 words per minute. For both students, reading the passage results in 10 chuckles and one roaring belly laugh at the end of the passage. Because he reads faster, Fred's rate of chuckles is 1 per minute, while Dave's rate of chuckles is half of Fred's, 1 chuckle per 2 minutes. Assuming that chuckles represent moderate rewards, Dave's rate of rewards for choosing to read the passage is half of Fred's, which suggests that Fred is much more likely to choose to read. To gain an understanding of how much more likely Fred is to choose to read, consider how much more likely you would be to choose one job over another if you received the same pay and benefits for 20 hours, as opposed to 40 hours per week.

Reward quality and delay also influence reward strength. If all else is equal, we behave so as to access rewards quicker (in an hour as opposed to a week), and high-quality rewards (e.g., 10-dollar bill) are preferable to lower-quality rewards (e.g., 5-dollar bill). In our example, belly laughs represent higher-quality rewards than chuckles. As Table 6.2 indicates, Fred gains access to this higher-quality reward in 10 minutes, while Dave's access is more delayed (i.e., 20 minutes). Thus, assuming both Fred and Dave understand the entire passage and access the same rewards for reading the passage, Fred's rate of moderate rewards

TABLE 6.2. Effects of Reading Speed on Chuckles and Belly Laughs, Assuming 100% Passage Comprehension

	Fred (fluent)	Dave (dysfluent)
Reading speed	100 words per minute	50 words per minute
Time to read the same 1,000-word passage	10 minutes	20 minutes
Chuckles per passage (moderate-quality reward)	10	10
Chuckles per minute of reading	1	0.5
Time required to read per chuckle	1 minute	2 minutes
Belly laughs	1	1
Belly laughs per minute	0.1	0.05
Sustained reading time needed to produce a belly laugh	10 minutes	20 minutes

(chuckles) for passage reading is double that of Dave's rate of rewards, and Fred accesses the higher-quality reward (belly laugh) in half the time that it takes Dave to experience a belly laugh. Thus, Fred may be more likely to choose to read than Dave because the reward strength is worth the effort.

For Table 6.2, we assumed that both Fred and Dave comprehended the entire passage. Researchers have repeatedly shown, however, that fluent readers tend to have higher levels of comprehension than dysfluent readers (Reschly et al., 2009). Table 6.3 describes how this may impact rates of reinforcement. Note that because Dave only comprehends half of the passage, his belly laughs are reduced to 5, which in turn means his rate of reinforcement is now one-fourth of Fred's, as he experiences 1 chuckle per 4 minutes of reading. To understand the importance of this, consider that on a comprehension exam, Fred would receive a letter grade of A and perhaps accompanying rewards (e.g., praise) for 10 minutes of work, while Dave would receive a letter grade of F for 20 minutes of work. Thus, it would come as no surprise that Fred would choose to read, while Dave may not.

Whereas strong readers may enjoy a beautifully written piece of work (e.g., finding that the flow of the language was "intoxicating"), slow readers may not be able to appreciate such well-written work because they cannot read rapidly enough to catch the nuances. For example, a beautifully written sentence may be difficult to appreciate when each word must be sounded out laboriously. Dysfluent readers may expend so much energy on decoding and comprehension that they are incapable of understanding subtle nuances that make reading a rewarding experience for others. Again, when he chooses to read, Fred receives access to rewards that Dave may not.

To make our points about choice and rewards, we have focused on belly laughs and chuckles. We read for other purposes as well, like to gain information (so we can pass an exam, operate our new 60-inch flat screen television, or learn new strategies and procedures

TABLE 6.3. Effects of Reading Speed on Chuckles and Belly Laughs, Assuming 100% Passage Comprehension for Fred (Fluent) and Only 50% Comprehension for Dave (Dysfluent)

	Fred (Fluent)	Dave (Dysfluent)
Reading speed	100 word per minute	50 words per minute
Time to read the same 1,000-word passage	10 minutes	20 minutes
Chuckles per passage (moderate-quality reward)	10	5
Chuckles per minute of reading	1	0.25
Time required to read per chuckle	1 minute	4 minutes
Belly laughs	1	1
Belly laughs per minute	0.1	0.05
Sustained reading time needed to produce a belly laugh	10 minutes	20 minutes

for doing our jobs). Being more likely to choose to read will increase the probability that Fred passes his exams and advances in his job. He may also be able to put together his new gas grill without blowing something up, and with less frustration (e.g., few cusses per minute).

3. Fluent Reading Is Less Effortful

When given the choice of two behaviors with equivalent rewards (quality, delay, and rate), we are more likely to choose the behavior that requires less effort (Friman & Poling, 1995). Because it is difficult to measure effort, especially cognitive effort (e.g., effort required to read a 1,000-word passage), researchers often measure time required to complete a task. Our prior analysis in Table 6.2 suggests that Dave, while obtaining the same rewards (10 chuckles and 1 belly laugh), had to expend twice as much effort to access these rewards. To understand how important relative effort is, consider asking a child which lawn he or she would like to mow for the same reward (e.g., $40)—a quarter-acre lawn or a full-acre lawn—or consider your own reactions to someone doubling your work hours and assignments for no increase in pay.

Slow readers may be less likely to choose to read than rapid readers because of the sheer effort involved when a skill is not proficiently employed. The effort slow readers must expend to comprehend written materials may make it less likely that they will choose to read assigned materials when there are alternative means of obtaining the information (Mace, Neef, Shade, & Mauro, 1996). For example, a dysfluent reader may be less likely to choose to read material that was assigned for homework and instead, rely on class lectures to assist him or her in comprehending it, willingly settling for a lower grade. Even when they are not expected to learn information from texts, slow readers are less likely to choose to read for pleasure because the amount of enjoyment they receive from reading may not be worth the high levels of effort that is required for them to read (Skinner, 1998).

Fluency-Induced Spirals

It is impossible to force someone to engage in cognitively demanding activities, including and perhaps especially reading. Rather, students must choose to read. Perhaps the most important thing to remember about choosing to read is that it enhances reading skills. Thus, those who choose to read become better readers. Unfortunately, as described above, better readers may be more likely to choose to read because it is more rewarding and requires less effort (Skinner, 1998; Stanovich, 1986). Consequently, educators have to remember that one size does not fit all with respect to choosing to read. Merely offering a little praise may influence strong readers to choose to read; however, the dysfluent readers in need of additional practice may require additional support (e.g., stronger reinforcement, higher rates of interaction with others, praise from others, being allowed to choose what to read) in order to influence them to choose to read (Skinner, Skinner, & Burton, 2009). Otherwise, weaker readers may get caught in a downward spiral in which weaker skills reduce the probability of choosing to read, thus hindering skill development, making it even less likely that they will choose to read harder material.

ASSESSING READING FLUENCY
USING CURRICULUM-BASED MEASUREMENT

As noted earlier, reading fluency can be assessed simply by having a student read a passage and recording correctly read words and errors during the first minute of reading. Curriculum-based measurement (CBM) for oral reading fluency (CBM-ORF) is a standardized format for assessing reading fluency; it is so named because performance measures are generally based on curricular materials. Strong reliability and validity data support the use of CBM for decision making about students' reading proficiency (Reschly et al., 2009; Shinn, 1989). Oral reading fluency is a sensitive indicator of growth and instructional effects (Fuchs, Fuchs, Hamlett, Walz, & Germann, 1993). Another advantage of CBM is that it is a low-budget and easy method for collecting high-quality information prior to and during interventions. Finally, there is a wide variety of materials available on the Internet to support your use of CBM. So, very little time needs to be invested in preparing material, just some thought about where you will choose your passages. In this section, we briefly explain how to obtain assessment materials, how to administer CBM-ORF, and how to interpret the results.

Curriculum-Based Measurement Oral Reading Fluency Assessment Materials

CBM-ORF materials can be accessed and downloaded on the Internet from the following websites: AIMSweb (*www.aimsweb.com*), DIBELS (*https://dibels.uoregon.edu*), and easy-CBM (*www.easycbm.com*). Each website requires an account, which provides access to the materials (usually as .pdf files), further training, and can even manage your data and provide you with data-evaluation reports (e.g., making normative comparisons to national samples or local samples). If you do not already have an account, we encourage you to examine all three CBM-ORF resources to see which one appears to be the best fit for your needs. All of them are readily incorporated into RTI programs, producing a variety of reports about individuals and groups of students.

In some cases, people may want to use their own set of assessment passages (e.g., from a commercially published basal reading series). This can be done at *www.interventioncentral. org*. Click the CBM Warehouse tab and then click the link to Oral Reading Fluency Probes to reach the CBM Passage Generator page. Passages can be copied or typed in. Readability indices can be selected to obtain an estimate of the passage's grade-level difficulty. (Be careful, though, because these readability estimates are notoriously unreliable.) The CBM Passage Generator creates downloadable .pdf copies of the passage and includes both an examiner copy (which includes a cumulative tally of the number of words per line of text in the right margin) and a student copy (contains no cumulative tally of words). Individuals wanting to create their own passages will probably want to use the basal reading series that is being used for instruction with the student to be assessed. It is important to carefully select appropriate passages. Poems, plays, and material with a lot of dialogue, headings, and subheadings do not lend themselves to continuous, fluent reading, and are therefore not suitable for CBM-ORF assessments. Instead, texts with continuous paragraphs should be selected. Also, many current reading series are constructed to expose students to a variety of cultures and therefore include a variety of foreign words and names. At least some students may not have had previous exposure to many of these words, and their decoding skills may not be helpful to them. Therefore, these passages should be excluded when selecting and developing passages. Finally, passages should not contain anything other than text (e.g., artwork or pictures), because these can either distract the student or provide additional clues that inflate their CBM-ORF score. It is best to keep the passage to one page. We recommend a passage length of 150 words with a clear, visible font size and type (e.g., 14-point Times New Roman).

Creating your own passages is obviously a lot more work, and may not really improve your results. Using the curriculum in which the student is being instructed is technically more "curriculum based," but the goal of instruction is to improve students' reading beyond the passages in which they are being instructed. Immediate performance improvements in the curriculum may be encouraging but do not guarantee that the student is generalizing newly acquired skills appropriately. Ideally, an effective intervention should impact a student's reading fluency in all passages of equal difficulty level. If intervention effects are observed in independent passages over time (i.e., equal in difficulty level but not directly taught to the reader), you can be much more confident about the effectiveness of the intervention. That's why we recommend that you use one of the commercially available products. They are not perfect by any means (for reasons stated below), but routine progress monitoring will give a better estimate of generalized growth in oral reading fluency over time.

CBM websites like AIMSweb and DIBELS have two types of materials: benchmarking and progress monitoring passages. Benchmarking passages are used for schoolwide screenings and initial assessments of students. As noted in Chapter 3, screening data can be used to evaluate the core curriculum and can also be used to identify students in need of further intervention. The benchmarking passages are useful for making normative comparisons, either to national norms or schoolwide norms, both evaluations that these websites allow you to perform. Progress monitoring passages are for ongoing assessments over time, which is why there is a larger number of them. These passages constitute your assessment "pool" of materials. For a CBM assessment, you will need either three benchmarking passages or three progress monitoring passages, depending on your purposes. We suggest that you conduct the assessment first at the level at which the student is being instructed. This will provide an indication of how well the student is functioning at that level. Be sure to bring both examiner and student copies. You will also need a stopwatch and the standardized instructions, which appear in Figure 6.1. Practicing the administration and scoring procedures is critical to accuracy, so a time investment is needed to learn how to administer and score reading fluency assessments. With initial assessments, we strongly recommend checking your scoring against other people's scoring before considering the results "official." If you obtain a high level of agreement, you can trust the results as being trustworthy. Each passage is scored for correctly read words and errors per minute. After all three passages are administered and scored, you should select the median (middle) score for correctly read words and the median for errors as the score for the session. Using the median corrects for

SPECIFIC DIRECTIONS FOR READING

Setting of Data Collection

The reading measures must be administered to students individually. Prepare two copies of each passage: a numbered copy for examiner use and an unnumbered copy for the student to read. You will need a stopwatch to keep track of time.

Directions

Say to the student: **When I say "start," begin reading aloud at the top of this page. Read across the page.** Demonstrate by pointing. **Try to read each word. If you come to a word you don't know, I'll tell it to you. Be sure to do your best reading. Are there any questions?**

Say **Start.**

Start your stopwatch when the student reads the first words and follow along on your copy of the story, marking the words that are read incorrectly. If the student stops or struggles with a word for 3 seconds, tell him or her the word and mark it as incorrect.

Place a bracket ( ]) after the last word read when 1 minute elapses. Have the student stop reading when it is convenient (e.g., at the end of the sentence) and thank him or her.

Count the number of words read correctly and incorrectly.

Scoring

The most important piece of information is the number of words read correctly. Reading fluency is a combination of speed and accuracy.

1. *Words read correctly.* Words read correctly are those words that are pronounced correctly, given the reading context.
    a. The word *read* must be pronounced *reed*, not as *red*, when the context is present or future tense (e.g., "He will read the book").
    b. Repetitions are not counted as incorrect.
    c. Self-corrections within 3 seconds are counted as correctly read words.
2. *Words read incorrectly.* The following types of errors are counted: (a) mispronunciations, (b) substitutions, and (c) omissions. In addition, words not read within 3 seconds are counted as errors.
    a. *Mispronunciations* are words that are misread: *dog* for *dig.*
    b. *Substitutions* are words that are substituted for the stimulus word; this is often inferred by a one-to-one correspondence between word order: *dog* for *cat.*
    c. *Omissions* are words skipped or not read; if a student skips an entire line, it is counted as one error only.
3. *Three-second rule.* If a student is struggling to pronounce a word or hesitates for 3 seconds, the student is told the word, and it is counted as an error.

FIGURE 6.1. Directions for CBM-ORF. The original directions indicate that each word should be counted as an error. However, this practice has changed since the first publication of the Shinn (1989) text. Adapted from Shinn (1989, pp. 239–240). Copyright 1989 by The Guilford Press. Adapted by permission.

outliers due to a poor passage, overfamiliarity with a passage or terms in a passage, or other types of error that might occur. Results can be recorded on a worksheet like the one found on *interventioncentral.org.* You can find a great worksheet by clicking the CBM tab and looking for the list of CBM forms. It is downloadable as a .pdf file. You will also find manuals with additional administration and scoring information on this page.

The big question at this point is What do the results mean? CBM-ORF data can be used to answer two questions: (1) Does the student's score indicate good or poor oral reading fluency, and (2) Is the student making progress? The first question has to do with identifying whether there is a problem in the first place, and the second question addresses the issue of intervention effectiveness. Thus, each is discussed in turn. By using the Reports function on AIMSweb or DIBELS, you will be able to answer the first question by making comparisons with other students. If your school or district uses these services, you can compare a referred student with other students in your school or district. You can also make comparisons with national norms through these services. To provide you with additional information, we have pulled together data and recommendations from several reports in the literature (see Table 6.4). There are three sets of recommendations for instructional or expected fluency levels. (Howell & Nolet, 2000, refer to their guidelines as expected fluency rates.) The second part of the table describes average fluency rates that have been obtained at various times in the Minneapolis, Minnesota school district. Specifically, the rates reported by Hasbrouck and Tindal (1992) are based on data collected on between 7,000 and 9,000 students. The actual scores are the medians for the 50th to the 75th percentiles. The rates reported by Marston and Magnusson (1988) are based on 2,720 students for each testing period (resulting in a total standardization sample of 8,160 students) in Minneapolis. (The numbers in parentheses are standard deviations. All numbers in the first two parts of the table were rounded to the nearest whole number.) A comparison of these figures reveals a relatively high degree of correspondence between fluency rates. Of course, they are based on students in the same geographical area. However, our experience with developing local norms and comparing these figures with others that have appeared in the literature suggests that these fluency rates are robust and give a good, general indication of the level at which the average student is reading.

For the following reasons, we suggest that you use these instructional placement recommendations and average fluency rates as guidelines only for what to expect. By triangulating information across sources and with increasing experience and perhaps local norms (Shinn, 1989), you will be able to judge good from poor performance. We advise against using this information as the basis of making hard-and-fast rules about student placement levels. Consider that when designing interventions, consultants tend to have little power over the level at which students are being taught. Teachers are often resistant to moving a child down in the curriculum because it would create yet more reading groups. Therefore, as a consultant, the best you may be able to do is to assist in developing an intervention at the current level at which the student is being taught. Besides, there is no guarantee that an intervention in the student's current instructional level is going to be any less effective than an intervention at a lower instructional level.

To address the question about student progress, a good rule of thumb is that the more frequently assessments are conducted, the more quickly you can arrive at a decision about the effectiveness of the intervention. To make a reliable decision, you must have sufficient data points. Good and Shinn (1990) found that 10 data points were adequate. By collecting data twice weekly, you get 10 data points in 5 weeks, when a decision can be made (Shinn & Hubbard, 1992). An example of a long-term growth assessment can be found in Figure 6.2. To conduct these assessments, you should choose passages randomly from the pool of progress monitoring passages (three per assessment), replacing the passages each time an assessment is done.

TABLE 6.4. Instructional Placement Recommendations, Average Fluency Rates, and Average CRW per Minute Increase per Week in ORF

Study	Grade 1			Grade 2			Grade 3			Grade 4			Grade 5			Grade 6		
	Fall	Win.	Spr.	Fall	Win.	Spr.	Fall	Win.	Spr.	Fall	Win.	Spr.	Fall	Win.	Spr.	Fall	Win.	Spr.
Instructional placement recommendations																		
Fuchs & Deno (1982)				30–49 CRW 3–7 errors			30–49 CRW 3–7 errors			50–99 CRW 3–7 errors			50–99 CRW 3–7 errors			50–99 CRW 3–7 errors		
Howell & Nolet (2000)	30–50 CRW < 4 errors			70–100 CRW < 6 errors			110–140 CRW < 8 errors			> 140 CRW < 8 errors			> 140 CRW < 8 errors			> 140 CRW < 8 errors		
Shapiro (2004)	40–60 CRW < 5 errors			40–60 CRW < 5 errors			70–100 CRW < 7 errors			70–100 CRW < 7 errors			70–100 CRW < 7 errors			70–100 CRW < 7 errors		
Average fluency rates																		
Hasbrouck & Tindal (1992)				53– 82	78– 106	94– 124	79– 107	93– 123	114– 142	99– 125	112– 133	118– 143	105– 126	118– 143	128– 151			
Marston & Magnusson (1988)	19 (36)	52 (50)	71 (39)	51 (41)	73 (44)	82 (39)	88 (40)	107 (41)	115 (38)	105 (42)	115 (41)	118 (43)	118 (40)	129 (43)	134 (40)	115 (39)	120 (37)	131 (39)
Average words per minute increase per week (slope)																		
Deno et al. (2001)	1.80 (.15)			1.66 (.09)			1.18 (.10)			1.01 (.05)			0.58 (.05)			0.66 (.04)		
Fuchs et al. (1993)	2.10 (.80)			1.43 (.69)			1.08 (.52)			0.84 (.30)			0.49 (.28)			0.32 (.33)		
Marston & Tindal (1995)	2–3			2–3			1.5–2.5			1.5–2.5			1.5–2.5			1.5–2.5		

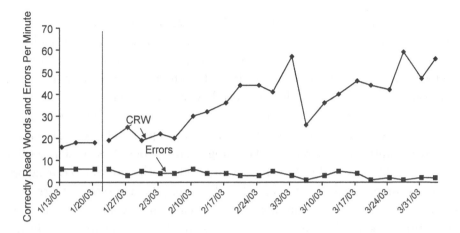

FIGURE 6.2. Example of long-term growth assessment for reading intervention.

When these data are used for progress monitoring purposes (question 2), it raises an additional question about how much growth a student should make. Table 6.4 contains estimates of growth in correctly read words (CRW) per minute per week in typical samples of students from three different reports (slopes of improvement). Deno, Fuchs, Marston, and Shin (2001) obtained performance increases of about 1.80 CRW per minute per week for the first graders in their sample. (The numbers in parentheses are standard errors.) You will see that students tend to make greater increases in fluency in the earlier grades than in the later grades. You will also note that there are some significant discrepancies across reports, and that there are no absolutes in this area either. Deno et al. (2001) also looked at seven reading intervention studies of students with learning disabilities. All of the studies reported significant growth in reading performance. Across these studies, the average weekly CRW per minute growth rate for the second- through sixth-grade participants was 1.39 CRW per minute per week. These figures may prove helpful to you in gauging the progress of students who are receiving reading interventions.

CBM-ORF is indeed a very good measure of reading proficiency and it measures an important skill. However, as with all assessments, it is not perfect, and error creeps in. For one, ensuring that passages are of equal difficulty level (an assumption of this type of assessment) is not easily done (Poncy, McCallum, & Skinner, 2011; Skinner, McCleary, Poncy, Cates, & Skolits, 2013). Readability formulas—a commonly used method for comparing passage difficulty levels—are notoriously unreliable. In fact, in some instances, the average standard error of measurement can amount to almost one full year of growth (Christ & Ardoin, 2009; Francis et al., 2008; Poncy, Skinner, & Axtell, 2005). This amount of error makes it difficult to validly evaluate the effects of interventions (Christ & Silberglitt, 2007; Christ, Zopluoglu, Long, & Monaghen, 2012; Christ, Zopluoglu, Monaghen, & Van Norman, 2013). Some change in oral reading fluency scores may be caused by poor or inconsistent administration and scoring procedures (Christ, 2006), but nonequivalent passages appear to account for more error than anything else (Poncy et al., 2005). Researchers have tried to enhance passage equivalence through a variety of procedures, and found that developing equivalent probes remains challenging (Christ & Ardoin, 2009; Christ et al., 2012). Until researchers determine how to reduce the error associated with oral reading fluency measures, caution should be exercised when interpreting oral reading fluency results based on only a few assessments. While increases in oral reading fluency may be an indication of improved reading skills, they may also be caused by measurement error.

CBM-ORF results can also be influenced by other extraneous factors that should be kept in mind. For example, asking students to read fast (as opposed to asking them to read to the best of their abilities) can increase oral reading fluency (Colón & Kranzler, 2006; Forbes, Maurer, Taylor, & Skinner, 2013). Merely showing students the stopwatch during oral reading fluency assessments has also increased oral reading fluency scores (Derr-Minneci & Shapiro, 1992). These increases were not just statistically significant; they ranged from one half to an entire grade level. Thus, increases in oral reading fluency may not always reflect improvements in other general or specific reading skills. They may occur as a result of the situation in which the student is being assessed.

Some educators have expressed concern that oral reading fluency is merely a measure of word calling and therefore unimportant relative to the goals of reading assessment. A series of investigations examined whether this was a legitimate criticism (Ciancio et al., 2013; Hale, Skinner, Wilhoit, Ciancio, & Morrow, 2012; Skinner, Williams, et al., 2009; Williams et al., 2011). In these studies, oral reading fluency and some other brief reading rate measures (e.g., reading comprehension rate, Maze fluency) were conceptualized as measures of oral reading speed. When assessment results were converted to rate by incorporating some measure of accuracy—including words read accurately (oral reading fluency), correctly selected words (Maze fluency), and correctly selected answers to comprehension questions (reading comprehension rate)—the investigators consistently found that the pure measure of reading speed embedded with oral reading fluency and similar measures accounted for much of the variance in broad reading skill development. What this means is that when people criticize oral reading fluency for being a measure of word calling or barking, it is critical to remind them that oral reading fluency is also a measure of reading speed. This answer seems to satisfy many educators who focus on enhancing students' fluency with basic academic skills. Underlying this criticism is often a concern about using oral reading fluency as a substitute for comprehension measures. In some instances, enhancing oral reading fluency scores may enhance comprehension scores, however, in other instances, comprehension deficits may have to be addressed with other procedures. For example, if students have limited vocabularies but strong oral reading skills, enhancing oral reading fluency scores are unlikely to address comprehension deficits, but enhancing vocabulary may improve comprehension (see Chapter 7).

Before we turn to oral reading fluency interventions, we want to issue a final note of caution about interpreting the results. Oral reading fluency deficits cannot be enhanced overnight. Rather, effective interventions typically require hard work (effort) and sustained and frequent applications of intervention procedures over a period of time. No matter how strong and appropriate CBM-ORF is as a measure of the student who concerns you, you should not expect to find improvements in general reading skills until empirically validated interventions have been applied over a long enough period of time to allow them to be effective (Christ et al., 2013). In other words, oral reading fluency interventions take time to work. Although it is good to gather data more frequently (it produces a more reliable trend), it is important to be sure you do not react too quickly to the results. Effects will take time.

EMPIRICALLY VALIDATED READING INTERVENTIONS

Although there may be many names for the different types of available reading interventions, they are easier to sift through when you understand that they are all variations on a small number of themes. After someone makes a procedural change, the intervention gets a new name and is described as a "new and improved" strategy. We present a manageable number of interventions that represent the fundamental principles that impact student learning. You may come across other intervention strategies in the literature, but we are confident that if you compare them with the ones presented in Table 6.5, you will see that they differ only in the degree to which they emphasize different components. One strategy might have more acquisition components, whereas another contains more fluency-building ingredients. Although we have adopted the popular names from the literature for the interventions listed in Table 6.5 and discuss them briefly below, we stress their features relative to the instructional hierarchy described in Chapter 2, so that you know when an intervention is likely to be more appropriate, that is, according to whether the student is having difficulty with accuracy, fluency, or generalization.

Repeated Readings

The procedure of repeated readings is presented first because it is the intervention that will work with the largest number of students. In this procedure the student reads the same passage multiple times. The student gets a lot of practice time and the procedure is simple. Repeated reading is perhaps the purest form of the "practice makes perfect" model of enhancing reading fluency. Various studies have shown that repeated reading is an effective procedure for enhancing reading fluency in general education students as well as students with disabilities (e.g., Blum & Koskinen, 1991; Dowhower, 1989; Samuels, 1979; Sindelar, Monda, O'Shea, 1990). This strategy is perhaps the best fluency builder, thanks to all the practice time it affords, and can help to correct situations in which there is a lack of sufficient practice, which may be the greatest weakness of many reading curricula. One weakness of repeated readings is that it is not appropriate when a student's accuracy is poor. If a student makes a lot of errors, repeated readings without other strategies that include modeling, prompting, and error correction might make things worse! Students could end up practicing errors. That said, it should be the core intervention strategy for virtually all reading fluency problems. For the student whose accuracy is poor, you should add other strategies (e.g., listening while reading and error correction) to make the practice more productive.

TABLE 6.5. Overview of Basic Reading Interventions

Type of intervention	Acquisition	Fluency	Generalization	Appropriate uses	Limitations
			Purpose of intervention		
Repeated readings	✓		• To reading words in context • Potentially to other texts with the same words	• Probably the most effective intervention with the most students, because it provides many opportunities to respond.	• Does not correct errors, so students may practice errors if an error correction component is not used. • Lacks an acquisition component for reading new words. However, students who are beyond acquisition and who have decoding skills may improve on some words "spontaneously" (i.e., without explicit modeling). • May be boring for some students if there is no performance feedback and contingent positive social attention for improvements.

Procedures

1. Present a text to the student and explain that you will have him or her practice reading the passage to help him or her get better at reading.
2. Have the student read the passage aloud three or four times, or have the student read the passage aloud for a preset amount of time (e.g., 2 or 3 minutes) three or four times.

Type of intervention	Acquisition	Fluency	Generalization	Appropriate uses	Limitations
Phrase drill error correction	✓		• This is a very strong error correction procedure, because students practice error words in connected text. Students are more likely to generalize correct reading of words when phrase drill is used than when error correction procedures do not have students practice words in context.	• This error correction procedure addresses errors effectively and encourages students to read each and every word correctly.	• This error correction is a bit more complex procedurally than other error correction procedures, and it takes more time.

Procedures

1. Have the student read a text while you underline or highlight error words.
2. When the student has finished reading the text, show him or her your copy with the underlined/highlighted words.
3. Read the error word correctly to the student (model).
4. Have the student read the phrase/sentence containing the error word aloud three times.
5. If a sentence contains more than one error word, model correct reading of all error words in the sentence first and then have the student read the phrase/sentence three times.

(continued)

TABLE 6.5. *(continued)*

Type of intervention	Acquisition	Fluency	Generalization	Appropriate uses	Limitations
		Purpose of intervention			
Performance feedback	✓		• May provide motivating conditions that help the student to want to read faster in the presence of the teacher/tutor, leading to generalized increases in reading when the teacher/tutor asks the student to read aloud.	• If the condition is motivating for the student, he or she takes an interest in trying to read faster.	• Students may mistake the purpose of reading as one of just trying to read faster. It is critical to stress the importance of reading words correctly and that this intervention component may help to make other reading easier, but will not, in itself, increase comprehension.

Procedures

1. Present the text to the student and explain that you will give feedback on how quickly and accurately he or she reads the passage.
2. Begin timing of the student when he or she says the first word. If the first word is pronounced incorrectly, correct the student and begin timing with the next word.
3. When the student has finished reading the text, give the student the following information: (a) how many words were read in the first minute, or (b) how much time it took to finish the story, and (c) how many errors he or she made.

Type of intervention	Acquisition	Fluency	Generalization	Appropriate uses	Limitations
Listening while reading	✓	✓	• Accurate and fluent reading of connected text is modeled for the student, increasing the chances that the student will be better able to read connected text containing similar words.	• This is a strong intervention for students who have high error rates and read slowly.	• Students may not pay attention or practice reading subvocally while the teacher/tutor is reading the story aloud. For this reason, students generally get fewer opportunities to respond.

Procedures

1. Present the text to the student and tell him or her that you will read the story aloud to help the student learn how to read the words. Tell the student to follow along with his or her finger.
2. Read the text at a comfortable reading rate while monitoring the student's tracking correctly with his or her finger.
3. Have the student read the passage aloud to you.

Type of intervention	Acquisition	Fluency	Generalization	Appropriate uses	Limitations
Strategic incremental rehearsal flashcard method	✓		• May produce generalized responding of isolated word reading, but will probably be less effective for text reading if the student does not practice newly acquired words	• When students are not responding to interventions in connected text (i.e., error rate is high and accuracy is poor), isolating words	• It is not a particularly strong strategy for producing generalized increases in reading fluency. • The procedures require practice and may be

(continued)

TABLE 6.5. (continued)

Type of intervention	Purpose of intervention			Appropriate uses	Limitations
	Acquisition	Fluency	Generalization		
			in text through other intervention components.	might help them to acquire more words. • Students get a lot of practice opportunities, and the task tends *not* to produce frustration because teaching of unknown words occurs in the context of many known words. Also, it gives the teacher/tutor ample opportunity to praise students and give positive feedback on performance.	confusing initially for teachers/consultants unfamiliar with them.

Procedures

1. Identify a pool of words the student cannot read ("unknowns"). This can be done either by having a student read texts and identifying error words, or by presenting words on flashcards from commonly used word lists and having the student say the words aloud, putting "corrects" and "incorrects" in separate piles. Set the "corrects" aside.
2. Present the first word from the pool of unknown words, read it to the student (modeling the correct response), and have the student read the word aloud.
3. Present the second word, read it to the student (modeling the correct response), and have the student read the word aloud.
4. Repeat steps 2 and 3 once.
5. Present each word once again for the student to read them aloud (without the model) and, if the student does not give the correct response in 2 seconds, read it to the student (prompt delay procedure). Repeat this step until the student can say the words without a delayed modeling prompt (i.e., within 2 seconds of presenting the word).
6. Now present a new word, read it to the student (modeling the correct response), and have the student read the word aloud.
7. Present the previously taught words (n = 2, items from steps 2-5) in random order.
8. Shuffle all three words and present them in random order, using the prompt delay procedure. If the student does not read a word correctly in 2 seconds, say the word, and have the student say the word aloud.
9. When the student responds correctly to all three words without the delayed modeling of the word, present a new word, read it to the student (modeling the correct response), and have the student read the word aloud.
10. Repeat this procedure for the remainder of the instructional session, "folding in" a new word each time the student is able to read all the other words without a delayed modeling prompt.
11. In new sessions, begin with previously instructed words to build fluency and continue to add words by folding them in when the student reads all previously instructed words correctly.

Although at first glance repeated readings may appear to be monotonous, our experience is that students generally like the intervention and are compliant with the procedure. One reason is that they usually get a lot of positive adult attention and encouragement for any improvement. (Be sure to praise the student for each improvement.) Students see themselves improve within passages and, because good effects are generally obtained, across passages. They see reading becoming easier and less effortful. We do, however, recommend strongly that you include a performance feedback component, such as telling a student how many words he or she read correctly in comparison to a previous reading. Students are more likely to be motivated by this kind of feedback. Again, because there is no acquisition component for words the student has not yet learned to read, we recommend that you include an error correction procedure, such as a phrase drill (see page 109) to bring the errors down across readings and reduce the risk of having students practice errors repeatedly. Finally, it is important to have students read aloud rather than silently, because students who are asked to read silently may not reread the passage (Chard et al., 2002; Hale et al., 2005). Furthermore, the student's reading performance can be measured across readings and monitored when the reading is done orally. These data can be used to monitor progress, provide fluency feedback, and encourage students to continue reading.

Figure 6.3 is a graph of performance feedback that can be used to enhance students' willingness to engage in repeated readings. A student's daily reading performance, wherein the student rereads the same passage three times each day, is displayed in bar graph form. The first shaded bar for each session represents the first student reading; the dark bar that follows represents the second student reading; and the white bar, the third reading for that day. The pattern of improvement shown in Figure 6.3 is fairly typical: Student performance almost always improves with each rereading. This improvement should be communicated to students, and they should be praised and reinforced for it. We have frequently found one

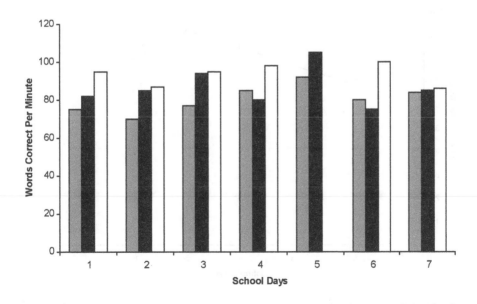

FIGURE 6.3. Example of repeated readings performance data.

of the easiest ways to positively reinforce improved performance is to give students written feedback (e.g., like the bar graph). Students typically love to share a graphic display like this with others (parents, teachers, the principal) who in turn provide praise. (This, by the way, is why Mom's refrigerator is perennially covered with artwork and other schoolwork!)

Generalized improvement in other texts may be observed because the student is practicing correct and rapid word reading in connected text. However, in one investigation that directly manipulated the amount of word overlap between what was taught and what was assessed, repeated readings did not produce such generalized increases (Rashotte & Torgesen, 1985). Yet, there have been instances in which generalization to noninstructed texts with high word overlap has been found with repeated readings (Daly, Martens, Dool, & Hintze, 1998; Daly & Murdoch, 2000). The bottom line is that there are no guarantees that generalized improvements will be observed. Studies that have yielded generalization increases (e.g., Daly, Martens, Kilmer, & Massie, 1996) have usually used multicomponent interventions (i.e., more than one strategy at a time). We suspect that the degree of generalization achieved with a particular student will be a function of his or her baseline skills prior to intervention and the strength of the intervention. Students whose problems are less severe and for whom attention and feedback are reinforcing are more likely to improve across passages with repeated readings.

Generalized student progress can be measured, to some degree, by assessing his or her reading improvement on previously unread passages. This can be done by assessing improved rates of words correct per minute during the first reading. The initial reading data (first shaded bar from each assessment) presented in the bar graphs of Figure 6.3 are presented as a line graph in Figure 6.4. These data show a less stable but increasing trend in the student's reading progress (reading rate on novel passages).

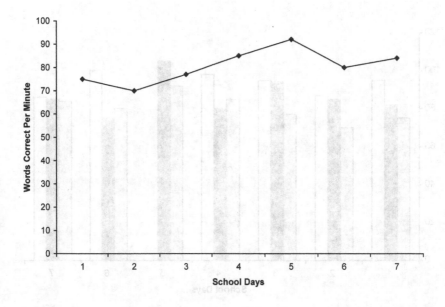

FIGURE 6.4. Example of a progress monitoring graph: repeated readings data.

Phrase Drill Error Correction

Reading errors reflect an accuracy problem. Error words should be treated as unlearned words, even if the student can get the word right from time to time. Unlearned words are words that have not been acquired. In response to errors, educators generally model correct reading of the word (an acquisition strategy), prompt a response from the student (practice), and provide feedback immediately for every response (an acquisition strategy). Feedback generally comes in the form of praise for a correct response (e.g., "Correct!") or correction (e.g., "No, the word is _____, say it again"). Intervention strategies that train students in the context of connected text (as opposed to training word reading in isolation) increase the likelihood of correct reading in texts (generalization; Daly, Lentz, et al., 1996; Daly & Martens, 1994). Phrase drill is superior to other error correction strategies (O'Shea, Munson, & O'Shea, 1984) for this very reason—it makes the student practice correct reading of the word in connected text (the context for reading). To use phrase drill it is necessary to have the student read an instructional passage at least once. Adding phrase drill to repeated readings makes for a very powerful intervention. When combining repeated readings and phrase drill for an individual student, we suggest that you do the phrase drill procedure after you have the student read the passage once. That way, the student practices correct reading of the words during the phrase drill procedure and also practices correct reading during the following two or three student passage readings that complete the repeated readings portion of the intervention strategy. Improving accuracy through error correction will make subsequent practice (and thus fluency training) more beneficial.

Performance Feedback

Performance feedback is primarily a motivational strategy that doesn't really teach students anything, except that it is important to read faster than they are currently reading, strictly a fluency-building issue. Many students like to try to beat their last score, and performance feedback might be rewarding, in itself. Using praise and encouraging statements may have even more rewarding value. If the teacher or tutor works with the student to graph his or her performance, the student can visually see increases and even gets a little math lesson as a part of the package! Results can be graphed for each reading of a passage (Figure 6.3) or for the first reading and the last reading (to make it simpler). Students are likely to see performance increases on a daily basis (i.e., from the first to last reading) and across sessions over time (as their initial reading performance increases). This tangible improvement is generally rewarding for those responsible for the intervention as well, as they get a visual representation of the student's performance over time. (There's nothing like hard data!) Performance feedback (Eckert, Ardoin, Daly, & Martens, 2002) works particularly well with repeated readings.

Performance feedback can be strengthened further through the use of rewards. Performance increases can be tied to access to privileges (e.g., extra free time, being line leader, reduced work load, having lunch with the teacher, not having lunch with the teacher), tangibles (e.g., selecting an object or toy from a treasure chest, much like at the dentist's office), and social praise from significant individuals (e.g., showing the student's reading score to the principal). In one study, performance feedback and access to tangible rewards were used to influence middle school students with behavioral disorders to choose which type of instruction they would receive (Daly, Garbacz, Olson, Persampieri, & Ni, 2006). The students had no obligation to choose to practice or do anything before they could try to go for a reward. Although reward criteria were different for students according to their skill level, the participants almost always chose the procedure in which experimenters had them practice, correct their errors, and model reading for them (on occasion). Performance increases in reading fluency across passages were found. In this study, performance feedback was critical to indicating to the students whether their practice was helping them and for determining whether they met their goals.

Modeling: Listening While Reading

Listening while reading (LWR) is another effective and simple procedure for enhancing oral reading. (This procedure also has been referred to as listening previewing [Rose, 1984b] and assisted reading [Hoskisson & Krohm, 1974].) Because LWR includes modeling by the teacher or tutor, it strengthens a student's reading accuracy. Modeling is a demonstration of how to perform a skill—reading words in this case. Effective modeling correct reading of words increases the chances the student will then read the words correctly when called upon to do so. During LWR, students first are instructed to read along silently as another reads aloud. The student then rereads the same passage aloud. LWR has been shown to enhance oral reading in students who have both intellectual and learning disabilities (Daly & Martens, 1994; Rose, 1984a, 1984b, 1984c). LWR has been used to enhance students' speed of accurate reading across passages and word lists (Freeman & McLaughlin, 1984; Skinner, Cooper, & Cole, 1997). The effect of LWR on fluency is probably more indirect and not as strong as those of repeated readings. The modeling component (i.e., reading to the student) is designed to help the student get the words right during subsequent practice (i.e., the student-reading portion of the procedure). However, the procedure provides fast-paced practice, and it may be the practice that strengthens learning.

Findings from several studies suggest that during LWR interventions, it is critical that the rate of oral presentation be slow enough so that the students who are following along have sufficient time to read silently, attempt to read, and use the model reading as accuracy feedback for the printed material (Skinner et al., 1993; Skinner, Cooper, et al., 1997; Skinner & Shapiro, 1989; see also Skinner, Logan, Robinson, & Robinson, 1997, for a review). It is best if oral readers do not read much faster than the students' current reading rate. Fluent readers who intentionally reduce their reading rates should avoid reading in a clipped, word-by-word fashion. Instead, they should read according to the rhythm of the material, pausing appropriately for punctuation marks and using inflection. The greatest problem we have found with this approach is that students may not pay full attention and therefore may derive limited benefits from the modeling. We expected the modeling to make it a strong procedure, but we have seen many students who do better with the repeated readings intervention than with the LWR intervention. Of course, the issue needs to be resolved on a case-by-case basis, and there are no strong predictors of how a student will do with the interventions, short of trying them both and seeing how he or she responds to each.

Teaching Words in Isolation

In general, students progress more when they practice reading connected texts, which is the natural context in which words appear. So, as noted above, the intervention strategies that train word reading in connected texts are more likely to promote generalization across texts. In some cases, however, the connected text creates too much "busyness" for a student to be able to learn individual words. Indeed, in some instances, teaching in context may create more confusion (Howell & Nolet, 2000). When this is the case, it may be useful to teach a student to read words in isolation. Taped words is generally appropriate when a student's word-reading accuracy is poor. Isolating the word individually and modeling correct reading of the words may be a necessary step before text reading will improve.

Taped Words

Taped-words procedures were developed by Freeman and McLaughlin (1984) and are used to teach isolated word reading. The procedure used involved printing a list of words in columns (e.g., 80 words, 2 columns of 40) and making an audio recording of the word lists being read very rapidly (e.g., 80 words per minute). The recording speed was thought to be critical because students may have modeled both accurate reading and reading speed. Students are then instructed to read the word list along with the tape. Researchers have found evidence that these procedures enhance word list reading accuracy and fluency in students with learning disabilities, intellectual disabilities, emotional/behavioral disorders, and ELs (e.g., Bliss, Skinner, & Adams, 2006; Freeman & McLaughlin, 1984; Shapiro & McCurdy, 1989; Sterling, Robinson, & Skinner, 1997).

To determine if students achieved the modeled reading rates after intervention, researchers slowed the rate of presentation (e.g., one word every 5 seconds) and compared learning across procedures. These studies suggest that students do not achieve the modeled reading rates, as word-list reading fluency improvements were similar when words were presented every second versus every 5 seconds (Skinner, Johnson, Larkin, Lessley, & Glowacki, 1995; Skinner & Shapiro, 1989; Skinner, Smith, & McLean, 1994). However, something interesting happened when words were presented at a slower rate (e.g., every 3–5 seconds): although students were still instructed to "read with the tape," when words were presented at a slower rate, many students began to attempt to read words before the tape. Additionally, they appeared to use the recording as feedback regarding the accuracy of their reading. For example, one student would read the word before the tape and then say "yes" when he heard the recording. In these instances, students had turned the tape-words intervention into something that resembled a flashcard intervention, which encouraged others to purposefully apply similar procedures to enhance basic math and reading skills (Bliss et al., 2006; McCallum, Evans, Friedrich, & Long, 2011; McCallum, Skinner, & Hutchins, 2004; Taylor, Skinner, McCallum, Poncy, & Orsega, 2013).

Flashcards

With taped words, students were required to read lists of words printed horizontally down a page. One concern with such procedures is that students may lose their place and mislearn words. One way to address this concern is to present only one word at a time with flashcards. Flashcard procedures have been shown to be very effective at increasing sight-word reading in students with disabilities (Browder & Xin, 1998). Like taped words, flashcards first build word-reading accuracy. However, because of the heavy practice component, it also builds word-reading fluency. Although flashcard sight-word instruction may seem like a very simple procedure, there are many decisions to be made when applying flashcard instruction.

A typical flashcard trial involves presenting the flashcard, providing some time for the student to respond, and then providing feedback on the response. If we start with this simple procedure, we are immediately faced with several considerations. First, we must consider how much time we should give the student to respond. This discussion may be dependent upon the specific word and other instructional strategies currently being applied. For example, consider two words (*chart* and *queue*). Because the word *chart* is a phonetically regular word, a student who is receiving phonemic instruction should probably be given a response interval that provides enough time for him or her to apply his or her phonetic skills and attempts to read this word. However, providing the same student with time to attempt to read phonetically irregular words may increase the probability that the student reads the word incorrectly and, thus, frustrate the student as he or she attempts to apply skills he or she has been previously taught but which do not apply in this case. Therefore, we may want to provide 3–5 seconds for students to attempt to read *chart*, but only 1 second for the student to read *queue* (Bliss et al., 2006; Yaw et al., 2011, 2012).

Staying with the above examples, we can now address the type of feedback we provide. Under both conditions, when a student reads the word correctly, immediate feedback should be provided. In some instances merely saying, "Correct!" is enough. In other instances, when teachers want to encourage the application of recently acquired phonemic skills, they may want to add labeled praise by saying, "Correct, nice job sounding out the word!" When errors are made on regular words, feedback may include some phonetic instruction (e.g., "The *ch* makes the /ch/ sound"). For irregular words, feedback should be quick, dispassionate, and corrective (e.g., "No, the word is *queue*"). In both cases, when errors are made students should repeat the word following the feedback. This repetition ensures that the last response they made was correct and increases the number of accurate responses students make with each session, a procedure that may enhance sight-word learning in students with disabilities (Belfiore, Skinner, & Ferkis, 1995; Ferkis, Belfiore, & Skinner, 1997).

When teaching irregular words to a student in a one-on-one context, another strategy may be to apply progressive time delay. With this procedure, you might show the flashcard and say the word simultaneously, with the student repeating the word as you continue to display the word. After finishing this procedure with a word set (say, five words), you would shuffle the flashcards and repeat this procedure, now giving the students 1 second to read each word before you say it. The next time through the set, you might allow 2 seconds before you read the word aloud. Eventually, you will find that students begin to say the word before you do. One of the primary advantages to this procedure is that students tend to make few errors because during early trials the correct word is provided before they can say it. They are also more likely to read the word correctly in subsequent trials because they have enough time; the earlier trials caused learning. Progressive time delay can also go in the other direction. With regular words, we may want to provide 5 seconds for students to respond on initial trials so that students have time to apply their phonemic skills. When the set of flashcards is repeated, reducing response intervals may encourage greater automaticity (Bliss et al., 2006; McCallum et al., 2004).

Researchers have also investigated computer-based flashcard instruction and found that it was effective for students with significant reading skill (Hilton-Mounger, Hopkins, Skinner, & McCane-Bowling, 2011; Kodak, Fisher, Clements, & Bouxsein, 2011; Yaw et al., 2011). The obvious advantage of computer-based flashcard instruction is that teachers do not need to monitor students individually. The disadvantage is that computers cannot adjust their procedures or feedback based on student responding. For example, a computer may not be able to observe a student attempting to apply phonemic skills and allow a bit more time for responding. Another disadvantage is related to computer-delivered feedback. In theory, voice recognition software should allow for the computer to immediately evaluate a student's sight-word reading. In practice, we have found that in too many instances, these evaluations are flawed, particularly when students have articulation problems, heavy accents, and/or speak softly.

Fortunately, it is fairly easy to develop a computer-based flashcard intervention that does not require programming or code. A method for creating flashcard items in PowerPoint is described in Figure 6.5 (based on Hopkins, Hilton, & Skinner, 2011). Prior to the session, the student should be instructed to read words aloud as soon as they appear on the screen. When a student starts the PowerPoint slides, a word first appears on the screen. He or she should attempt to read it. Next, an audio recording of the word plays after a slight delay (e.g., after 5 seconds), providing the student with feedback on his or her accuracy and a model for correct reading. The word remains on the screen for a brief moment (e.g., 1.5 seconds) to provide the student time to repeat the word in front of the word display. After the word disappears, a new word appears and the process is repeated. We recommend that you have the student practice the same words at least twice in a single session.

Researchers have manipulated response intervals (how long student have to respond before the recording is played). Learning across different response intervals (1-second, 3-second, and 5-second intervals) was similar (Black, Forbes, Yaw, & Skinner, 2013; Yaw, 2013). However, because the briefer intervals reduced instructional time, students learned at a much more rapid rate during the 1-second computer-based flashcard procedures. Also, students appeared to prefer shorter (1-second) response intervals (Yaw et al., 2012). Consequently, while it may be tempting to develop procedures that allow plenty of time for students to respond, these delays may reduce learning because they reduce the overall number of word presentations over time. Additionally, some research suggests that long delays may reduce student attention and learning (Hawkins, Skinner, & Oliver, 2005).

Materials:

Computer, Microsoft PowerPoint

Selecting Unknown Words:

Words can be presented on a computer or on handwritten index cards. Several criteria have been used. We recommended initially presenting all words for 2 seconds without assistance to determine whether the student can read the word or not. Any words not read correctly within 2 seconds should be considered unknown and included in the pool of words targeted for instruction.

Preparing PowerPoint Slides:

1. Open PowerPoint and create the first slide "Start"; when the student clicks, the intervention will begin.

2. Create target-word slides. Press and hold the *CTRL* key, then press the *M* key. When a new slide appears with two text boxes, eliminate the bottom text box by clicking it and then pressing the delete key. Click the remaining text box, drag it to the middle of the screen, and type the target word. This first slide can serve as a template for all additional slides.

3. Create recordings for each slide. If your computer does not have an internal microphone, plug one into the audio jack. Go to the *Insert* menu, and select *Sound* or *Movie/Sound* and a dialog box will appear with the following options: PLAY, STOP, and RECORD. To make a recording, click RECORD and say the word immediately, click STOP, and then click OK. **Do not select automatic play.** When a *speaker* symbol appears on the PowerPoint, drag it to the bottom of the slide. You may double click the speaker to check the recording.

4. Slide intervals. Five-second intervals are recommended: 3 seconds to read each word plus 0.5 seconds for the recorded response plus 1.5 seconds to allow the student to repeat the word. To set these intervals, click the *Animations* menu and, under the advanced slide options, deselect *Mouse Click* and select *Automatically after* and then type in 5 seconds.

5. Audio recording intervals. In our example, we wanted to allow the student 3 seconds to read the word; therefore, after the word appears on the screen, we want to set a 3-second auditory delay. To do so, select the *speaker* symbol, right click and select *Custom Animation*, and click *Add Effect*, then *Sound Action,* and finally *Play*. To set the response interval or delay between the word and the recording being played, right click the new *Sound Animation* icon and select *Timing*. When the *Play Sound* dialog box appears, use the dropdown button beside *Start* and select *With Previous*. Type in *3* beside *delay* and then click *OK*.

Making Additional Slides:

You now have your first template slide. You can test it by viewing the slideshow. Next, create new slides by copying these slides. Once you have a pool of slides, they should be saved under a template file. This file can then be used to create new word pools (different words for different students), randomly sequenced words, and repeating words lists (repeat each list of 15 words four times instead of two times). As words are learned, they can be deleted and replaced with new words. It is also possible to use the slides to create computer-based assessments that involve each slide being presented for 2 seconds.

FIGURE 6.5. Creating flashcards. Based on Hopkins, Hilton, and Skinner (2011).

Other researchers have suggested that students will learn more from flashcard instruction if 70% or more of the words are known. Despite two meta-analytic studies that suggest such procedures work (Burns, 2004; Burns, Zaslofsky, Kanive, & Parker, 2012), we do not advocate using such procedures because they can take so much additional time. In fact, researchers who measured how much learning occurs per minute of instructional time found evidence that including too many known words reduced, as opposed to enhanced, learning rates (Forbes, Maurer, et al., 2013; Joseph, Eveleigh, Konrad, Neef, & Volpe, 2012; Joseph & Nist, 2006). The flashcard interventions used in these studies almost universally neglected to include prompting strategies like modeling and delayed modeling prompts.

Kupzyk, Daly, and Andersen (2011) added modeling and a prompt delay procedure (modeling after 2 seconds) to a method called incremental rehearsal. By including acquisition strategies, Kupzyk et al. (2011) were able to use all unknown items in their flashcard condition (now called "strategic incremental rehearsal"), which made the instructional sessions more efficient and produced faster word acquisition and better maintenance than the traditional incremental rehearsal flashcard procedure. This strategy is described in Table 6.5. Strategic incremental rehearsal is efficient because the instruction only needs to target unknown reading words and includes heavy doses of prompting to be sure students can give correct responses to unknown words right away.

Generalization is a concern with computer-based flashcard procedures. There is evidence to suggest that learning to read words on the computer can generalize to reading handwritten index cards (Yaw et al., 2012), typed sentences (Joseph & Nist, 2006), and typed passages (Cazzell et al., under review). However, generalization across formats did not always occur. Furthermore, being able to read a word aloud does not guarantee that students will know the meaning. Be careful to not assume that students will be able to read instructed words in texts. We suggest you have them practice the words in connected text after learning how to read them in isolation.

THE CONTEXT FOR READING INTERVENTION: PUTTING THE COMPONENTS TOGETHER

You now have some ideas and some steps to follow for creating reading interventions. The problem is figuring out which strategies are most appropriate for each student. Psychology has had a long love affair with attempting to predict successful interventions. Unfortunately, the practice went way beyond the data, and researchers and practitioners alike forgot to check the outcomes before coming up with complicated processes for prescribing interventions (Kavale & Forness, 1999). There are no sure ways to predict which strategy or combination of strategies is going to work. You simply have to choose them and try them. That's why long-term progress monitoring is so critical to this whole enterprise. Each case is essentially a new experiment, and there will be differences in circumstances both within and across cases. What is highly effective for one child might not be effective for another child, and what works at one time with a child might not work as well at another time. Therefore, we acknowledge that the best we can do is give you some guidelines that may save you time in the long run. It is your responsibility to monitor the intervention carefully and make adjustments, as necessary.

The best way to improve students' reading is by making them read! You may be thinking that this is an overly obvious suggestion. However, one of the characteristics of poor classroom instruction is a lack of active student responding (i.e., student reading in this case). Often, students who are having difficulty learning to read spend less rather than more time reading in the classroom. Intervention sessions should be characterized by a lot of active student responding. Students should spend most of the time reading something. Students who are not actively reading aloud during instruction should be engaging in activities that prepare them to read aloud (e.g., following a model of good reading so that the passage becomes easier to read). Such sessions should not be too long; students are likely to become fatigued and frustrated if sessions last more than about 20 minutes, in general. Of course, some students won't be able to sustain attention even that long. You will need to monitor each child carefully.

We also suggest that you attempt to integrate intervention procedures with current ongoing instruction as much as possible. For instance, repeated readings can be handled by a tutor or willing parent before or after a child reads a story in reading group. Folding-in words can be taken from reading passages, and so forth. View these intervention strategies as ways to supplement what is currently happening in the classroom. There are exceptions to this rule, however. We have seen examples where a teacher is willing to revise classroom instruction procedures altogether because he or she recognizes that more children will benefit. In this case, ongoing instruction is changed to fit the chosen intervention strategies. Perhaps, for example, the teacher is willing to do repeated readings with the reading group through a choral reading exercise (i.e., all students reading aloud together). Another situation arises when a student's skill level is significantly below the current instructional level—for example, a third-grade student receiving second-grade instruction but still showing significant deficits in phoneme segmenting abilities or phonics skills. The intervention should probably target these prerequisite skills. You may want to work with the teacher to see if he or she can modify work demands (e.g., seatwork) so that the student is working on material that is at a more appropriate level.

Another approach to strengthening instruction is to supplement the instruction delivered by the teacher with an intervention that is carried out with the aid of technology, by the student (self-managed interventions), a peer, someone at home, or another adult (e.g., a volunteer tutor or an available paraprofessional; Lentz, Allen, & Ehrhardt, 1996). If a peer or a volunteer is trained to do repeated readings, LWR, or error correction with the target student, tutoring sessions can occur before the student arrives in reading group, making him or her more capable of benefiting from the instruction the teacher is delivering. Alternately, the teacher can assign passages or words to be reviewed through one or more of the interventions outlined in Table 6.6 after instruction for practice and more in-depth error correction. Teachers need not bear all the burden of instructional interventions. Utilizing available resources wisely can help to improve the impact of the teacher's instruction.

TABLE 6.6. Prioritizing Intervention Components

Student's skill level	Increasing intensity————————————▶				
Fluency	RR	PF	PD		
Acquisition	RR	PF	PD	LWR	SIR
Phonics acquisition	RR	PF	PD	LWR	PWI

Note. RR, repeated readings; PF, performance feedback; PD, phrase drill; LWR, listening while reading; SIR, sequential incremental rehearsal; PWI, phonics words taught in isolation.

Prioritizing Intervention Strategies

When choosing which intervention to use, you need to balance effectiveness with cost efficiency (in terms of time and resources). In many cases, a simpler intervention is a good starting point. Avoid making recommendations to a teacher for interventions that are cumbersome and difficult to manage—unless, of course, they are absolutely necessary. If a simpler intervention does not work, then try a more complex one (which might involve nothing more than adding intervention components, as opposed to changing the intervention entirely). That said, the ground rule is: Start with a simpler intervention that is likely to be effective most of the time. The intervention of repeated readings fits this requirement well. Repeated readings often is the strongest fluency-building intervention of those discussed in this chapter. The other strategies support or enhance the efficacy of repeated readings.

If you start with just having the student read aloud as one would do with repeated readings, you can observe his or her patterns and gauge his or her instructional needs. Are errors high and the fluency rate low? If so, the student's accuracy is poor and strategies like modeling, error correction, and practice in isolation might be necessary. Are errors low, but reading is still slow? If so, the student's fluency is poor and he or she would benefit most from practice (e.g., repeated readings) and motivational strategies like performance feedback and maybe even an explicit reward program. Table 6.6 presents our recommendations for how you might prioritize the choice of additional intervention strategies. You will want to vary intervention components depending on the student's skill level. If a student is at more of an acquisition level than a fluency level, then there are additional steps you probably should take. A more significant problem occurs when a student is struggling with basic phonics and having difficulty reading even the simplest texts. The table characterizes this skill level as "phonics acquisition." An intervention plan is presented in the next section for this special case. Another factor to consider is the intensity of the intervention—that is, how much time can (and should) be put into individual reading sessions. The more intense the problem (e.g., there is a very large discrepancy with peer levels), the more intense the intervention should be. Because there are no sure predictors of intervention effectiveness, it is generally safe to start with a lower-intensity intervention and modify it if it doesn't work, rather than starting with a very intense intervention that may have some unnecessary steps. Intervention components are presented in Table 6.6 in terms of recommended levels of increasing intensity.

As you consider how much time, effort, and complexity intervention strategies are likely to add to an intervention session, you may discover that some of them really don't "cost" much. For example, performance feedback is easily added to repeated readings at very little cost in terms of time and effort—and there may be a big payoff for the student if he or she finds the improvements rewarding or if it leads to other rewards (e.g., the tutor praising the child). Although we highly recommend this strategy, a glaring weakness of it is that sometimes students end up practicing their errors. Therefore, although phrase drill is a bit more involved in terms of the time it adds to the intervention and the need for more careful supervision, it may be a worthwhile and important addition to an intervention comprising repeated readings plus performance feedback.

If the student is really struggling or has a low fluency rate, you probably want to add some acquisition components. LWR is a relatively simple addition to an intervention plan and is easier to do than folding in. We suggest that you add LWR first. If the student continues to have difficulty mastering some words, then start doing the sequential incremental rehearsal flashcard procedure. You may go through some or all of these interventions and discover that the student is not responding, or you may figure out early in the process that the student hasn't mastered basic phonics skills. In that case, you might want to try something different (a recommendation is presented in the next section). Before these types of problems are addressed, we draw your attention to Worksheet 6.1 at the end of this chapter, which can help you select an intervention package. You can use this form to record critical information about the case and to guide your selection of various intervention components. Figure 6.6 shows a sample worksheet that has been filled in for Malinda, a third-grade student. In this example, Malinda is presumed to have a fluency problem, and repeated readings and performance feedback are selected as interventions.

When You Can't Go Lower in the Curricular Basal Series

Figure 6.7 presents an intervention that can be used when a student is learning basic phonics skills. Although this protocol targets short-vowel sounds, it can be modified for any other type of phonic skill (e.g., long-vowel words). Just change the rule in steps 1 and 2 of Part I (the phonics lesson) to reflect the skill being taught. A variation of this intervention was used by Daly, Martens, et al. (1996) to produce generalized increases in reading fluency for high-contact-overlap passages. The intervention has been changed to include a phrase drill component and performance feedback, which were not a part of the original study. The basic sequence of instruction was configured to reflect strong instructional design principles (Grossen & Carnine, 1991): The phonics skill is taught in isolation first, with opportunities to apply and practice the skill in the context of connected text. Throughout the session the student receives modeling, practice, error correction, and performance feedback. This intervention may prove particularly useful when there is no systematic teaching of phonics in the classroom.

Classwide Peer Tutoring

Repeated readings and LWR are effective procedures for enhancing reading fluency. These procedures are likely to be more effective when (1) students are reading from material that is not too difficult, (2) feedback and reinforcement are provided for improved performance, and (3) procedures are implemented frequently so that students have many opportunities to respond. One program that incorporates all of these components is classwide peer tutoring (CWPT). CWPT is a group intervention that can increase the skills of many students at one time and is therefore an efficient intervention, if it is acceptable to the teacher.

CWPT programs have been developed for reading, mathematics, spelling, and content areas (Greenwood, Delquadri, & Carta, 1997). These programs are designed to enhance student skill development by eliciting high rates of active academic responding in all stu-

Student Name: *Malinda*   Date: *1/30*

Grade: *3rd*

Step 1. Identify student needs.

Baseline student data:

Two assessments in fourth-grade basal reader; median CRW = 50, errors = 3 (1/28/13); median CRW = 46, errors = 5 (1/30/13). Teacher notes Malinda often appears unmotivated to read.

Suggest that student is struggling with:

    (Fluency)   Acquisition   Phonics acquisition

Step 2. Select intervention strategies.

What is the simplest yet potentially appropriate package to begin with?

Skill level	Increasing intensity →				
Fluency	(RR)	(PF)	(PD)		
Acquisition	RR	PF	PD	LWR	SIR
Phonics acquisition	RR	PF	PD	LWR	PWI

Note. RR, repeated readings; PF, performance feedback; PD, phrase drill; LWR, listening while reading; SIR, strategic incremental rehearsal; PWI, phonics words taught in isolation.

Malinda needs practice and may increase motivation with performance feedback. Error rate is high and needs to be reduced.

Step 3. General considerations.

How can the selected intervention procedures fit with current instruction, or vice versa?

Mom has agreed to supervise her at night and conduct PD after first reading. Malinda and Mom will graph the results together. They will practice upcoming stories in the curriculum. That way, she will come to reading group well prepared.

FIGURE 6.6. Example of a completed worksheet for selecting an intervention package for Malinda.

dents within a classroom setting (Greenwood, Delquadri, & Hall, 1984). The program uses peers to supervise and provide feedback for responding, a game-like format in which rates of accurate oral reading are reinforced, and weekly progress evaluations that can be used to make educational decisions for individual students.

CWPT has been shown to increase academic engaged time and reading fluency in both general education students and students with disabilities (Kamps, Barbetta, Leonard, & Delquadri, 1994; Otis-Wilborn, 1984). The program is also associated with lower dropout rates, increases in performance on standardized achievement test scores, and reduced spe-

Overview:

1. Teach a phonics lesson.
2. Train phonics words in isolation: model plus prompt responses.
3. Have students practice phonics words in passage: model, repeated readings, error correction, performance feedback.

Materials Needed:

Instructions for administration
Instructional word list
Phonics passage
Stopwatch
Pen or pencil

Procedures:

Part I: Phonics Lesson

1. Say, "TODAY WE ARE GOING TO LEARN WORDS THAT CONTAIN THE [STATE LETTER SOUND] SOUND."
2. Present the word list to the student and say, "THESE WORDS ALL CONTAIN THE [STATE LETTER SOUND] SOUND BECAUSE . . . THE VOWEL STANDS BY ITSELF IN THE WORD AND IS SHORT."
3. Say, "I WILL READ THE WORDS TO YOU. I WANT YOU TO POINT TO THE WORDS AS I SAY THEM AND SAY THEM TO YOURSELF."
4. Read the words out loud to the student, as the student points to the words.
5. After reading the list to the student, say, "NOW I WANT YOU TO READ THE WORDS TO ME. IF YOU ARE NOT SURE OF A WORD, I WILL HELP YOU."
6. Tell the student to begin reading at the top of the list.
7. If the student does not read a word within 3 seconds, say the word for the student and have the student repeat the word (saying "Repeat after me!" if the student does not repeat the word spontaneously).
8. Have the student read the entire list, while you correct errors each time they occur.

Part II: Listening while Reading

1. Present the instructional passage to the student, saying, "THIS IS A STORY WITH A LOT OF WORDS THAT HAVE THE [STATE LETTER SOUND] SOUND. I WILL READ THE STORY TO YOU. PLEASE FOLLOW ALONG WITH YOUR FINGER, READING THE WORDS TO YOURSELF AS I SAY THEM. THE STORY IS CALLED. . . ."
2. Read the entire story at a comfortable reading rate, being sure that the student is following along with his or her finger.

Part III: Student Reading, with Error Correction and Performance Feedback Provided

1. Have the student reread the passage, saying, "NOW IT'S YOUR TURN TO READ THE PASSAGE. PLEASE BEGIN READING HERE [POINT TO THE BEGINNING] AND TRY TO READ EACH WORD. IF YOU COME TO A WORD YOU DON'T KNOW, I'LL TELL IT TO YOU. WHEN YOU ARE DONE, I WILL TELL YOU HOW QUICKLY AND ACCURATELY YOU READ THE PASSAGE."
2. Begin timing the student when he or she says the first word. If the first word is pronounced incorrectly, correct the student and begin timing with the next word. Underline or highlight error words as the student reads aloud.
3. If the student hesitates for more than 3 seconds, point to the word in the student's copy of the story, say the word, and underline the word.
4. When the student has finished reading the text, tell him or her either (a) how many words he or she read in the first minute or (b) how much time it took to finish the story and (c) how many errors he or she made.
5. Next, show the student your copy of the passage, with its underlined/highlighted words. Read each error word correctly to the student (modeling). Have the student read the phrase/sentence containing the error word aloud three times. [If a sentence contains more than one error word, model correct reading of all error words first and then have the student read the phrase/sentence three times.]
6. Have the student read the passage two more times. (That is, repeat steps 2 and 3 two more times. Omit underlining of error words.)

FIGURE 6.7. An intervention plan for students with poor accuracy and poor phonics skills (short-vowel words).

cial education placement rates (Greenwood, 1991a, 1991b; Greenwood et al., 1984; Harper, Maheady, Mallette, & Karnes, 1999). A protocol for CWPT is presented in Table 6.7. Further information about implementing CWPT can be obtained at *interventioncentral.org* (see also Chapter 2).

The CWPT program has several advantages over more traditional oral reading programs. In a class containing 15 students, a teacher may call students to a specific area of the room, have them sit in a circle, and take turns reading aloud (small-group round-robin reading). With all the time required for transition, students may be reading aloud and receiving feedback, reinforcement, and error correction for only 1 minute (often less). However, by using peers to provide this feedback, students can engage in such behavior for 10–15 minutes in the same time period.

A second component to this program is that rewards, in the form of points, are delivered contingent upon rate of accurate responding. Additionally, in the game-type format, an unknown number of points is needed to win the game each day, and the mystery is highly motivating. All students are encouraged to do their best, of course. Fluent readers can help their team win by reading even more rapidly and accurately. Those with reading skill deficits can also contribute to their team's success by doing their best, which may make the activity more rewarding for them. Team compositions are changed frequently. Thus all students have an opportunity to be on a winning team.

The program incorporates both repeated reading and LWR. Although dyads read and reread the same material, the material can be varied across groups of students with regard to difficulty and length. Length is of particular interest. For slower readers, passage length can be reduced so that while the tutee reads aloud, he or she has the opportunity to reread

---

TABLE 6.7. Classwide Peer-Tutoring Procedures

1. Use CBM data to determine students' highest instructional level.

2. Divide class into two teams each week.

3. Within each team assign students to dyads based on CBM results; students in each dyad should be reading from the same material.

4. Each student takes a turn reading aloud to team members for a fixed amount of time (10–15 minutes). As one student reads aloud (tutee), the other student (tutor) follows along, awarding points for correctly read sentences and immediately correcting errors (e.g., skipped line, mispronunciation).

5. If a student finishes the selected passage before the allotted time expires, he or she begins to reread the passage.

6. As students are reading, the teacher moves around the room giving bonus points for implementing procedures accurately and reading words that students are unable to decode.

7. After time is up, students switch roles and repeat the procedure.

8. Points are totaled.

9. Individual student points and team points are publicly posted; winning teams are announced each day, often followed by a round of applause.

10. This procedure is typically implemented 4 days per week; on the fifth day progress data are collected by having students read aloud for 1 minute (CBM procedures).

the material several times. This strategy should boost these students' total points and may improve their reading skills. Furthermore, CWPT provides an excellent format for LWR because students reading at the same instructional level read the material silently while serving as tutors. Thus, the tutee may not be reading too fast or too slow, but at just the right speed to enhance the reading skills of the tutor who is following along and scoring.

When first implemented, CWPT is likely to require additional time as students learn the system. Additionally, classrooms are likely to get noisier, and some students may cheat (inflate points) or argue among one another. However, teachers who implement this program consistently find that they are able to adapt to the noise level and address these other concerns.

A final issue concerns the public posting of students' performances. Posting the low points of dysfluent readers is not recommended because it may encourage peers to compare their individual performances (i.e., points earned). Such comparisons are unlikely to be favorable to dysfluent readers. Instead, educators should post each team's performance with a focus on improvement.

CONCLUSIONS

This chapter gives an overview of the importance of, measurement of, and interventions for oral reading fluency. The intervention and measurement strategies are presented with guidelines for use, when appropriate. It is essential, however, that you adapt these methods to your local needs. Students have different fluency levels before intervention, and schools have different priorities and ways of organizing intervention efforts. The ultimate test of the utility of these interventions is whether they produce measurable increases in performance. With ongoing assessment, you will be able to determine whether the methods you are employing are meeting that standard. When the data suggest that something is not working, procedures should be revised until an effective plan is developed. It is worth repeating here that long-term monitoring of progress is the best test of the effectiveness of any intervention plan.

 Students with reading skill deficits may approach all reading activities cautiously because of their history of failure. When working with these students, it is helpful to approach all activities with an upbeat attitude. Do not dwell on or punish errors or mistakes. Instead, attempt to keep scheduled activities moving along rapidly. When the student's performance improves, do provide feedback along with praise. Remember, students who associate reading activities with success and other positive experiences may be more likely to choose to read, as opposed to avoiding reading activities. The more frequently students choose to read, the greater their fluency is likely to become. As students become more fluent readers, they are more likely to choose to read in the future. This upward spiral is the goal of all procedures designed to enhance fluency.

Selecting an Intervention Package

Student Name: _____ Date: _____

Grade: _____

Step 1. Identify student needs.

Baseline student data:

_____

_____

_____

_____

Suggest that student is struggling with:

    Fluency   Acquisition   Phonics acquisition

Step 2. Select intervention strategies.

What is the simplest yet potentially appropriate package to begin with?

Skill level	Increasing intensity ⟶				
Fluency	RR	PF	PD		
Acquisition	RR	PF	PD	LWR	SIR
Phonics acquisition	RR	PF	PD	LWR	PWI

Note. RR, repeated readings; PF, performance feedback; PD, phrase drill; LWR, listening while reading; SIR, strategic incremental rehearsal; PWI, phonics words taught in isolation.

Step 3. General considerations.

How can the selected intervention procedures fit with current instruction, or vice versa?

_____

_____

_____

_____

When will the intervention be carried out and for how long each time? (Student should be reading actively during most of the session. Sessions should probably last no longer than 20 minutes.)

_____

_____

_____

_____

_____

CHAPTER 7

Vocabulary

Vocabulary knowledge is an essential component of academic success. Research has repeatedly documented that students with larger vocabularies tend to be better readers and have better code-based skills (Cunningham & Stanovich, 1997; Ouellette, 2006; Scarborough, 1998; Snow et al., 1998; Verhoeven, Van Leeuwe, & Vermeer, 2011). It stands to reason that students who struggle to understand the words in a text will be unable to extract meaning from what they read. It has been suggested that readers need to know 90–95% of the words in a passage to comprehend its meaning (Anderson & Freebody, 1981). The connection between vocabulary knowledge and other language and literacy-related skills is well documented, with word knowledge being predictive of both phonological representations and irregular sight words for young learners as well as comprehension for older learners (Ouellette, 2006). In addition, students' word knowledge impacts their ability to comprehend instruction in class, read unfamiliar texts, and write, as well as categorize and synthesize new knowledge (Baumann, Kame'enui, & Ash, 2003). Taken together, these findings suggest that vocabulary instruction is an important component to literacy success. In this chapter, we review what is currently known about good vocabulary instruction, and provide strategies for intensifying instruction to meet student needs across grades.

WHY IS IT IMPORTANT TO TEACH VOCABULARY?

Given the previously described connection between vocabulary and other reading-related skills, vocabulary instruction should be a central task of teachers in both the early and later grades. However, explicit teaching of words is rare in the early grades. When it does occur, it has been described as brief and superficial by Kucan (2012). The most common

124

approach to vocabulary instruction is incidental word learning, where words are learned in the context of a story with little explicit attention dedicated to exploring word meanings (Beimiller, 2001). Storybooks have a greater number of rare words than regular speech. The following is an example from the storybook classic *George and Martha*, written by James Marshall in 1972: "George carefully poured the rest of his soup into his loafers under the table." Most students would not be familiar with the word *loafers*; however, in listening to this storybook, students who are familiar with many shoes in the shoe family (e.g., slippers, high-heels, boots, and tennis shoes) may easily integrate this word into their existing repertoire of known shoe types (Cunningham & Stanovich, 1998; Hayes & Ahrens, 1988). However, it is less likely that these students will encounter this word again in common speech and thus it is hard to know whether its meaning will be retained. Brief exposure to words in storybook contexts can be a missed opportunity. For students to benefit from being exposed to these new and unfamiliar words contained in text, they must have a sufficient knowledge of the adjoining words; in other words, a prerequisite for learning incidentally is that students know the words that provide contextual clues for figuring out a novel word's meaning (Coady, 1993).

That you can only learn new words casually if you already have a relatively large vocabulary creates a paradox that can explain the significant differences in word knowledge among children from different socioeconomic backgrounds (Hart & Risley, 1995; Moats, 1999). Children who come from lower socioeconomic backgrounds are exposed on average to less rich oral language early on and in turn their growth in vocabulary increases at a slower rate than children who have been exposed to rich oral language environments—as they may not benefit from words learned in context as significantly as their peers with larger vocabulary repertoires—with cumulative effects for their academic trajectory (Anderson & Nagy, 1992). For example, a student will have a difficult time understanding the meaning of the novel word *drenched* used in the storybook if the teacher defines *drenched* as being "sopping wet," when the student has never heard the phrase *sopping wet*. In such a case, the student will lose an opportunity to learn the word *drenched* and the expression *sopping wet*, as well as potentially miss out on understanding the story's meaning. By contrast, a student who does know what sopping wet means will have extended his or her network of words that describe being thoroughly wet, thereby developing a more in-depth and discriminant understanding of how these words are used and how they may differ in their shades of meaning. The growing vocabulary discrepancy between learners with and without large vocabularies makes simply providing a language-rich environment in school insufficient for closing the gap between these different word learners. In fact, such an environment may exacerbate rather than decrease differences in vocabulary size, as some students will be able to take advantage of incidental word exposure and others won't (McKeown, 1985; Shefelbine, 1990). This concept of *the rich get richer and the poor get poorer*—the idea that early achievement influences later achievement—has been referred to as the *Matthew effect* in reference to a verse in the Gospel of Matthew. To address this challenge, it is critical that a shift in practices around vocabulary instruction occurs that moves from casual exposure to explicit instruction. Several strategies that incorporate explicit instruction are provided in this chapter, but we begin by elaborating on the benefits of explicit instruction.

Explicit vocabulary instruction provides a potential opportunity to (1) minimize the discrepancies between word learners and (2) support related literacy skills such as listening and reading comprehension. Explicit vocabulary instruction involves the direct teaching of high-utility words in a consistent and reliable manner, so that word meanings are defined clearly and similarly across word exposures for the purpose of establishing strong word connections (refer to Table 7.1 for some examples; Beck et al., 2013). Explicit teaching of a target word should (1) incorporate both contextual and definitional information about a word's meaning, (2) provide multiple contexts in which the word is used, and (3) support deep processing of words through comparing and contrasting relationships between different words and their relationship to each other (Baumann et al., 2003; NRP, 2000; Stahl, 1986).

Explicit vocabulary instruction has been found to be generally effective for improving reading comprehension according to the NRP (2000), with two studies on specific explicit vocabulary interventions documenting improvements in students' vocabulary on standardized vocabulary measures, not just words taught. Indeed, the value of explicit instruction is demonstrated not only by gains in target word knowledge but also through reading comprehension and generalized vocabulary measures (Marulis & Neuman, 2010). Furthermore, vocabulary training programs can also help students make better inferences about the meanings of words and thus make them more likely to determine the meaning of unfamiliar words (Nagy, 2007). Table 7.2 provides a summary of the benefits associated with explicit vocabulary instruction.

TABLE 7.1. Explicit Vocabulary Teaching: Ingredients and Examples

Explicit teaching ingredients	Examples using *drenched*
Contextual and definitional information about target word's meanings	Provide students with a definition of the word *drenched*. • "*Drenched* means very wet." Explain situations when one might be "drenched" and contexts in which the target word could be used. • "Let's think about how we might get 'drenched.' What are some ways we might get 'very wet'? Maybe after a thunderstorm, your clothes are all wet from the rain. Your clothes are so wet that it's like you went swimming in your clothes! Now say to the person next to you, 'I am drenched from the thunderstorm!'"
Multiple contexts in which the word is used	Give students different examples of how the target word is used. • "You can be 'drenched,' very wet, from water. For example, 'I was drenched from the rain.' You can be 'drenched' with sweat. 'I was drenched with sweat after running around the gym with Raphael.'"
Support deep processing of words through comparing and contrasting relationships between different words and their relationship to each other	Compare different words that are similar and different from the target word. • "I spilled juice on my shirt at lunch; would I be drenched? No, 'drenched' means very wet, not just a little wet." • "What are other words that are like the word *drenched* that mean 'very wet'? Yes, *soaked* or *sopping wet* also mean 'very wet'!"

TABLE 7.2. Why Explicit Vocabulary Instruction Is So Beneficial

- It levels the playing field for students who have smaller vocabularies and may be less likely to learn words through incidental word exposure.
- It increases students' ability to comprehend text because they can understand the words being used in the text.
- It heightens students' word awareness; they are more conscious and attentive to words they hear in their environment and thus more likely to learn words beyond the target vocabulary.
- It supports students' inferences about new words increasing the likelihood that they will be able to figure out the meaning of new words on their own.

Given these strong arguments for increasing explicit vocabulary instruction in schools, this chapter focuses on the specific strategies that support target word learning using this approach. This special emphasis on explicit vocabulary instruction reflects the growing need to provide practices that are maximally beneficial for a variety of word learners. We discuss types of activities that facilitate a variety of levels of support, word strategies, and chosen words for the purpose of adequately addressing gaps in vocabulary and preventing later challenges in reading across diverse genres. To address this challenge, this chapter provides evidence-based vocabulary instruction strategies, including tips for how to pick words to teach and examples of programs that integrate these practices. Of course, instruction is not complete without good assessment to drive instructional decisions. Thus, we also explore options related to assessment of vocabulary skills. Finally, recommendations are included with regard to how to intensify instruction for struggling students and tailor instruction to be more responsive for diverse learners.

INSTRUCTIONAL STRATEGIES FOR INCREASING VOCABULARY

In the following section, we describe evidence-based strategies for teaching vocabulary. We begin with an overview of all-purpose best practices for improving vocabulary and then delve into age-specific practices, as well as examples of materials and programs that have been used with younger and older learners.

To begin, the NRP (2000) provided several recommendations for vocabulary instruction based on expert opinion and a thorough review of the literature. These five recommendations are provided in Table 7.3, along with accompanying examples of how we suggest you might put these recommendations into practice.

Strategies for All Students as Word Learners

There are multiple word-learning strategies that are maximally beneficial to all types of word learners. For example, readers are strongly advised to provide *friendly definitions* of words: definitions that are easily accessible to students. Returning to the example of the word *drenched* used earlier in this chapter, instead of telling students that *drenched* means

TABLE 7.3. Recommended Strategies for Explicit Vocabulary Instruction

Recommendation	Ideas and examples for classroom application

Provide direct instruction.	• Provide clean and consistent definitions of target words.
	  ○ Example: *stumble*: "If someone is stumbling, he or she is almost falling."
	• Include good models presented by the teacher.
	  ○ Example: "I *stumbled* while walking through the snow. I almost fell onto some ice!"
	• Review the target word.
	  ○ Example: "I am going to say a sentence. Can you tell me the word that could finish the sentence? A man had trouble walking, and he almost _____ down the stairs."

Repetition and multiple exposures in rich contexts.	• Provide opportunities to hear the word in a model sentence as well as in a story. • Say the word in sentences. • Use multiple exposures to contrast the word with related words or address multiple meanings in different contexts. ○ Example: "The man in the story stumbled upon the treasure; he came upon the treasure by accident. How is this use of *stumble* the same or different from the example we talked about yesterday with the man who almost stumbled down the stairs?"
Restructure tasks for low achievers/ at-risk achievers.	• Offer small-group instruction where target vocabulary is reviewed in more detail. • For younger students, provide picture cards of the target vocabulary. • For older students, provide a handout of friendly definitions or example sentences of the target words.
Present activities that actively engage.	• Provide opportunities to make personal connections to words. • Discuss a word in relation to an experience students have had or something the word reminds them of. • For younger learners, make vocabulary activities into a game where students provide group responses, thumbs up or thumbs down, yes/no to incorrect or correct examples of the target words. • For older learners, provide an interesting text on a topic that is relevant and engaging (e.g., an article on same-sex schooling or the use of electronic media) in order to stimulate student motivation through personal interest in the topic.

Employ a variety of instructional methods for optimal results.	• Integrate vocabulary activities . . .
	  ○ with read-aloud discussions.
	  ○ using multimedia with accompanying video or audio.
	  ○ in the context of word organizers and games with a word web.
	  ○ in small heterogeneous- or homogeneous-ability groups.

Note. Based on NRP (2000).

"sopping wet," teachers should provide a definition that is understandable to the student, such as "*drenched* means really wet." Students should be familiar with all of the words in the definition and should understand their meaning. These definitions provide an opportunity for students with varying levels of vocabulary to understand word meanings (Beck et al., 2013).

Another strategy is to provide students with *examples, nonexamples,* and *synonyms*; students begin to understand how target words are used in a variety of contexts and to see how different words are connected and related to each other. In so doing, students are better able to experience more in-depth word processing, where they are not merely memorizing the definition of a word but instead are coming to understand its meaning in conjunction with other words and concepts and increasing their propensity to use the word and make it their own.

For example, teachers can create *semantic maps* and list relevant information about the word or provide descriptions of words through categorization. In an activity for kindergarteners and first graders, with a semantic map for the word *drenched*, the teacher might use a semantic map something like the one in Figure 7.1 and begin by saying:

> "Today, let's talk about the word *drenched. Drenched* means very wet. I want you to think of ways you can get really wet. I am going to write on the board your ideas about how you can get *drenched*, or really wet, inside and outside of the house."

For examples outside the house, students might list a thunderstorm or stepping in a puddle; for inside the house, students might list taking a bath/shower or spilling juice on themselves at the dinner table. The teacher can list these in the semantic map and help students think about the differences between *drenched* and just wet (e.g., a thunderstorm might get you *drenched* but not a few rain drops) as well as about synonyms: "Yes, you were soaked! *Soaked* is another word for *drenched*. It also means 'very wet!'" Semantic maps also create great opportunities for students to make personal connections to words, or discuss how these words may be relevant to them. For example, a student might mention how he or she loves stepping in puddles and getting really wet, even though his or her parents might not like that behavior very much! Indeed, research shows that students who make personal connections to words retain their meanings longer than words with which they do not make these connections (Beck et al., 2013).

Finally, a complete package of vocabulary instruction should also include attention to features such as pronunciation (phonological representation) and how the word is written (orthographic representation; Kucan, 2012). For younger students in particular, cues to attend to sounds in words can be a critical component to correct pronunciation and general understanding about how words work. Rhymes, clapping syllables, and sound manipulation games (e.g., "What else can we turn *cat* into? That's right—*bat, sat, fat, mat, pat*") are

Drenched	
Inside	Outside
• Bath time	• Thunderstorm
• Spilling a big bowl of soup	• Jumping in puddles
•	•
•	•

FIGURE 7.1. A semantic map example for the word *drenched*.

key activities to support learning about how words sound and work. As students get older, instructional emphasis on spelling and extension to morphology (units of meaning in words) and syntax (word forms associated with specific aspects of speech) should increase, and often are built into typical spelling or grammar programs. Together, these instructional strategies can be referred to as *metalinguistic* in nature, that is, they constitute instruction that supports the ability to reflect and manipulate the structural features of language including both written and spoken language (Nagy, 2007). Word learning is multifaceted; grasping the definition of a word requires an understanding of syntax, relationships between words, and word parts (i.e., prefixation, suffixation). Helping students develop their metalinguistic abilities (e.g., making them word conscious) can also be a useful aspect of vocabulary instruction that has been strongly linked to reading comprehension, particularly for older learners (Nagy, 2007).

In summary, strategies that include (1) friendly definitions, (2) semantic maps/word charts, and (3) metalinguistic activities offer appropriate options for all word learners and can be integrated into a complete literacy program. Each of these strategies can be used for younger and older learners, with some adaptations. In the next section, we delve into specific instructional needs associated with younger and older student populations.

Strategies for Young Word Learners

Most differences between children with relatively low vocabularies and their peers with high vocabularies have already occurred by the end of grade 2 (Biemiller & Slonim, 2001). Thus, it is important that early education experiences include an emphasis on building vocabulary as one strategy for preventing later academic failure. Research on vocabulary instruction for young learners supports the use of explicit vocabulary strategies for this age group (Beck & McKeown, 2001; Coyne, Simmons, Kame'enui, & Stoolmiller, 2004). In fact, some research has suggested that it takes at least 12 exposures to learn word meanings (Beck & McKeown, 2003), which makes it highly important to include both early and systematic plans for vocabulary instruction. The general recommendations discussed in Table 7.3 offer a foundation with regard to structuring plans for explicit vocabulary instruction. Providing a consistent definition for a target word when presenting and modeling the word—as well as providing multiple opportunities to hear, say, and use the word—are all necessary parts of the exposure needed for students to integrate a new word into their repertoire (Stahl & Nagy, 2006). However, in planning vocabulary instruction, a central question to ask before you begin teaching words to young learners is *which* words should be targeted.

Which Words Do I Choose?

Decisions regarding which words should be targeted in explicit vocabulary instruction can be daunting given the vast array of types of words that might be considered (e.g., high-frequency words, words with important structural features, content-specific words; Kucan, 2012). One strategy for word selection comes from Beck et al. (2013, p. 65). These researchers apply a metric used in the popular story "Goldilocks" for determining what words to teach: "not too difficult, not too easy, but just right." This phrase assists in grouping words into three tiers. Figure 7.2 presents a visual overview of tiers, including a brief description and examples. Tier One words (too easy for most but not all students) are common sight words and are largely composed of simple nouns and verbs (e.g., *hat, house, eat*). Tier Two words (just right) are in general use but would not be considered words that are common or frequently used (e.g., *glimmer, wade, chef*). Finally, Tier Three words (too difficult) are both rarer and conceptually more difficult. For Tier Three words, young students may not have a handle on their meaning yet, and these may be words that are limited to specific contexts. These words can be more difficult because students must learn the word and the concept at the same time (Graves, 1986; Nagy, Anderson, & Herman, 1987), as opposed to words in which the concept is already known and only the label must be learned.

Using the "Goldilocks" strategy, target words should be "just right" and thus likely will be primarily comprised of Tier Two words. Importantly, unlike Tier One-type words such as high-frequency word lists, a singularly agreed-upon "Tier Two word list" is not available. Decisions regarding selection of words must be made by the teachers, and often this must be completed using supplementary materials, given that beginning-reader texts are typically focused on decoding skills. Thus, word emphasis is often placed on Tier One-type words, such as those that occur with high frequency, which means that less time is devoted to rich vocabulary. Chosen words should reflect those that are likely to appear across written and oral texts that students will encounter—that is, high-utility words. As noted by Kucan (2012), these are the words that are perceived to provide the most "mileage" or "traction" for students in expanding their learning. More specific recommendations for Tier Two selection might be based on balanced consideration of (1) importance and utility, (2) instructional potential, and (3) conceptual understanding. Table 7.4 provides an overview of each point along with questions to consider.

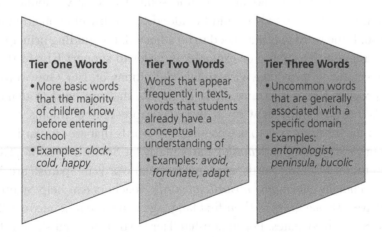

FIGURE 7.2. A tiered system for selection of target words. Based on Beck, McKeown, and Kucan (2013).

TABLE 7.4. How to Select Tier Two Words

Importance and utility: words that are characteristic of mature language users and appear frequently across a variety of domains.
- Is the word important for comprehending and writing about related ideas?
- Does the word appear frequently in the texts and contexts to which students are exposed?

Instructional potential: Words that can be worked with in a variety of ways so that students can build rich representations of them and their connections to other words and concepts.
- Is the word *not* ordinarily used or heard by students in daily language?
- Can the word be used in a variety of ways to maximize learning and connections to other words?

Conceptual understanding: words for which students understand the general concept but provide precision and specificity in describing the concept.
- Do students have knowledge/experiences that help them understand the word?

Note. Based on Beck, McKeown, and Kucan (2013) and Kucan (2012).

When selecting words we return to James Marshall's *George and Martha* series. For example, in *George and Martha: The Complete Stories of Two Best Friends*, think about which words you might select as Tier Two words (e.g., *dentist, handsome, furious, scarcely, tightrope, confidence, wobble, restored, suspense, pride, tarantula, wicked*). We would choose *handsome, furious, confidence, suspense, pride,* and *wicked* because these are words that are central to the George and Martha stories, and teaching these words will help students talk about, think about, and eventually write about the important concepts in the stories. Furthermore, many of these words can be conceptually related (e.g., *pride, handsome, confidence*) to help students build strong semantic understanding and word networks. For example, you might reserve a more in-depth discussion of words like *tarantula* for a unit on spiders!

Careful consideration regarding word selection becomes even more critically important for ELs, given that these students may find some Tier One vocabulary words to be a challenge and, thus, these words should be added to the list of explicitly taught words. However, although the word lists may need to be adjusted, the guiding principles for teaching vocabulary remain the same. For example, in order to support ELs in the classroom, these learners should be provided with simple definitions of Tier One words. Bilingual teachers can provide ELs with translations for words that are hard to demonstrate, for example, words that frequently show up in everyday expressions or idioms (e.g., *Once upon a time*). Another useful strategy is to use cognates, or words that are similar in sound, spelling, and meaning (e.g., *familia* and *family*). Particularly for Spanish-speaking ELs, cognates can be very useful for teaching words, as many common words in Spanish are Tier 2 words in English (e.g., *enorme/enormous, absurdo/absurd*). Teachers can help Spanish-speaking students who have a strong grasp of their first language make the link between Tier 1 words in English and Spanish cognates. For unfamiliar Tier 2 words in English or a student's first language, teachers can preteach these words to ELs and provide rich oral discussions about the target word's meaning using small-group instruction where ELs have more opportunities to hear, say, and use the word in context.

Word Learning in Action

As previously discussed, there are general strategies of explicit vocabulary instruction that apply to all word learners (see Table 7.5). However, one example of an approach particularly helpful for young learners can be found in Beck and McKeown's (2001, 2003) "Text Talk." This approach uses read-alouds that are accompanied by extensive vocabulary activities and use of student background knowledge about text topics.

An example of the interactions that might occur between teachers and students using Text Talk is provided in Figure 7.3 using the Tier 2 word *absurd*. In this example, students are given multiple opportunities to be exposed to the meaning of *absurd*; they are provided with a definition of *absurd* and modeled responses that include the word *absurd*. The teacher provides an example as well as nonexamples of the meaning of *absurd* to help students deepen their understanding of its meaning. These kinds of interactions around words in text can help students master the target words and also make them better word learners in general (Nagy, 2007).

These word learning strategies are crucial for improving the vocabulary development of young learners. As students shift from learning to read in the early grades to reading to learn in the later grades, they are faced with new curricular challenges. These new academic expectations require different vocabulary instructional aims and curricular goals necessary for keeping students in sync with content instruction. In the next section, we address the vocabulary challenges of older students who attend secondary school.

Strategies for Older Word Learners

Academic success for adolescent learners is contingent upon successful reading comprehension (Biancarosa & Snow, 2004), with vocabulary being a central component of reading for understanding. Indeed, the relationship between reading comprehension and vocabulary is reciprocal, with greater word knowledge contributing to better comprehension and better comprehension and more frequent reading providing increased opportunities to learn new and unfamiliar words in text through reading (Anderson & Freebody, 1981). Unlike their younger peers who are learning to read, older word learners are reading to learn (Chall, 1996). The expectation in the later grades is that content-area knowledge is gained from reading discipline-specific texts (e.g., textbooks, novels, historical documents). This shift in expectations brings forth a new set of challenges with regard to vocabulary instruction.

Foremost among these challenges is that students must have sufficient knowledge of *academic language* (Bailey, 2007; Lesaux, Kieffer, & Faller, 2010; Snow, 2010) in order to take advantage of texts. The language of school is different from everyday language. Language used in informal contexts uses referents, gestures, and assumes shared knowledge, all characteristics that are highly dependent upon the discussion context. By contrast, the academic language of text is meant to be context independent or decontextualized; its meaning resides with the text and uses specific norms such as highly complex grammatical structures (e.g., "Fossilization is the process by which something turns to stone," a phrase using a

TABLE 7.5. Different Aspects of Word Knowledge

Explanation	Example
Incrementality	
Knowing a word happens over time due to repeated exposures to that target word. Each and every time we encounter a word and use it, we develop a stronger and more developed understanding of the word's meaning, allowing one to use the word flexibly across contexts.	Teachers might include activities in which students raise their hand or fill out a worksheet to determine whether the student (1) has never seen the word, (2) has heard it but doesn't know what it means, (3) recognizes it in context, or (4) knows it well. Teachers could also have students try to determine the meaning of a word from a sentence (i.e., figuring out the word's meaning through context) and then discuss how this one exposure can provide some information about a word's meaning but that there is much more to know.
Multidimensionality	
Knowing a word means understanding different aspects of the word's use (morphological uses, types of speech, such as how to use it as a verb, noun, or adjective), knowing how it differs from related words (antonyms and synonyms), and being familiar with the words with which it commonly co-occurs.	Morphological and syntactic difference activities might include helping students identify the differences among *strategy, strategic,* and *strategizing* and word co-occurrence patterns such as *pick you up* versus *picking on you.*
Polysemy	
Knowing a word means understanding that it may have multiple meanings across different contexts (e.g., *cup, pair*) and may be different when used figuratively.	Semantic map activities that visually show words' multiple meanings, or engaging in activities about puns or jokes that highlight words' multiple meanings (e.g., *bug* as a virus vs. *bug–insect* distinction).
Interrelatedness	
Knowing a word means understanding its association with your existing knowledge set, or how it connects to what you already know about the word, or categories that the word may be part of that are part of your background knowledge.	Preteaching vocabulary words before reading a text and having students brainstorm about word meanings that they will find in the text is a particularly useful activity for supporting students in making these connections.
Heterogeneity	
Knowing a word means understanding how it functions, in other words, one must understand how to apply words in a range of contexts.	Creating activities to help students understand how a word functions depends on what kind of word it is. Trying to teach students how to use words like meanwhile or *moreover* would require different activities than the word *hypotenuse.* The former words could be taught with sentence frames with blanks for students to fill in the appropriate conjunction, and the latter could include a worksheet with various diagrams of different shapes.

TEACHER: In the story, when the fly told Arthur he could have three wishes if he didn't kill him, Arthur said he thought that was absurd. That means Arthur thought it was silly to believe a fly could grant wishes. When something is absurd, it is ridiculous and hard to believe.

If I told you that your teacher was going to stand on his or her head to teach you, that would be absurd. If someone told you that dogs could fly, that would be absurd.

I'll say some things, and if you think they are absurd, say, "That's absurd!" If they are not absurd, say, "That makes sense."

"I have a singing cow for a pet." (absurd)
"I saw a tall building that was made of green cheese." (absurd)
"Last night I watched a movie on TV." (makes sense)
"This morning I saw some birds flying in the sky." (makes sense)

If I said "let's fly to the moon this afternoon," that would be absurd. Who can think of an absurd idea?

[When a child answers, ask another if he or she thinks that was absurd, and if so, to tell the first child, "That's absurd!"]

FIGURE 7.3. An example of Text Talk for the word *absurd*. Based on Beck and McKeown (2003).

structure that is far less common than those used in informal speech). Even the breadth of words used is different. For example, varying one's word choice is a staple of good writing but is less common in colloquial conversations where using the same word may be used for emphasis (e.g., saying "totally" multiple times across sentences; Schleppegrell, 2001). This means that students are not only learning new concepts and new labels for concepts, but in order to do so, they must understand how these words are applied in academic contexts and across disciplines. For example, the word *analyze* has a different meaning when conducting a mathematical or statistical analysis than it does when a student is asked to analyze the intent of a character in their English/language arts textbook. As a result, students who are highly successful in communicating in informal contexts may still struggle in school (Bailey, 2007).

Which Words Do I Choose?

Despite the shift to more discipline-specific texts, the process of selecting words as described for young word learners is similar for secondary students. That is, target words should reflect words that (1) are used frequently in text, (2) help students accurately access text, and (3) students can connect with personally. General all-purpose academic words (i.e., words that focus on analysis, process, and interpretation) that occur across content areas are particularly relevant for older learners as they fit these three criteria and are likely to appear across subject-area texts. A highly useful list of all-purpose academic words has been provided by Coxhead (2000), and can be found at *www.uefap.com/vocab/select/awl.htm*. The list is arranged alphabetically by headwords, or words that are most frequently used in word families. The 570 headwords are listed along with a link to the definition, as well as additional words within the family. For example, the first headword to appear is *abandon*, with associated family words including *abandoned, abandoning, abandonment,* and *abandons*. All-purpose academic words can help students access academic language across the content areas. Content-area teachers should teach students how these words are used and applied in their specific area as well as provide rich opportunities for students to use, read, and write about the word.

As with young word learners, the first step for integrating explicit vocabulary instruction in classrooms with adolescent learners is determining which high-utility words to focus on. This decision should to a large extent be based on course texts, with an eye toward words that will facilitate student comprehension of text. In addition to using texts as a guide to choosing appropriate academic words, speaking with other content-area teachers about words that can be taught across the content areas is also useful. Cross-disciplinary coverage of the same words facilitates what we know to be research-based vocabulary strategies: repeatedly exposing students to words and providing varied opportunities to use words in speaking and writing. In this case, this strategy is accomplished through the repetition of words across the content areas (Lawrence, White, & Snow, 2010). The second step is supporting depth of word knowledge around discipline-specific vocabulary. Central to this aim is determining which discipline-specific words to explicitly address through exposure to text, hands-on activities, and examples and nonexamples, as well as identifying activities for listening, reading, writing, and speaking the target words. Figure 7.4 is a flowchart of moving through this decision-making process.

Teaching prescribed sets of target words benefits students in that they gain additional word knowledge incrementally, and the process of learning new words exponentially impacts their word growth through developing students' word consciousness. It is important to pro-

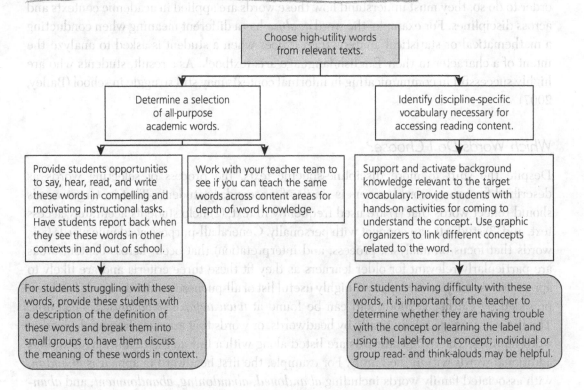

FIGURE 7.4. Making good instructional decisions for teaching academic language.

vide these students with engaging and motivating contexts and texts for learning new words in order for them to make word learning their own. Next we review several programs that have been identified as useful strategies for teaching all-purpose academic words.

Word Learning in Action

Each of the programs reviewed here incorporate the guiding recommendations for explicit vocabulary instruction. In particular, the programs have students focus on a set of words across content areas during the same week in order to promote greater exposure and deeper word knowledge.

Word Generation was created by the Strategic Education Research Partnership (SERP, 2011). It offers a secondary school program with weekly units that provide students with five high-utility target words (see Figure 7.5 for an example). The target words are used in passages across the content areas and present a controversy or debate for discussion. You can access and download for free Word Generation materials at *http://wg.serpmedia.org* (SERP, 2011).

The program's target words are applicable for a variety of discipline-specific settings, with teachers using the same weekly words across subject areas. Similar to the recommendations presented at the beginning of this chapter, this technique is intended to (1) provide multiple exposures to target words, (2) give opportunities for students to understand how words are related, and (3) allow students to develop depth of word knowledge. In Figure 7.5, we provide an example of a weekly schedule for integrating the five target words across subject areas with students reading, listening, speaking, and writing about the words. For example, using this program in an English/language arts classroom, students would participate in engaging debates and exercises using the morphological components of the target words. In science class, students would conduct experiments that relate to a controversy being discussed and that make use of the weekly target words. Students in math class would

---

Word Generation

This program is designed to be flexible enough to accommodate local variations; however, each week should begin with the introduction of the passage and end with the open-response writing activity. Any variation within the week is optional and should be decided upon by the implementation team. Most importantly, all content-area teachers should be implementing at least one of these activities a week.

ELA	Science	Math	Social Studies	ELA
• Establish word meanings • Comprehend the gist of the passage	• Establish science version of the definition • Analyze data in fictional micro-experiment	• Apply the words in the context of math problems • Discuss and solve math problems	• Students take position on the issue • Teacher facilitates classroom debate	• "Taking a stand" essay

FIGURE 7.5. An example of a middle school program for vocabulary knowledge. From *http://wg.serpmedia.org/WordGenOverviewLowQ.pdf*. Reprinted with permission from Matthew B. Ellinger.

be tasked with having to solve word problems that incorporate the target words, and in social studies they would have to take a position on the controversy, defend their position in front of their peers, and hear peer rebuttals, all using the target words. Last, students would be given the opportunity to conclude the week in English/language arts class with a written assignment to articulate their position using the target words.

Another program that emphasizes academic all-purpose vocabulary for secondary school students across text genres (e.g., information and persuasive), and which specifically targets ELs, is Academic Language Instruction for All Students (ALIAS). ALIAS is an instructional approach that incorporates sustained text-based vocabulary instruction for 18 weeks, with eight 2-week units comprising 8-day lesson cycles with two 1-week review units (see Figure 7.6 for a visual of the ALIAS activities schedule). Each week is made up of 4 days of instruction with 45 minutes a day dedicated to eight or nine academic target words used with informational text and persuasive text (from *Time for Kids* magazine). ALIAS uses explicit instruction of vocabulary knowledge and word-learning strategies (Lesaux et al., 2010).

ALIAS focuses on the lexical as well as grammatical aspects of learning vocabulary and was created to be easy to implement in an English/language arts classroom. This program is intended for use during typical 90- or 120-minute English/language arts programming, and is an example of how explicit vocabulary instruction can be incorporated into existing English/language arts or content-area routines. Activities in this program include word charts where students fill in syntactic forms of the target words (e.g., *analysis, analytic, analyze,* and *analytically*). However, this same strategy could be used across disciplines to help students with words like *abolition* and *abolitionist* in the case of a social studies classroom and similarly for science concepts.

Days 8 and 9	How to use the word precisely in extended writing		
Day 7	The meaning of the word in different contexts	How to use the word to write and talk about other topics	
Days 5 and 6	The different word parts inside the word and their meanings	The different forms of the word and how they are used	
Day 4	Multiple meanings for the word	How to represent its meaning graphically	
Day 3	Its meaning in the article	How to use it to talk about the article	
Day 2	What I already know about its meaning	Its dictionary definition	
Day 1	How to spell it	What it looks like	What it sounds like

FIGURE 7.6. Activities by day in the ALIAS program. Reprinted with permission from Nanie K. Lesaux.

Putting It All Together

In this section, we have reviewed general strategies for teaching vocabulary for all word learners, challenges and strategies specific to younger and to older learners, and example programs that put these research-based practices into action in whole-group settings. Here, we condense this information into a framework for planning and implementing good practices in vocabulary instruction. Figure 7.7 presents a task sequence for vocabulary lesson planning that includes (1) selecting the target words, (2) preparing user-friendly definitions, (3) designing engaging activities that use words in multiple contexts, and (4) providing follow-up activities to reinforce learning.

Case Example

Abby is a 6-year-old student in kindergarten. Her teacher reports that she is engaged and pays attention during large-group story reading, but that she rarely participates in story discussions. When her teacher explicitly asks Abby questions during storybook reading, Abby does not respond in full sentences, but rather provides one- or two-word answers. Her teacher also notes that Abby has trouble with suffixes; for instance, when reading a story about a kitchen, Abby was unable to produce "cooked" as the past tense for "cook." Abby has provided correct past-tense suffixes for words in previous lessons, although somewhat less frequently than her peers. When assessed using the Peabody Picture Vocabulary Test—Fourth Edition (PPVT-IV; Dunn & Dunn, 2007), Abby scored in the 40th percentile for children her age.

The results from the PPVT-IV indicate that Abby's receptive vocabulary skills are somewhat lower than those of her same-age peers, and her teacher's report of Abby's language skills suggests that Abby may require some additional vocabulary instruction, preferably tailored around words used in the current lesson, that is, high-utility words that will help improve her comprehension of the storybooks the class is reading. Instructional recommendations for Abby's teacher might include providing additional opportunities for use

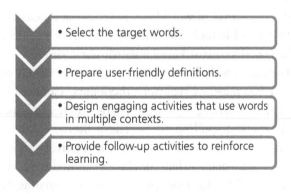

FIGURE 7.7. Task sequence for vocabulary lesson planning.

of target words with varying morphological endings, as well as additional scaffolding and repetition. More specifically, once target words are identified, Abby's teacher can provide friendly definitions of the words along with sample sentences, as well as opportunities for Abby to hear and repeat the target words in sentences prior to the introduction of the story. For example, her teacher noticed that she struggled with the word *comforting*. So, Abby's teacher gave Abby additional sentences with the word *comforting* to practice such as "Playing with friends is *comforting* when you feel lonely" and "It is *comforting* to be with your family." Abby's teacher also presented pictures of examples of comforting activities (e.g., a picture of a cat on a child's lap) she found on the Internet as prompts for Abby to come up with her own sentences.

Now that we have completed our review of explicit instruction for all word learners, it is important to turn our attention to recommendations for intensifying instruction for those students who are not meeting core expectations. However, understanding which students are in need cannot be done without data to drive those decisions. Thus, we first review information relevant to vocabulary assessment, which we acknowledge has been an under-researched area to date.

ASSESSING VOCABULARY KNOWLEDGE

On average, students learn about 1,000 to 3,000 words during a typical school year. However, this estimate reflects the average student, with many students falling below this number. Low-income students, ELs, and students with language and literacy difficulties tend on average to fall below this average estimate (Snow et al., 1998). In order to create appropriate instruction for these learners—so that they do not fall further and further behind their peers—educators must determine what students do and don't know when it comes to learning, differentiating, using, and retaining words. This is where the importance of good assessment comes into play; however, unique challenges from those in other areas of literacy exist for vocabulary assessment.

Determining a student's level of word knowledge is not an easy task. This task is complicated by the fact that word knowledge is neither an all-or-nothing matter (e.g., there is great variability in how well you can know a word) nor a discrete skill that once learned is mastered for life. Instead, vocabulary encompasses an enormous area for mastery—just consult the more than 1,500 pages of *Webster's* dictionary. Contrast this with the manageable and measurable task of learning to distinguish between 44 phonemes, 26 letters of the alphabet, and several hundred spelling rules! These literacy skills are conceptually and developmentally discrete, can be mastered within a relatively short period of time, and are easily measured with assessments that are closely aligned to the instructional practices in which they are learned. Take, for example, the task of learning to write one's name—practicing writing your name involves assessment of the same skill. Although the process of mastering such a skill may involve trial and error (e.g., writing a *p* instead of a *b*, missing vowels, writing one's name backward), once the skill is mastered, there is little variability in performance thereafter. By contrast, vocabulary has been referred to as falling within a "large problem space" in that vocabulary is far more difficult to measure, develops slowly over long periods of time, and is multicomponential (Snow & Kim, 2006). A visual picture defining literacy skills in terms of small or large problem spaces can be found in Figure 7.8. To elaborate on vocabulary as being a larger problem space, word knowledge is not one isolated skill; it requires an understanding of meaning, but also syntactic and morphological aspects of a word's nature, as well as how it is spelled and pronounced. In addition, vocabulary knowledge is a lifelong pursuit. For example, when one of the authors recently taught a lecture on vocabulary development to graduate students, 78% of the students indicated they had never previously heard the word *sesquipedalian.* All of us are lifelong word learners, being exposed to new words regularly and increasing the depth of our understanding of a word each time it is used in a different context (e.g., the word *record* can refer to an object for listening to music, or a piece of evidence from the past, or to inscribe something). As such, vocabulary is a large problem space, growing incrementally over time and with varied exposure. Although skills defined as falling within a small problem space (such as oral reading fluency) may require an instructional focus on automaticity and accuracy, vocabulary is best taught through repeated and varied experiences with words across language modalities (i.e., reading, writing, speaking, listening). The incremental nature of vocabulary knowledge makes it especially important for teachers to use sensitive measures of vocabulary depth and growth to better understand mastery.

The What *and* How of Sensitive Vocabulary Assessments

The bottom line in vocabulary assessment is that focus on development and use of teacher- or researcher-constructed instruments of vocabulary growth is encouraged (NRP, 2000). This recommendation represents an attempt to provide educators with more context-

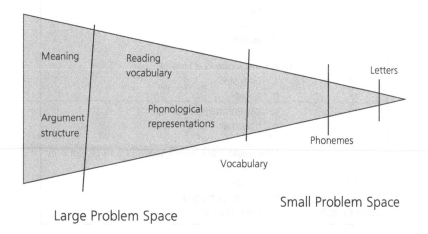

FIGURE 7.8. Problem spaces for literacy development. Adapted from Snow and Kim (2006). Copyright 2006 by The Guilford Press. Reprinted by permission.

specific assessments that would better mirror classroom practice as well as allow teachers to better understand incremental growth in language development specifically and more generally. However, the design of sensitive instruments by teachers requires an understanding of the different aspects of word knowledge. It is important for intensifying instruction to distinguish among students who (1) understand the concept, (2) can use the word, (3) understand the concept and its corresponding label, and (4) understand the word in context. For example, when we say "The computer has a bug," we are referring to a virus, not an insect. In the case of words with multiple meanings, vocabulary knowledge as well as comprehension skills are required. This distinction is important to teach to students who may not have adequate depth of word knowledge.

Nagy and Scott (2000) propose five different elements of word knowledge that are used in reading. These different aspects of word knowledge can be useful for thinking about what types of assessments will be informative. Table 7.5 draws heavily from this work conducted by Nagy and Scott and shows these different aspects of word knowledge. Teachers eager to provide students with support need to know where students fall across these stages and the depth of word knowledge students possess across the five elements of word knowledge. For example, when assessing incrementality, one might try to assess students' levels of word depth by asking students to discriminate the meaning of the target word in a more fine-grained manner. For example, Figure 7.9 demonstrates how students could encounter the same test item stem across examples of increasing complexity.

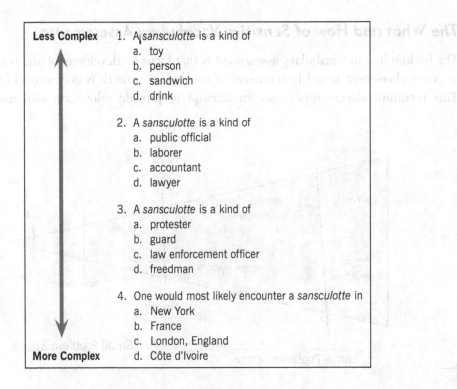

FIGURE 7.9. Items for incrementality. Based on Stallman, Pearson, Nagy, Anderson, and Garcia (1995) and Pearson, Hiebert, and Kamil (2007).

What Standardized Norm-Referenced Vocabulary Assessments Can Tell You

We have elaborated on how vocabulary is not a monolithic skill set. Thus, the assessments used to measure word knowledge should be interpreted with care and with attention to the information they can impart about both breadth and depth of word knowledge separately; this is especially true in the case of widely used standardized measures of vocabulary. The PPVT-IV is one of the most common standardized measures of vocabulary and is often used as a screening measure for students to receive supplementary services or to be flagged as those who may have language and literacy difficulties. The PPVT-IV provides useful information about students' *receptive vocabulary*, with each test item asking students to look at a set of illustrations and point to the picture that best represents the meaning of the word said by the examiner. The PPVT-IV is a norm-referenced and individually administered test—results are calculated by sorting students based on where they fall in relation to the sample on which the test was normed. This standardized measure is an informative measure of students' breadth of word knowledge, but fails to address multiple aspects of vocabulary knowledge such as productive vocabulary.

The PPVT-IV is considered to be simple and efficient, and typically requires only 11–12 minutes to administer. The age-based norms provide specific information regarding typical student functioning, in order to determine if a student's receptive vocabulary achievement is higher, lower, or similar to that of their same-age peers. However, the lack of subscales limits the utility of the PPVT-IV for targeting specific areas for intervention.

By contrast, the Expressive Vocabulary Test–2 (EVT-2; Williams, 2007) is an *expressive vocabulary* test that presents students with a picture and asks them to respond with a one-word answer to a question about the target picture (e.g., to provide a label or a synonym that connects to the picture). The EVT-2 was, in part, developed to be used as a complement to the PPVT-IV, as the same sample was used to norm both the PPVT-IV and the EVT-2. This conorming may therefore facilitate score comparisons between the PPVT-IV and the EVT-2 in order to build a more complete profile of a student's vocabulary achievement. Like the PPVT-IV, the EVT-2 may be administered in a brief session, requiring on average only 10–20 minutes to administer.

The EVT-2 separates items into two types—home and school—in order to provide further detail regarding students' strengths and challenges with expressive vocabulary. However, the EVT-2 manual points out: "The divisions of these topics into the *home* and *school* categories is somewhat arbitrary" (Williams, 2007, p. 31); therefore, caution must be used when interpreting this part of the instrument. The EVT-2 also divides words into the three-tiered system recommended by Beck et al. (2013) to help determine with which type of vocabulary students are most adept or require additional assistance.

Neither of these standardized measures provides information on whether these vocabulary skills can transfer to reading or writing the target words or distinguish them from other related words. Both the standardized and teacher-developed measures described here provide a piece of the puzzle for understanding what students know about words and the varied or circumscribed situations in which they can apply their knowledge. Using the

PPVT-IV as a general screener and creating assessments that reflect some of the five aspects of vocabulary useful for reading will support instructional decisions about what students still need to be able to do to be successful word learners and users and whether they will need instruction that is more intensive than what is provided to the whole class. As is true with all tests, these aforementioned products should only be administered and interpreted by individuals with appropriate training in student assessment.

INTENSIFYING VOCABULARY INSTRUCTION IN A MULTI-TIERED FRAMEWORK

Intensifying explicit vocabulary instruction can easily be folded into whole-class instruction. One of the most common practices for vocabulary instruction in whole-class formats is embedding word discussions in story read-alouds: an ideal space for learning new words. Indeed, a wealth of research documents the language-development benefits of listening to stories (Elley, 1989; NRP, 2000; Robbins & Ehri, 1994; Senechal & Cornell, 1993). Active engagement in these shared reading activities that include explicit vocabulary instruction and discussions about words has been shown to increase student language development for a diversity of learners, especially those students who might ordinarily lose out on incidental word learning in story reading alone (Penno, Wilkinson, & Moore, 2002). Storybook reading provides a wonderful opportunity for rich oral language experiences that allow students exposure to a variety of words they might not ordinarily encounter. However, it is likely that some students may continue to struggle to learn new words even with explicit instruction during activities such as storybook reading. For students who still struggle, a useful option is differentiated small-group instruction for students of homogeneous developmental levels (Stahl, 2011). A benefit of *small-group* homogeneous instruction is that it provides these students not only with more opportunities to interact with words and process words deeply, but most importantly it allows the teacher to provide students with more in-depth *modeling, scaffolding*, and *feedback*. To provide examples of these three key elements within supplementary, small-group intensive vocabulary instruction, we draw from an intervention developed and evaluated by Dr. Coyne at the University of Connecticut. The supplementary intervention designed by Coyne and colleagues incorporates the key elements of extended vocabulary instruction previously discussed, such as multiple encounters and contexts to learn target words, and explicit teaching of target words (e.g., including examples and nonexamples of word use, personal connections to word meanings; Beck & McKeown, 2003; Coyne, McCoach, & Kapp, 2007; NRP, 2000). This supplementary intervention is conducted in conjunction with strong whole-class instruction that includes these same features and uses the same target vocabulary words weekly. This small-group intervention is differentiated from its whole-classroom counterpart by its small-group format, with three to four students engaging in daily vocabulary learning for 20-minute sessions while interventionists provide scripted *modeling, scaffolding*, and *feedback*. Figure 7.10 provides examples of each of these aspects of Tier 2 instruction and we discuss each in detail below as well.

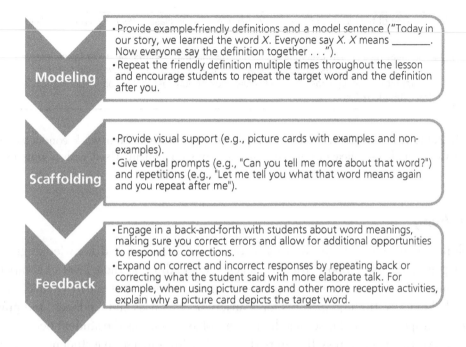

FIGURE 7.10. Strategies for teaching vocabulary words in Tier 2 settings.

Modeling

Modeling improves accuracy, in this case accurate word-level knowledge. Providing students with clear and consistent definitions is especially important for students who require more intensive instruction. Students need multiple opportunities to practice using vocabulary words, preceded by clear and consistent definitions explicitly demonstrated by the teacher. For example, an intervention teacher might say:

> "One of the magic words we learned in the story was *drenched*. Everyone say *drenched*. *Drenched* means really wet. Everyone say, '*drenched* means really wet.'"

In the following excerpt, we see that the teacher, after showing a picture illustrating the target word, repeats the word and provides a clear example sentence that uses the word, which she will repeat during the lesson. She might continue with:

> "This picture can help us remember what *drenched* means. In the picture you can see that the boy is really wet from the hose. Look at how the boy is spraying his brother with the hose, making him all wet! Do you see that the boy looks really wet?" [Students answer, 'Yes!'] Now I'm going to talk about the picture using our magic word *drenched*. 'The boy is *drenched*!' Everyone say, 'The boy is *drenched*.' [Students respond as a group.]"

Check out Figure 7.11 for another example!

> TEACHER: One of the magic words you have been learning in class is *fleet*. Everyone say *fleet*.
>
> STUDENTS: *Fleet!*
>
> TEACHER: *Fleet* means fast. Everyone say, "*Fleet* means fast." (*Shows the anchor picture.*) This picture can help us remember what *fleet* means. In the picture you can see that the rabbit is running across the field. Wow, look at how fast that rabbit is running! Does this rabbit look fast?

FIGURE 7.11. An example of modeling. This example is drawn from work conducted by Dr. Michael Coyne and his colleagues at the University of Connecticut. Used with permission from Michael Coyne.

Scaffolding

Scaffolding allows students to progress in their understanding and knowledge gradually, receiving more or less support from the teacher depending on their level of competency. Scaffolding can be thought of as responsive instruction that strategically delivers modeling, guided practice through prompts for a variety of responses and feedback, and praise to strengthen responding, and modifies these forms of assistance as the student becomes more proficient. As students progress, the support is slowly withdrawn so that students can begin to apply skills and strategies independently. Thus scaffolding responses vary based on the level of mastery by the student. Concrete scaffolds, beyond providing additional sentence frames or models, might include pictures, gestures, examples, and nonexamples in order to provide concrete representations of word meanings. For example, an intervention teacher might say:

"Let's play a game about our magic word *drenched*. I'll show you some pictures. If you think the picture shows something really wet, or *drenched*, put your thumbs up like this and whisper, 'That's *drenched*!' If the picture doesn't show something *drenched*, put your thumbs down like this and don't say anything."

In this example, the intervention teacher provides students with picture cards to scaffold their learning the meaning of the target word and support their deep processing of the word across a variety of images that do and don't represent *drenched*. Furthermore, using the "thumbs up or down" approach with such a small group of students allows intervention teachers to quickly assess which students are struggling to understand the meaning of the target word. Figure 7.12 provides some additional examples of scaffolding.

Feedback

Teachers can increase opportunities for exchanges and interactions with individual students and maximizing opportunities for immediate and individualized feedback by organizing students into small groups of three or four. Giving students explicit corrections, including requests for sentence elaborations, helps students improve their accuracy with word knowledge through better understanding of mistakes and confirmation of correct word use. These interchanges give students multiple opportunities to practice their developing knowledge,

If the student says a *sentence without the target word*, say:	**Great sentence! Can you say it again using our magic word?** If not, model a sentence and ask the student to repeat it.
If the student says a *very short sentence*, say:	**Great job telling about the picture! Can you tell me a little more?** If not, model a sentence and ask the student to repeat it.
If the student *cannot say a sentence on his or her own*:	Model a sentence and ask the student to repeat it. For example: **Can you say . . . ?**

FIGURE 7.12. Examples of scaffolding. These examples are drawn from work conducted by Dr. Michael Coyne and his colleagues at the University of Connecticut. Used with permission from Michael Coyne.

which is crucial, as repeated practice is often difficult to deliver in the context of whole-class instruction. For example, a teacher might say:

"If you put your thumb up like this and said 'That's *drenched*,' you're right! The bear in this picture looks really wet, or *drenched*. 'The bear in the river was *drenched*.'"

In the event that students do not provide appropriate responses for target words, teachers return to missed vocabulary and concepts later in the lesson to provide delayed and varied practice. This type of ongoing, guided practice provides learners with the support and feedback they need to develop rich decontextualized knowledge of word meanings. Check Figure 7.13 for an additional example of feedback. Providing spaces for increased student–teacher interactions with opportunities for individualized feedback enhances students' active engagement with words. This increased participation and talk is a centrally appealing and effective aspect of small-group supplementary instruction.

It is important to note that in a multi-tiered framework, consistent and careful communication across all tiers of instruction is crucial for student progress and development. In the example program provided, supplementary instruction remained in sync with whole-class instruction, using additional small-group strategies to build on the vocabulary being learned in the homeroom classroom. Without strong, core instruction (Tier 1), it is difficult to differentiate a child who truly needs more intensive support from a student who simply hasn't been exposed to quality instruction. Supplementary instruction (Tiers 2 and 3) does not and should not replace core instruction; it is in addition to quality core instruction. Indeed, more intensive instruction can only be as good as the preventative core instruction

TEACHER: If you put your thumb up like this and said, "That's fleet," you're right! The kids in this picture look fast, or fleet. "The fleet boys ran out of the water."

TEACHER: If you put your thumb down like this, you're right! The turtle doesn't look fast, or fleet. The turtle moved very slowly over the ground.

FIGURE 7.13. Examples of feedback. These examples are drawn from work conducted by Dr. Michael Coyne and his colleagues at the University of Connecticut. Used with permission from Michael Coyne.

that accompanies it. Solid core vocabulary instruction should include the best practices we have reviewed in this chapter: daily opportunities for rich interactive discussion about vocabulary words, clear and friendly word definitions, exposure to words across varied contexts with rich opportunities for students to interact with words, and structured opportunities to review target words. All of these activities can begin during a storybook read-aloud and then continue throughout the day woven throughout other activities. For those students requiring more intensive supports, these activities can then be extended with more explicit modeling, scaffolding, and feedback in the context of a supplementary small-group context, and repeated with more frequency and scaffolding using increased opportunities for student participation in the context of individualized vocabulary support. Vocabulary intervention poses some unique challenges relative to other components of reading. Figure 7.14 describes a conundrum teachers face, with a recommendation for how to proceed.

These same principles as described for classroom storybook reading can also be applied to content-area classrooms. Core practices of providing students with rich opportunities to interact with words, explicit definitions of words, and experiences analyzing relationships between words (e.g., word webs and word charts) are still appropriate and feasible to intensify in content classrooms. Again, small-group instruction with its more focused opportunities to provide modeling, scaffolding, and feedback are crucial for all ages and content areas, although the focal activities in the content areas differ (e.g., learning the word *photosynthesis* during a demonstration with class plants, learning the word *moor* in the context of an Emily Dickinson poem). Examples of focal activities to support word learning in small-group contexts in the content areas might include small homogeneous-ability groups focused on derivations (e.g., What does *photosynthesis* mean? What does *synthesis* mean? How is it used in other contexts? How is this use related to the word *synthesize*?), summary writing, or story grammar elements. In each context students are provided with more intensive and applied opportunities for language use with feedback.

Intensifying Vocabulary Instruction for English Learners

Quality vocabulary instruction for native English speakers is also useful for ELs. In a multitiered framework, these same instructional practices (*modeling, scaffolding,* and *feedback*)

Both *breadth* of words (i.e., number of words you know) and *depth* of word knowledge (i.e., how well you know words) are important for vocabulary growth and for reading comprehension. Increased exposure to many words increases the likelihood that students will be able to extract meaning from text. However, for students who struggle with certain aspects of word learning such as morphology or appropriate syntactic usage, in-depth instruction on specific words is central to students' successful use of these words. There are still many debates in the research literature about which should be privileged in these small-group settings. Given the rare and important opportunities for increased teacher–student interactions around words in these contexts, we recommend that teachers spend considerable time on developing students' depth of understanding of target words as well as making sure during these word-based discussions that students continue to be exposed to a variety of words through depth activities.

FIGURE 7.14. A Tier 2 conundrum: Breadth or depth of vocabulary knowledge in intensifying instruction?

are equally important for EL language development. What is different about instructing these learners is the crucial role of allotting teaching time to English language development. Instructional time devoted to English language development has been found to be particularly useful for ELs (Fien et al., 2011). Ideally, teachers across tiers should identify both content and language goals explicitly so that they can adequately track EL progress in these two areas separately, so they are not conflated.

Examples of modifications that can easily be made in the context of whole-class instruction include picture supports, preteaching target words before the lesson, native language use, outlines of text or lectures in advance, and stimulating student background knowledge about the word, as well as sentence frames. The latter is particularly useful for ELs for whom grammar and syntax may be particularly challenging when learning and using a new word (Echevarria & Vogt, 2011). Figure 7.15 provides a list of potential modifications for ELs.

All of these strategies are examples of modifications to instruction that are especially useful with ELs. Supplemental small-group instruction, like the example provided above, should give students more opportunities to practice and receive corrective feedback. Indeed, the modifications listed should be used in greater frequency and intensity in the context of small-group contexts.

Case Example

Leo is a Spanish-speaking EL whose family recently moved to the United States from the Yucatán Peninsula in Mexico. Mrs. Chan—Leo's third-grade teacher—notices that during their story discussion on the Arctic and Inuit people, Leo is having trouble understanding

Picture supports	Show students an example picture of the target word (e.g,, a picture of a cheetah running to depict the word *fleet*). Provide students with a visual (e.g., a plant diagram with directional arrows explaining the process of photosynthesis).
Preteaching target vocabulary	Before the instructional activity begins, teach students about the words they will encounter in the activity and write them on the board so students can refer back to the conversation during class.
Native language use	Provide students with a first-language definition of the word or synonyms/cognates for the word and give them an example sentence in their first language.
Outlines	Let students review an outline of the lecture or activity for the lesson before the class formally begins so they have a better sense of the purpose, goals, and structure of the lesson and the intersection of content and language goals.
Background knowledge	Help students connect what they already know about related topics or areas to the target words.
Sentence frames	Support students' grasp of grammar and syntax for the target words by providing sentences for them to fill in using the target words. The word _____ reminds me of _____. I think _____ is different than _____ because _____.

FIGURE 7.15. Modifications for ELs.

the story because he is unfamiliar with the topics and ideas being discussed in the text. Leo explains to Mrs. Chan after the lesson that he has never seen snow before. To support Leo's learning during this lesson, Mrs. Chan provides pictures and videos of snow, ice, and the work of indigenous peoples to illustrate the story and its vocabulary. When viewing the video, Mrs. Chan stops the video periodically to review vocabulary highlighted in the film. She writes the words in big letters on a piece of paper for Leo to keep with him during their next storybook reading. Mrs. Chan helps Leo construct a word web with the class using *snow in the center, and encourages the class to fill the web with semantically related words (e.g., snowflake, snowstorm)*. She occasionally repeats an English word with its Spanish equivalent so Leo can use his Spanish knowledge to help him understand and make connections between the different words. After the activity, Mrs. Chan works with Leo to review the words in the web and clarify any novel vocabulary.

CONCLUSIONS

In this chapter, we have reviewed general evidence-based practices for improving vocabulary development, including strategies that are particularly relevant during different developmental and curricular milestones. We have also made an effort in this chapter to identify research-based programs that incorporate quality vocabulary instruction and included explicit examples of these vocabulary principles in action. In accordance with the larger aim of this book to provide instructional strategies in the context of a multi-tiered framework, we have focused attention on how to carefully interpret vocabulary assessments for the purpose of providing responsive instruction. In this vein, we provided suggestions for how teachers might create their own assessments to more closely track student vocabulary mastery. We ended this chapter by discussing possible options for intensifying vocabulary instruction for students who continue to struggle with word learning.

We want to conclude this chapter by emphasizing that learning new words during a vocabulary lesson is valuable because it results in deeper understanding of the target words, accelerates vocabulary development more broadly, improves later reading comprehension skills, and bolsters academic success over the long term. Furthermore, these kinds of intensive vocabulary activities increase student word consciousness, whereby students are more interested in words generally, attend to how they are used, and understand their central role in learning and communicating (Stahl & Shiel, 1999). A classroom rich in explicit intensive vocabulary instruction has the potential to provide students with a new word today and a new attitude and passion for learning words tomorrow.

CHAPTER 8

Reading Comprehension

In earlier chapters we focused on developing prereading skills and fluent reading. These foundational reading skills undergird reading comprehension, but they do not guarantee successful reading comprehension. Decoding skills and word fluency are necessary but not sufficient for helping students understand what they read and make meaning of text content (Skinner, Neddenriep, et al., 2002; Snow, Porsche, Tabors, & Harris, 2007). This chapter focuses explicitly on the knowledge and skills necessary for successful comprehension as well as strategies that support these abilities when prior instruction has not been effective.

The primary reason we read is to gain knowledge, for personal enjoyment, and to facilitate our ability to learn independently (Shanahan et al., 2010). Individuals who read rapidly and comprehend text easily are likely to choose to read more, and thus read more frequently (Skinner, 1999). And, with more frequent reading individuals become more skilled readers (Stanovich, 1986). By contrast, students who have trouble reading avoid it because they don't understand what they read and in turn lack frequent exposure to text and fall further behind. The purpose of this chapter is to present reading comprehension strategies that can be used to intervene with students having reading comprehension difficulties who may need more intensive support. First, let's examine what reading comprehension is to provide a context for the strategies that are described later in the chapter.

WHAT IS READING COMPREHENSION?

In 1999 the RAND Reading Study Group (RRSG, 2002) was tasked by the office of Educational Research and Improvement of the U.S. Department of Education with addressing the most pressing issues in literacy. Reading comprehension—the central focus of their report—was defined by the RRSG as "the process of simultaneously extracting and constructing meaning through interaction and involvement with written language (p. xii). The group highlighted multiple areas that influence successful comprehension: the reader, the activity or purpose for reading, the text, and the contexts in which reading and learning occur. They emphasized diverse reader characteristics, including motivation, cognition, genre knowledge, and existing knowledge. Task characteristics such as purpose and choice, and text-specific characteristics such as vocabulary and syntax, all influence a student's ability to read for understanding. Moreover, students acquire literacy not only in the classroom but also in their homes and communities. The social and cultural practices they engage in beyond the school walls can provide a rich context for the development of literacy (RRSG, 2002). In this chapter we focus specifically on reading activities and texts as they relate to comprehension interventions, but we encourage the reader to also keep in mind the larger cultural and linguistic contexts in which students function so that they can be drawn on to help students understand what they are reading. Figure 8.1 presents the RRSG's heuristic for reading comprehension, with reading comprehension represented at the center, depicting the interconnected relationship among all of these different elements of reading, each influencing students' abilities to comprehend text. In order for students to be able to understand what they read, multiple skills are necessary. We provide a list of six skills that support successful comprehension in Table 8.1. This list is not exhaustive but provides a useful baseline for supporting students' skills for comprehending text. Table 8.1 lists each of these abilities along with ideas for how to support their development in the classroom.

The first skill focuses on *foundational reading skills* and more specifically word-level abilities. Strong decoding skills and the ability to use sight words for fluent reading is a prerequisite of successful reading comprehension (Snow et al., 1998). Automatized foundational reading skills allow students to focus their cognitive energy on extracting the meaning from the text as opposed to focusing on lower-level skills that may be particularly taxing for students' memories. The second ability is *word knowledge* (vocabulary), which is the gateway to making meaning. Students who are unable to comprehend the words in the

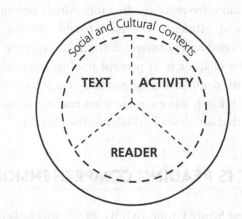

FIGURE 8.1. The RRSG's (2002) interactive view of reading comprehension. Copyright 2002 by the RAND Corporation. Reprinted by permission.

TABLE 8.1. Knowledge for Successful Comprehension

Foundational reading skills. Students should have solid decoding skills and knowledge of sight words. Providing students with activities to increase their word-reading skills and fluency will help automatize these lower-level skills.

Word knowledge. Strong vocabulary skills are necessary for comprehending text. Providing students with instruction in vocabulary activities (described in Chapter 7) as well as exercises that involve listening comprehension builds their oral language skills, which can strengthen text reading when accompanied by adequate instruction in other areas.

Background knowledge. Knowledge of a diversity of concepts including discipline-specific concepts (e.g., World War II in social studies or pollination in science) as well as more general concepts (e.g., the relationship between cause and effect) are useful for improving students' understanding of the meaning of a text. Providing students with rich curricular materials and activities that promote broad conceptual knowledge development is crucial!

Comprehension-specific cognitive strategies. A specific skill set required for comprehension is knowledge of various cognitive strategies that can be used in different reading contexts. Providing students with a diverse repertoire of strategies and then teaching them when and how to use them across different texts will enable students to read a variety of types of texts in content areas (e.g., with social studies texts students should monitor their reading by asking themselves questions about cause and effect, turning points, and other questions central to the work of historians; c.f., Buehl, 2011; Mandell & Malone, 2007).

Reasoning skills. Complex texts require that students utilize thinking skills that facilitate their making inferences and connections across sentences and text themes so that they can better understand the author's intended message. Providing students with models of how to think through text can teach them how to reason effectively.

Motivation and engagement. Motivation to read is a central component of successful comprehension, as students are unlikely to activate or make use of the cognitive skills at their disposal if they are not motivated to do so. Providing students with real-life purposes for engaging in reading activities and books on topics that interest them motivates them to continue when they are faced with challenging text.

Note. Based on Shanahan et al. (2010).

text cannot understand the meaning of sentences that contain unknown words (Beck et al., 2013). The third skill is *background knowledge* about concepts. This knowledge, be it about subject-specific concepts or more broad general knowledge, allows students to integrate what they read with what they already know. Another important skill set is a repertoire of cognitive strategies that can be used in different reading contexts to help students stop, think, and reflect on what they are or will be reading so they can extract meaning from the text (Palincsar, & Brown, 1984). Reasoning skills are also necessary for successful reading comprehension; students' abilities to think through the logic of the text and use their analytic skills are an integral part of making meaning of text (Brown, Pressley, Van Meter, & Schuder, 1996). Last, but certainly not least, motivation to read—the specific purpose(s) for reading—is an important ingredient for effective reading (Guthrie, Wigfield, & Perencevich, 2004). Students who are motivated to read will persist in reading during a more challenging text, will read more frequently (strengthening their comprehension skills), and are more likely to apply cognitive strategies to a reading task because they want to understand the text (Turner, 1995; Wigfield & Guthrie, 1997).

READING ACTIVITIES APPROPRIATE FOR THE READER

Due to the complexity of all of the skills that go into reading comprehension, instruction and intervention methods are not as easily broken down into accuracy, fluency, and generalization components as many of the earlier skills are. The strategies that are available teach the student how to engage the text in a way that goes beyond mere word reading. The student who wants to learn from a text should approach it with expectations and be seeking clues about what the text might be saying. He or she should read the text with ongoing questions about the content that stimulate thoughts about meaning and relationships to other ideas. He or she should also be able to analyze the text following reading to extract information that might not have been fully understood or exploited when first read. Thus, this section describes specific reading comprehension activities that can be used prior to, during, and after reading depending on the kind of more intensive instruction students need (see Table 8.2). Although the timing of the strategies described below differs, they all essentially teach the student to extract meaning from the text by adding structured prompts for how to engage the text. All of these strategies essentially model analytic thinking. If they make the student successful and there is sufficient practice with the strategies, one would anticipate that the strategies can be progressively withdrawn so that the student learns to prompt him- or herself independently.

Teachers may choose to begin using comprehension strategies individually and then slowly introduce additional strategies or they may choose to introduce several strategies simultaneously. Research to date is inconclusive regarding the optimal means of introducing comprehension strategies and so teachers are encouraged to integrate them in ways that work best in their classroom (Shanahan et al., 2010). Regardless of how these strategies are introduced, the goal is to have students be able to use multiple strategies while reading, as that is what successful readers do. In order to explain how to integrate these strategies into a normal lesson plan we review examples in isolation; however, these strategies could be introduced together as a multiple-strategy approach in cases where teachers find this more appropriate for their students or the text being read. The strategy activities listed in Table 8.2 are organized according to when they can be used—prereading, during reading, or postreading (i.e., when the student has finished reading). Some strategies combine prereading, during-reading, and/or postreading procedures.

Prereading or Previewing Comprehension Activities

Previewing or prereading procedures clarify the purpose for reading and enhance comprehension. Previewing activities may enhance comprehension by drawing on prior knowledge related to the material. Students may read to confirm, support, accentuate, or disconfirm prior knowledge. Previewing procedures can help students to generate questions or hypotheses about the subject covered. Reading the text then resolves these questions or hypotheses. Previewing activities enhance the speed and accuracy of reading, thereby reducing the time and effort required for reading (Rousseau & Tam, 1991). Finally, previewing activities may heighten students' interest in material, thus encouraging their reading.

TABLE 8.2. Reading Comprehension Strategies

When to use the strategy	Strategies
Prereading	Clarify the purpose of reading.
	Help the student to estimate the general content of the text by noting title, date of publication, author, and scanning the text.
	TELLS (Title–Examine–Look–Look–Setting strategy).
	Preteach vocabulary.
	Preteach concepts through semantic maps or story grammar.
	Carefully choose reading material and allow student choice of reading material (with some restrictions).
During reading	Promote frequent and sustained reading.
	Consider story grammar for fictional text.
	Use outlines and study guides for expository text.
	Apply strategic note taking for expository text.
	Use time lines and flowcharts for expository text.
	Make conflict charts.
	Use visualization for fictional text.
Postreading	Use summarization for both types of text.
	Use question-and-answer relationship training.
Combined strategies (prereading, during reading, and/or postreading)	Strategic note taking
	SQ3R
	Multipass
	POSSE
	Using rewards

Clarifying the Purpose of Reading

Being a strategic reader requires goal-directed reading; to support targeted reading teachers can provide students with an understanding of the purpose for reading specific material before beginning to read (Duke & Pearson, 2002). When educators assign reading materials, they are likely to increase the probability of students choosing to read if they clarify the purpose or function of reading. Furthermore, providing a reading goal helps engage students and focuses their attention on relevant aspects of the text for comprehension. In so doing teachers can help students avoid what researchers have labeled "seductive details" in texts, that is, tangential story features and facts that may actually distract students from more central aspects of the text useful for extracting meaning (Garner, Brown, Sanders, & Menke, 1992). In almost all instances, the purpose requires students to comprehend what they read and enhances the probability of students choosing to read and keep reading. Thus, in most instances, educators should do more than merely assign reading; they should also specify the purpose for the reading.

Helping Students to Estimate the General Content of the Text

READING TITLE, DATE OF PUBLICATION, AND AUTHOR

Students can be taught several procedures that allow them to estimate the general content of the text. Reading the title of a text may allow students to activate prior knowledge related to the title and content. While the title can provide clues regarding content, other pre-reading activities may also help students form hypotheses regarding content. For example, checking the date of publication may help students understand the author and historical context in which the text was written. Also, identifying the author and providing information about the author may provide additional cues regarding content (Miller, 1982).

SCANNING THE TEXT

Next, students can flip through the text in order to gain an understanding of the content and nature of the text. Sections, subheadings, and subtitles provide additional information related to content. Illustrations, figures, tables, or graphs provide additional information regarding the scope and sequence of the text (Idol-Maestas, 1985). Students can also scan the text to determine the length of the text and/or each section of the text. This can allow students to set goals for when reading requires multiple sessions. For example, students may scan a science text and determine that they will read and take notes on one section before dinner. These intermittent goals can help maintain reading (Chan, Cole, & Barfett, 1987).

Scanning the text can also be used to allow students to identify important words or unknown words. For example, many content-area texts (e.g., biology texts) make this process easier by highlighting (e.g., printing these in bold letters the first time they appear) words, phrases, or terms that are likely to be unknown by students. However, even when these additional cues are not provided, students can be taught to scan the text and identify words that appear to be important and are unknown (Idol-Maestas, 1985).

Scanning also can be used to answer questions regarding the general nature of the text and its structure. For example, students can scan to determine whether the material is expository or narrative. Because different kinds of texts are read differently, knowing whether the material is factual or fictional is likely to influence the student's reading. For example, when reading a fictitious narrative, the focus is usually on characters and settings. Additionally, the reader may not have access to any prior knowledge of the characters that can be used to enhance comprehension. When reading factual, expository text, the focus is usually on text structure and involves constructing and revising summaries while reading (Duke & Pearson, 2002). The student's prior knowledge may be used to assist with comprehension.

The TELLS (Title–Examine–Look–Look–Setting) Procedure

TELLS is an acronym for a previewing procedure designed to enhance comprehension of stories (Idol-Maestas, 1985). Table 8.3 provides an overview of the steps for using the TELLS procedure. A blank, reproducible form that can be used with students appears in

TABLE 8.3. Steps for the TELLS Previewing Procedure

• T	Title	What is the title of this story? Does it give a clue as to what the story is about? What do you think it is about?
• E	Examine	Look at each page of the story to find clues about the story. What did you find?
• L	Look	Look for and write down important words, such as ones that are bold or used frequently. What do they mean?
• L	Look	Look again through the story for hard words—words you do not know. Write them down. What do they mean?
• S	Setting	Write down clues about the setting, such as the place, date, and time period. (Hint: These clues are often found in the beginning of the story.)
FACT or FICTION?		Is this a true story (fact)? Or is this a pretend story (fiction)?

Worksheet 8.1 at the end of the chapter. While the TELLS procedure can be used with individual students, it may actually be best to train students to use these procedures in a group format.

The first step in the TELLS procedure is to teach students to read the *title* and form clues as to what the story is about. A teacher may introduce the reading material by announcing the title and asking students what they think the story is about and why they think this. During this instruction, it is critical that teachers avoid providing evaluative feedback regarding their responses. What is critical is for students to learn that they can form hypotheses about content by merely reading the title. This first step should encourage students to read in order to confirm or disconfirm their hypotheses.

The second step is to *examine*. Here the student is taught to look through each page of the material skimming for clues. Clues embedded in the title will give information regarding the general content and confirm or disconfirm readers' hypotheses or the clues will cause readers to develop new more complex hypotheses regarding the content of the text. Clues include illustrations, sections or subtitles, and figures or graphs. Other clues include the structure and layout of the text. For example, text with many quotes and a hand-drawn color picture of a dragon may suggest a fictional story, whereas text with many headings, subheadings, and figures and a black-and-white photograph of a living lizard may suggest that the material is factual.

During the third stage, *look*, students are taught to scan for important words. In this step, students can be taught to look for clues for important words in bolded or italicized font, for example. Students should also be taught to look for words that are used frequently. Illustrations and captions may also help students identify important words.

When an illustration depicts a particular event, there may be important words surrounding that event. When a word from the title is repeated frequently in the text, this may be a clue that this is an important word to know and understand while reading the material.

During the fourth stage, students are taught to *look* for hard words. Hard words can be a variety of different kinds of words. These can be words they don't readily recognize. Sometimes students may not recognize or know the meaning of a printed word, but may recognize the words once they hear it pronounced or use their decoding skills to pronounce the word. In other instances, students may not know the meaning of a word, even though they can accurately read the word. Students need to be instructed on how to skim page by page through a text looking for these hard words.

In the fifth stage, students are taught to skim for clues about the *setting* of the story. Students should look for clues like places (e.g., city names), area descriptions (e.g., a park in the heart of downtown), dates, or references to time periods (e.g., a few weeks before Christmas or before the invention of electricity). Students should be instructed to focus their attention on the beginning of the story since most settings are described early in the text.

After the TELLS acronym is complete, the student answers one question regarding the general nature of the story. From the clues gathered during the TELLS procedure, the student should be able to predict whether the text is a true story (fact) or a pretend story (fiction).

Preteaching Vocabulary

The first step in preteaching vocabulary is to identify words to teach. Many reading curricula and content-area texts (e.g., science texts) have lists of vocabulary words that can be taught prior to reading. Additionally, educators can scan material to identify key words that are high-utility words. These key words are words that are important in understanding the phrase or passage and are useful for talking about the text content (Rousseau & Tam, 1991). Finally, students can be asked to scan material and identify unknown words that appear important (Idol-Maestas, 1985).

Procedures such as providing a definition, having a student look up the word in a dictionary, or giving a synonym or antonym can enhance vocabulary (refer to Chapter 7 for more strategies). Teachers may use the word in a sentence and/or ask the student to use the word in a sentence. Alternately, the teacher may have a student read a brief section of text where that word is used and have him or her attempt to use context cues to discern the meaning of the word.

There are some concerns with preteaching vocabulary. Students may forget the definition of words as they are reading. Because students with reading skill deficits often read slowly, they are likely to have to maintain this information for a longer period of time, as they will not arrive at new words as quickly as others. Further complicating matters is that students with reading skill deficits may have cognitive processing deficits that make it difficult to remember or recall newly acquired information as they read (LaBerge & Samuels, 1974; Lesgold & Perfetti, 1978; Lesgold & Resnick, 1982; Wong, 1986).

There are several solutions to these problems. After students have initially learned the meaning of a word, context cues may help them recall the meaning of the word. Providing students with a list of these words and brief definitions or synonyms can be used to aid comprehension. Finally, providing sufficient opportunities to practice using new vocabulary words prior to asking students to read text containing these words can enhance the probability of the students remembering definitions as they read (Gravois & Gickling, 2002).

Another procedure that educators often use is to provide students with a dictionary and encourage them to look up unknown words that they come across while they are reading.

While this method is often used, it has several limitations. First, having students look up words in a dictionary has not been shown to be very effective (Bos, Anders, Filip, & Jaffe, 1989). In many instances, it disrupts reading and interferes with comprehension, as the cognitive effort and time required to look up words in the dictionary causes their understanding of previously read material to deteriorate (Stanovich, 1986).

Looking up words in a dictionary also reduces time available for students to read and build their comprehension skills. Requiring students to look up words in the dictionary makes reading more effortful and can decrease students' motivation to read. Therefore, when students are reading for comprehension, it is appropriate for educators, peers, siblings, parents, or others to provide synonyms or brief definitions of words rather than requiring the reader to look them up in the dictionary.

In some instances, students may use their knowledge of word parts to determine meanings of words. For example, understanding prefixes and suffixes and root words may help students understand the meaning of words. Additionally, providing students with other information about words (e.g., whether it's a noun or a verb) may assist with comprehension. Again, this should be done prior to reading for comprehension, as teaching this material will disrupt their continuous reading and adversely affect comprehension.

Preteaching Concepts

Teaching new words in isolation can be effective, but prereading procedures that teach more detailed concepts and multiple words or phases may cause greater increases in comprehension (Bos et al., 1989). Graphic or advanced organizers and semantic maps may assist students with learning concepts and understanding written text. These are typically graphic representations of information that is contained in the text. These materials can provide students with information that enhances comprehension levels and reduces the time and/or effort required to comprehend the material. Such tools may also activate prior knowledge and highlight goals or purposes related to reading the material.

Before discussing the procedures for preteaching concepts, it is important to note that these materials should supplement but not replace the text. If advanced organizers contain all the pertinent information in the text, then there is no reason or purpose for reading the text. All students, especially students with poor reading skills who require more time and effort to read, may be more likely to choose *not* to read the text. Instead, they could merely study the advanced organizer.

SEMANTIC MAPS

Graphic or advanced organizers most often associated with content-area texts are semantic maps or semantic feature analysis charts. These organizers can be used prior to reading or during reading exercises. In order to use these graphic organizers as a prereading instructional method, educators must create either a semantic map or semantic feature analysis chart. Both of these graphic organizers are relationship charts. The steps used by Bos et al. (1989) to create these charts are summarized in Table 8.4.

TABLE 8.4. Steps in Constructing Semantic Graphs

1. Read assigned text.
2. List key concepts and vocabulary.
3. Review concept list for the all-inclusive idea (e.g., chapter topic).
4. The all-inclusive idea becomes the title of the semantic graph.
5. Organize entries on the concept and vocabulary list into categories (e.g., characteristics, steps in a process, examples of the main concept, functions).
6. The main concept for each category becomes a coordinate concept.
7. Place the coordinate concepts along the top line of the semantic graph or in the medium-sized circles of a semantic map.
8. The supporting concepts and vocabulary for each coordinate category become the subordinate concepts.
9. Place subordinate concepts along the left-hand column of the graph or in the small-sized circles underneath the coordinate circles in the semantic map.
10. Fill in the relationships between the coordinate concepts and the subordinate concepts on the graph, or fill in the relationship lines between the coordinate concepts and the subordinate concepts on the semantic map.

Note. Data from Bos, Anders, Filip, and Jaffe (1989).

The first step in developing a relationship chart is to read the assigned material and complete a content analysis. The content analysis consists of several steps during which special attention is given to textual cues (e.g., titles, subheadings, highlighted words, figures). First, the teacher must list the key concepts and vocabulary. This list is then evaluated to determine which idea seems to be all inclusive. The all-inclusive topic is considered the superordinate concept (e.g., topic of the chapter) and is used as the title of the graphic organizer. The remainder of the concepts list is then organized into categories. For example, the concepts can be organized into categories of characteristics, functions, examples of the main concept, or steps in a process. The main concepts for each category become the coordinate concepts. The remaining concepts are considered the subordinate concepts or supporting ideas of the coordinate concepts. Those concepts that don't fit into a coordinate category, but are considered important to comprehending the text, should be added to another portion of the prereading curriculum. Once all the concepts are labeled by categories, the educator develops the semantic analysis chart or semantic map. In the chart, the superordinate concept is the title of a grid chart. The coordinate concepts are placed along the top of the grid and the subordinate concepts are listed along the left side of the grid (see Figure 8.2). In the map, the superordinate concept is the largest circle along the top of the page (see Figure 8.3). The coordinate concepts are then medium-sized circles directly attached to the superordinate concept. The subordinate concepts are placed in smaller circles attached to each coordinate concept.

When using a semantic graphic organizer as a prereading technique, the relationship chart can be completed or reviewed during group instruction prior to reading the assigned material. The instructor can leave the relationship chart blank or the relationship lines in the map circles off and then help guide the students to the correct relationships. In this way,

(Superordinate Concept) How Fossils Are Made			
	What are fossils?	Things that can become fossils	(Coordinate concept)
How we learn about dinosaurs	x		
Dinosaurs (subordinate vocabulary)		x	
Hardened tracks or footprints	x	x	
Animals or plants (subordinate idea or concept)		x	
Teeth, bones, or shells		x	

FIGURE 8.2. Example of a semantic analysis chart. Data from Bos, Anders, Filip, and Jaffe (1989).

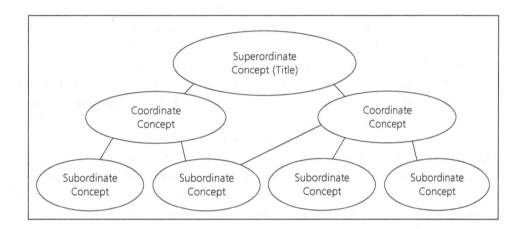

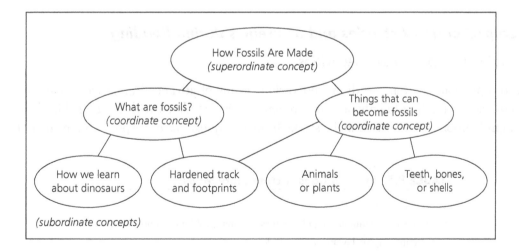

FIGURE 8.3. Example of a semantic map for an expository text. Data from Bos and Anders (1990) and based on a story from Granowsky (2000).

the educator is aiding the students in the activation of their prior knowledge and increasing the students' involvement with the concepts and vocabulary. The instructor can also use the semantic graphic organizers as a prereading technique by providing a completed relationship chart and then reviewing the chart with the students. Worksheets 8.2 and 8.3 at the end of the chapter can be used for preparing a semantic analysis chart and a semantic analysis map, respectively.

STORY GRAMMAR

A commonly used advanced graphic organizer is a story map. Story mapping is a graphic representation of story grammar. Story grammar is the common pieces of a narrative story (i.e., setting, character, problem, events, and solution). In order to develop a story map, the educator first must read the narrative text (see Table 8.5 for the step-by-step procedure). While reading, a list is created that includes the setting, character(s), problem(s), event(s), and solution(s). This list is then compiled into graphic form (e.g., a story map).

Each piece of story grammar should be taught in a prereading exercise. When introducing these concepts, the educator can assist the students in looking up each piece of the story. Once these parts have been taught, students are provided with a graphical representation of story grammar (Bos & Anders, 1990). These graphs can take on a variety of forms including maps, illustrations, or charts (see Figures 8.4 and 8.5 for examples).

When introducing the story grammar concepts, the graphs can be given with all or some of the information provided and reviewed prior to reading. Then the students are instructed to read the story in order to confirm or disconfirm the story map and fill in the blanks. Once a story grammar has been introduced, the graphs are usually left blank for the students to fill in while reading the story.

Comprehension Activities and Strategies during Reading

Reading Comprehension Activities

In the previous section, we discussed various forms of advanced organizers that can be used prior to reading to enhance comprehension. For students with reading skill deficits, comprehension activities that make students answer questions or respond to the content *as*

TABLE 8.5. Steps in Constructing Story Maps

1. Read assigned text.
2. List story grammar (i.e., characters, setting, problem, events, solutions).
3. Create graphic layout (see examples).
4. Place title for each portion of the story grammar in the desired location.
5. Place correct information in the appropriate graphic location.

Note. Data from Bos and Anders (1990).

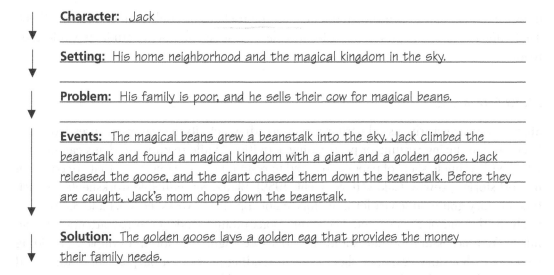

Character: Jack

Setting: His home neighborhood and the magical kingdom in the sky.

Problem: His family is poor, and he sells their cow for magical beans.

Events: The magical beans grew a beanstalk into the sky. Jack climbed the beanstalk and found a magical kingdom with a giant and a golden goose. Jack released the goose, and the giant chased them down the beanstalk. Before they are caught, Jack's mom chops down the beanstalk.

Solution: The golden goose lays a golden egg that provides the money their family needs.

FIGURE 8.4. Example of story grammar in chart form. Data from Newby, Caldwell, and Recht (1989).

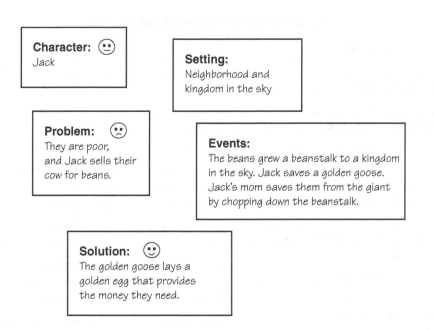

Character: Jack

Setting: Neighborhood and kingdom in the sky

Problem: They are poor, and Jack sells their cow for beans.

Events: The beans grew a beanstalk to a kingdom in the sky. Jack saves a golden goose. Jack's mom saves them from the giant by chopping down the beanstalk.

Solution: The golden goose lays a golden egg that provides the money they need.

FIGURE 8.5. Example of story grammar in map form. Data from Newby, Caldwell, and Recht (1989).

they are reading have been shown to enhance comprehension (Robinson & Skinner, 1996). The following are examples of ways to provide additional support to students while they read.

STORY GRAMMAR

Story grammar was discussed earlier as a prereading activity. These procedures have also been used as during-reading or postreading activities. While reading, students can be provided with a simple sheet of paper and asked to respond to basic questions that are common in most stories (Newby, Caldwell, & Recht, 1989). Blank, reproducible worksheets for each type of story grammar (chart form or story map) appear in Worksheets 8.4 and 8.5 respectively, at the end of the chapter. These questions prompt students to pay attention to the information necessary to understand the story (see Figure 8.6 for an example). Providing students with a story grammar sheet prior to reading provides a purpose for reading and allows students to form hypotheses about the material based on their scanning of pictures, titles, and so on. Having students complete this sheet *as they read* can help them consolidate, store, and maintain information.

MORE COMPLEX STORY GRAMMAR QUESTIONING

1. Who is the story about? _____
_____

2. What is the boy's job? _____
_____

3. What problem does he have? _____
_____

4. What does he do to try to get money for the family? _____
_____

5. What happens when he brings magical beans home? _____
_____

6. Where did he meet the giant? _____
_____

7. How was the giant killed? _____
_____

8. What happens in the end? _____
_____

9. Could Jack have done something different to get money? _____
_____

10. What might have happened to Jack if his mother had not cut down the stalk? _____
_____

FIGURE 8.6. Example of a more complex story grammar in question form. Data from Grossen and Carnine (1991).

When teaching students to use story grammar, teachers should gradually give greater responsibility to students over time. Teachers should first teach students how to use the story grammar correctly, then observe students' independent use of the story grammar, and finally fade the use of the story grammar so that the student independently comprehends the material. Demonstration, practice, and feedback should be used to teach the student the correct application of the story grammar. When students apply it correctly, they can be asked to respond to items verbally as material is being read or by filling out sheets as they read. As the story grammar is being faded out, students would not be given a copy of the story grammar or asked to fill in their responses as they read. Educators could still assess the student's comprehension by delivering the questions from the story grammar after the student has finished reading (Newby et al., 1989).

Story grammars are effective and especially useful with younger students whose reading curricula are often composed of multiple simple stories that have limited characters and plots. As students' reading comprehension skills are enhanced, story grammar prompts can be altered to include more complex items such as (1) type of conflict (e.g., man vs. nature), (2) foreshadowing (e.g., What do you think will happen next and why do you think this?), and (3) general themes (e.g., persistence helps accomplish goals).

In these examples, structured prompts or questions are provided and students are to respond as they read. However, following some forms of previewing students can also develop their own prompts or questions prior to reading. These self-generated prompts may be particularly useful for narrative or story reading. Having students write their own questions ahead of time and use these prompts as guided notes may enhance overall comprehension equal to or more than prestructured prompts (Schumaker, Deshler, Alley, Warner, & Denton, 1982). Examples of self-questions may include "Will Johnny get caught?"; "How will he cross the bridge?" These self-generated prompts can also be used to support small-group activities. Teachers can create what, where, and why index cards and have students generate their own questions and ask their peers questions about the story in small groups (Shanahan et al., 2010).

EXPOSITORY TEXT

As with story grammars, a variety of advanced organizers and visual graphic displays that are used to enhance comprehension of expository text prior to reading can also be incorporated into reading activities. Outlines, study guides, strategic notes, timelines, and flowcharts can be systematically inserted into text and students can be prompted to respond to comprehension questions as they are reading.

OUTLINES AND STUDY GUIDES

Outlines or study guides are prepared in advance of the reading assignment. These aids are distributed to students when the reading is assigned. Students read the text and follow along with the outline. Some outlines contain all the pertinent information, and students read these as a prereading activity. These can also be used as a postreading activity (e.g., study aids). One major limitation to these procedures is that sometimes students will choose to merely read these summaries as opposed to reading the text, which can actually hinder comprehension if the outline or study guide discourages students from actually reading assigned text (McDaniel et al., 2001). However, with other outlines students respond to items as they are reading. One example includes questions that students answer as they read. These questions are generally provided in the same sequence as they are presented in the text. Both questions and answers should be brief so as not to cause unnecessary disruptions in student reading.

Framed outlines have many similar characteristics in that prompts and responses are typically provided in the same sequence as in the text. Framed outlines are constructed with brief prompts focusing on key information (e.g., brief sentences). Students are typically required to make brief responses to these prompts. Figure 8.7 provides an example of a framed outline in which students are required to fill in the blanks as they read (Lovitt, Rudsit, Jenkins, Pious, & Benedetti, 1986).

STRATEGIC NOTE TAKING

Rather than providing brief, one-word responses, students may be required to make more general notes, a technique referred to as strategic note taking (see Figure 8.8). Taking notes, however, often requires much time and energy and may end up disrupting reading. Thus, these procedures are often used with more advanced readers who can easily move back and forth from writing notes to reading. When used with less skilled readers, these time-consuming activities are probably more appropriate at the end of the reading session.

TIMELINES AND FLOWCHARTS

Two other forms of *during-reading* activities are timelines and flowcharts. Both timelines and flowcharts are useful for enhancing comprehension in content areas when an understanding of linear events is important. Both forms include prompts based on the sequence of events. Timelines provide prompts based on a chronological sequence of events. They help students translate narrative text by requiring them to respond in order to complete summaries of discrete events covered in the text. Figure 8.9 provides an example of a timeline.

We learned about dinosaurs from their   *fossils* . A fossil is left by a   *plant or animal* . Fossils can be leaves, shells,   *eggs, or skeletons* . Some fossils are the hardened tracks of   *footprints*   left by a moving   *animal* . When an animal or plant dies, it can become covered with   *mud or sand* . As time goes by, the plant or animal becomes covered by   *many layers*   of mud or sand. After   *thousands*   of years, the   *bottom*   layers harden into   *rock* . The dead   *plant or animal*   also hardens into   *rock* . This is how   *fossils*   are formed.

FIGURE 8.7. Example of a framed outline for a third-grade basal reading selection on fossils. Based on a passage from Granowsky (2000).

FOSSILS

I. Fossils are left by . . .
   A.
   B.

II. Fossils can be . . .
   A.
   B.
   C.
   D. skeletons.
   E. hardened tracks or footprints left by a
      moving animal.

III. When a plant or animal dies, what happens?
   A. It becomes covered by mud or sand.
   B. As time goes by . . .
      1.
      2. Dead plant or animal hardens into rock.

FIGURE 8.8. Student copy of strategic note taking. Based on a passage from Granowsky (2000).

Flowcharts can cover chronological events or sequential physical events. For example, a flowchart may describe the sequence of blood flowing through the heart.

CONFLICT CHARTS

Conflict charts can be used during reading to aid with comprehension of nonlinear concepts. With this simple procedure students are required to list support for conflicting arguments or conclusions. For example, as students are reading, they could be asked to list the pros and cons of nuclear power on each side of a sheet of paper.

STUDENT COMPREHENSION STRATEGIES DURING READING

We have reviewed activities that support reading comprehension and accompanying reading strategies that support *activating prior knowledge* and knowledge of story structure and

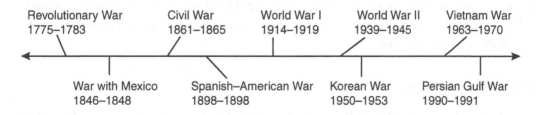

FIGURE 8.9. Example of a historical timeline for U.S. wars.

main ideas through *questioning*. We next review other comprehension strategies particularly useful during reading to help support reading comprehension.

CLARIFYING AND MONITORING

A useful strategy for enhanced comprehension is having students learn to monitor their comprehension and attend to when they are not understanding aspects of the text. For example, Baumann, Seifert-Kessel, and Jones (1992) taught third graders a very simple think-aloud strategy. Specifically, students were taught to ask themselves, "Does this make sense?" Mastropieri et al. (1996) taught middle school students with learning disabilities to do the same thing. Specifically, after reading each sentence students were taught to ask, "Why does that make sense?" After students were taught to make these responses out loud, they were then encouraged to respond in their head. Also useful is encouraging students to restate what they have read in their own words and reread the parts of the story that they have not understood (Shanahan et al., 2010).

VISUALIZATION

Another strategy that may enhance comprehension is visualization. Forming a cognitive picture or representation of what students have read may help comprehend material (Alesandri, 1982). Various procedures have been used to prompt or train students to use visual imagery. The simplest procedure is to tell students to form a picture in their mind (Alesandri, 1982). Pictures can also be used as prompts to assist students in developing visual images (e.g., Giesen & Peeck, 1984). Chan, Cole, and Morris (1990) used a storyboard format (i.e., sequence of pictures) to attempt to teach students with learning disabilities to form sequential, as opposed to static, visual images. Carnine and Kinder (1985) had fourth to sixth graders with comprehension skills deficits first make pictures in their mind of events that happened in a story as they were reading. The following day, students were encouraged to close their eyes and form pictures. When they finished, students drew pictures of the images. Results of all these studies suggest that these visualization procedures enhanced comprehension.

Brandoff-Matter (1989) described several procedures that she used to help students visualize. First she told students to close their eyes and picture what was being said as material was read aloud. She then asked them specific questions, such as "Where are you?" (e.g., setting) and "Who is talking?" (e.g., characters). Additionally, she described an object and asked students to indicate what object was being described. These exercises, designed to enhance visualization skills, may be necessary for students to successfully use visualization to enhance comprehension.

DRAWING INFERENCES

An additional strategy that helps students comprehend text is supporting their ability to make inferences about the text, that is, students should be able—in the presence of missing information in the text—to extrapolate from the information that is present and deduce the meaning of the text content. For example, a story describing an interchange among a pig, a cow, and a goat, is likely occurring on a farm. While the text may not explicitly say the setting, existing clues in the text support this inference. Teachers can help students generate this information by having them look up words they don't know that may help them draw appropriate text-based conclusions. A study by Hansen (1981) compared students who received explicit instruction on inference making, those who received explicit instruction on activating prior knowledge, and those who received no strategy instruction at all and found that the former was the most effective for increased reading comprehension gains.

We have reviewed five strategies that research shows support reading comprehension for students in the elementary grades: *predicting/activating prior knowledge, questioning, visualizing, monitoring/clarifying,* and *drawing inferences.* A sixth strategy, *summarization,* is addressed in the following section on comprehension strategies after reading.

Postreading Comprehension Activities

After students have finished reading, a variety of activities can be used to enhance comprehension. These include teaching the summarization strategy, structuring student discussions about the text, identifying the relationships between comprehension questions and the answers in the text, and rereading. Students are more likely to have success using these procedures if they are applied immediately after they have finished reading. These postreading activities can also be used to assess comprehension. Additionally, student performance on these postreading procedures provides educators with an opportunity to reinforce reading comprehension.

Summarization

When reading content-area text (e.g., science text), the goal is for students to acquire information that is needed for subsequent activities (e.g., to complete a laboratory assignment; understand the applications of a theory; pass an exam; or better understand subsequent reading material, lectures, or demonstrations). Summarization procedures are often used as a postreading activity to enhance comprehension and maintenance of expository text. While some students may develop effective summarization skills without specific instruction, students with reading skill deficits may need to be taught effective summarization skills. For example, researchers have taught students to write down the main ideas using their own words (Macon, 1991), try to organize the ideas into related groups (Fahmy & Bilton, 1990), reduce the main ideas as concisely as possible, and use an outline form to indicate main ideas and subideas (Anderman & Williams, 1986).

Nelson, Smith, and Dodd (1992) demonstrated how to intensify instruction by teaching students with learning disabilities a summarization skills strategy. The first seven steps focused on identifying and organizing the main ideas and important information. These steps required students to:

1. Write down the main idea.
2. Write down the important things the writer had to say about the main idea.
3. Review the text to check their understanding of the main idea and the important things related to that main idea.
4. Write down the main idea or topic that they wanted to write about in their summary.
5. Order important things (from step 2) by how they want to write about them.
6. Review the text and their notes to see if there is any important information left out or any unimportant information they can leave out.
7. Write the summary.

After written summaries were completed, the focus shifted to clarifying and revising these summaries. First, students reread their own summaries and revised them if there was anything that was not clear. Second, peers read each other's summaries and indicated anything that was not clear. This feedback was used to make final revisions of the summaries. The authors of this study also provided a summary skills study guide that included all nine steps with space to write down the requested information. Results of their study showed that this summary strategy instruction produced increases in reading comprehension scores and improved summary writing (Nelson et al., 1992).

Most effective summarization strategies are highly structured and students receive specific instruction on completing these summaries. D'Alessio (1996) investigated a similar, less structured summarization strategy that incorporated a retelling technique. In this procedure, students were instructed to recreate a portion of the text that they had just read or someone had read to them. While this general procedure could easily be used across text, D'Alessio (1996) found that merely having students retell without any specific instruction as to how to re-create the text or summarize the reading did not result in increased reading comprehension scores. Thus, it appears that students must be taught how to complete summarization procedures and the steps should be clear and structured.

These techniques can be adapted for use with narrative stories. Instead of recording main ideas and grouping them by relationships, the students can be instructed to record the main characters and his or her actions. These actions can be grouped by goals, relationships to other characters, and/or actions. Thus, students would be creating a type of story map, like the one that was described earlier in this chapter. In this manner, the story mapping would be considered a during- and postreading technique since the recording of main story elements occurs during reading but the relationship grouping or mapping occurs after reading has finished.

Question-and-Answer Relationship Training

Question-and-answer relationship (QAR) training was based on the original research from Pearson and Johnson (1978) who proposed that answering comprehension questions was not an isolated task but a relational task among the readers, the reader's background knowledge, and the text (Raphael, 1986). The relationships between comprehension questions and answers were originally placed into three categories: Text Explicit, Text Implicit, and Script Implicit. Raphael (1984) modified these three categories and labeled them "Right There," "Think and Search," and "On My Own." These categories were further modified into two categories with four subcategories (Raphael, 1986). The two new categories include "In the Book" and "In My Head." Under "In the Book," the two categories include "Right There" (i.e., an explicit answer in the text) and "Think and Search" (i.e., an implicit answer is in the text but you have to find it, sometimes in multiple locations). Under the "In My Head" category, there is "Author and You" (i.e., an answer comes from the student with some clues from the author) and "On Your Own" (i.e., the answer comes from within the student).

Teaching the QAR program to students follows the model–lead–test procedure. The teacher shows the students how to identify the location of the answer for a comprehension question. The teacher involves the students in the process of answering a comprehension question (i.e., guided learning). The students are then gradually given more independence to apply the QAR strategy to the answering of comprehension questions (Sorrell, 1990).

In the training phase of QAR, short (e.g., two to four sentences) text passages are used for each comprehension question. After students have acquired the skills, text passage length should be increased. Another teaching technique includes providing lines after each comprehension question for each of the four categories of questions. The student would then be asked to record the answer to that question followed by the type of question (e.g., "Right There"). The original author of QAR (Raphael, 1984) trained students in this program over several days using booklets with text passages, comprehension questions, QAR categories, and samples. Studies using the QAR program for training reading comprehension question relationships have found increased comprehension scores (Raphael, 1984, 1986).

Graham and Wong (1993) adapted the QAR program for use in comprehending literature. The three-H strategy was made to simplify the mnemonic for students who are reading disabled. The new three-H strategy is an alliteration that may assist students in remembering cues for how to search text for meaning. The QAR categories were replaced with "Here," "Hidden," and "In My Head." These labels correspond with the text explicit, text implicit, and script implicit (e.g., student's own knowledge base) categories from Pearson and Johnson (1978).

Training for the three-H strategy is similar to the QAR program. It includes modeling of the strategy with a teacher using a think-aloud, overt guidance by the instructor as the student uses the strategy, faded self-guidance as the student continues to use the strategy, and covert self-instruction as the teacher's assistance is faded completely. Graham and Wong (1993) found that average and poor fifth- and sixth-grade readers who were taught the three-H strategy scored better on comprehension questions than a nonstrategy control group.

Combining Procedures

Some interventions combine several of the techniques already discussed. Additionally, they involve prereading, during-reading, and postreading comprehension activities. We review several of them.

Strategic Note Taking

Strategic note taking can be used at all three stages. Worksheet 8.6 displays a strategic note-taking form that requires students to complete sections before, during, and after reading. The top of the page provides space for the student to identify the topic of the reading material and any previous knowledge of that topic prior to reading. The next section instructs the student to take notes in clusters or groupings as he or she is reading. This cue is designed to help students with organization and to identify relationships among ideas. A quick summary of the section pertaining to those key ideas is requested. The steps of clustering ideas and summarizing are repeated throughout the reading assignment. When finished reading, the student is cued to list five main points and describe them. This postreading summarization activity provides an overall but less detailed summary of the entire text.

SQ3R

The SQ3R study approach was designed for expository texts (Robinson, 1946). The acronym stands for "survey, question, read, recite, and restate." First, students *survey* the passage. They then formulate *questions* about the titles and subheadings they read during the surveying. This allows students to activate prior knowledge. It also provides a purpose for reading to answer those questions. Next they *read* (R1) the passage for the first time. During the reading, the student can answer the questions generated prior to reading. This can be done in writing, verbally, or cognitively (i.e., in his or her head). After reading, the student is instructed to *recite* (R2) certain content in the passage and make notes of the answers to the questions previously generated. A final review is conducted when the student *restates* (R3) or summarizes the content (Schumaker et al., 1982).

Multipass

The multipass strategy was developed in response to mixed research results using the SQ3R (Schumaker et al., 1982). This technique incorporates the skills of *survey, size-up,* and *sort out*. Each of these skills is considered a subcategory and each requires a separate pass through the text. In the first pass, the students are asked to *survey* the text for the main ideas and the chapter organization. In this step, students are instructed to read the titles, the introductory paragraph, illustration captions, and the summary paragraph. The student must also review the chapter's relationship to other adjacent chapters and paraphrase all the information gathered during this first pass through the text.

The second pass through, *size-up*, involves four steps designed to help the student gain specific information from the text without reading it from beginning to end. Prior to starting the steps, the student is encouraged to read the comprehension questions at the end of the chapter to see which facts appear to be the most important to remember. The steps include (1) looking for textual cues such as bold-font print, subtitles, or italics. The reader then (2) turns the cue into a question (e.g., the subtitle "Civil War" might be "Who Won the Civil War?" or "Who Fought in the Civil War?"). In the third step, (3) the student "skim reads" the surrounding text to answer the questions just generated. Finally, (4) the student is asked to paraphrase the answers to the questions without looking back in the book. When this pass through is complete, readers are encouraged to paraphrase all the facts, concepts, and ideas from the chapter that they could remember.

The third and final pass through is designed as a comprehension monitoring technique. In this step, the student reads all the comprehension questions at the end of the chapter. If a question could be answered immediately, a checkmark is placed next to it. If the student couldn't answer the question immediately, he or she was trained to look up the answer using the information about text structure already gained. Once the question is answered, a checkmark is placed by it.

POSSE

POSSE utilizes a variety of reading strategies while reading expository material (Englert & Mariage, 1991). POSSE is usually taught with modeling and guided learning methods. Students scan the material and then *predict* ideas based on his or her background knowledge. Students are encouraged to brainstorm about the passage's topic. After predicting, the students *organize* their thoughts into a structure similar to the text. Students are prompted to categorize and group ideas together. A semantic map may be used to facilitate this process. Then, the students begin reading and *searching* for the text structure and any cues as to text content. After reading (or intermittently), students *summarize* the main ideas and subordinate ideas. Students are encouraged to generate questions about the main ideas as they read to help facilitate the summarizing process. Finally, students *evaluate* their own comprehension by (1) comparing their summarizations and semantic maps from the organize section with the text, (2) clarifying any unclear points and answers to questions generated in the summarize section, and (3) predicting what will be discussed in the next section using cues from the text or the revised semantic map.

Formats for teaching multiple strategies beyond those reviewed here also include reciprocal teaching (Palincsar & Brown, 1984), transactional strategy instruction (Brown et al., 1996), informed strategies for learning (Paris, Cross, & Lipson, 1984), and concept-oriented reading instruction (Guthrie et al., 2004).

TEXT CHOICES

The activities to use and strategies to teach will be influenced by the genre, level, and content of the curricular texts chosen. Choosing authentic and appropriate text is central to the success of these activities. Thus, we review here suggestions for choosing texts to serve comprehension goals.

What Texts Should Teachers Choose?

Several variables influence what students should read when reading for comprehension. For example, comprehension is enhanced when students know at least 93% of the words (Hargis, 1995). This does not mean that harder material should be avoided entirely. In fact, in many instances this may not be an option. Instead, the previewing procedures described earlier can be used to enhance students' knowledge of words before they are asked to read the material. Additionally, concept maps may make it simpler to comprehend material, thereby freeing up the student to concentrate more on difficult texts. This is particularly important when students are asked to read material that is above their instructional level.

Pretesting children using CBM procedures described in Chapter 6 may help you in selecting material that is neither too difficult nor too easy. Because both accurate and rapid reading enhances comprehension, such procedures are recommended (Fuchs et al., 2001). Most reading curricula are carefully designed so that passages are progressively more difficult. Text length is also gradually increased. However, for students with reading skill deficits, special efforts may be needed to shape the amount of material they can read and comprehend during a particular session. Students may be asked to read less material than peers during a session. Educators can then use shaping procedures to gradually increase the amount of material they read and/or the time they spend reading during a particular session (Skinner, Skinner, & Armstrong, 2000).

What Are Appropriate Self-Selected Books?

When a student's reading level is established and the goal is to have students read in order to practice and enhance their comprehension skills, students can be assigned reading or be allowed to choose from options. For example, an entire class may be asked to read a specific story as part of a lesson designed to enhance vocabulary, understanding of plot structure, and foreshadowing. In other instances, the purpose of the assignment is not related to gaining specific information. Rather, students are reading to enhance their reading skills and their attitudes with respect to reading. In these instances, it is often appropriate to allow students some choices regarding what they will read. For example, during sustained silent reading time, students may be able to choose which material they will read.

Allowing students to choose the material that they will read has been shown to enhance the probability of reading and decrease the probability of problem behaviors (Cosden, Gannon, & Haring, 1995; Dunlap et al., 1994; Dunlap, Kern-Dunlap, Clarke, & Robbins, 1991; Dyer, Dunlap, & Winterling, 1990). Students are more likely to choose to read material associated with (1) higher-quality rewards, (2) more immediate rewards, or (3) higher rate of rewards (Neef, Shade, & Miller, 1994). Preference, however, will be idiosyncratic. Thus, one student may find reading about snakes very rewarding, whereas another student is bored with the topic. Providing choices allows students to choose material that interests them. Additionally, students may have preferences for specific authors, writing style (humor vs. history), or format (plays vs. story). While providing choice can allow students to choose reading material that is most rewarding to them, students must be able to accurately assess the material (i.e., content, style, format) in order to make these choices. Thus, prior to providing choices, educators can encourage students to use the scanning procedure described earlier to help them select material.

In general, whether students find reading something highly rewarding is partially dependent on whether students are able to comprehend the material. Thus, when providing choices, it may be important to limit options to material that is written at or near their instructional level. However, in some instances, students with a strong interest in a particular content area also have enough background knowledge to read and comprehend material in that content area, even when the material is written above their instructional level. When students choose material written slightly above their current reading level, educators should carefully monitor their progress (i.e., comprehension, reading rate, interest) and provide necessary assistance (e.g., prereading concept teaching) to reduce the probability of them becoming frustrated with the material.

With respect to reinforcement rate, rapid readers are likely to comprehend better (Skinner, 1999). All readers are likely to expend less effort and read material more quickly when they read material that is easier (i.e., at their mastery level). Thus, another concern with providing choices is that students may repeatedly choose to read material that is too easy, which can limit growth in their comprehension skills, thereby reducing their overall reading skill development (Skinner, Wallace, & Neddenriep, 2002). When this is a concern, educators should attempt to limit options and offer choices only of material written at the student's instructional level. However, because students with reading skill deficits are likely to have had fewer positive interactions with written material, occasionally allowing students to choose to read brief, but interesting material that is written at their mastery level gives them successful reading experiences and can improve their attitudes toward reading.

Sometimes young children and students may repeatedly choose to read the same material. Anyone who has ever read to young children knows how much they love to have a favorite story read over and over again (sometimes to the parent's dismay after the 50th reading!). Indeed, many adults reread favorite books or stories. Rereading helps comprehension and builds language skills. Students are often encouraged to reread material that they had difficulty comprehending. (We regularly recommend this strategy to our graduate students who sometimes have to tackle dense texts.) There are, however, two primary concerns with rereading. The first concern is that rereading material may not enhance comprehension as much as reading new material. The second concern is that if the student is rereading material silently, it may be difficult to discern whether the student is actually reading at all. Thus, if a student were oriented toward a text and turning pages at appropriate intervals, most would conclude that the student is reading silently. However, the student could be thinking about the cookies he or she is going to have for lunch. Comprehension questions can be used to assess whether silent reading is reading. But, correct answers to comprehension questions may reflect what the student learned from previous reading and not the content of the text being read this time around. Therefore, it may be best to avoid letting students choose to reread material until a specific amount of time has passed or until they have read other material. Rereading a favorite story can even be made contingent on reading a new story.

A final concern that parents often have is when their children repeatedly choose material on the same topic (e.g., about sports or dragons), written by the same author (e.g., Stephen King), material written in the same format (e.g., short stories) or material from the same series (e.g., Hardy Boys, Harry Potter). When children pick up a book, bug you to purchase it, or save their own money to purchase the book, they are clearly reading for their own reasons. Whenever possible this should be encouraged, not discouraged. Remember that one of the most important ways to develop reading skills is to read. Again, this does not mean that parents cannot encourage children to read diverse material, but they should avoid discouraging students from reading specific materials they independently choose to read.

REINFORCING READING COMPREHENSION

Although some strategies like self-selected books may be motivating enough, it is important to be aware of ways of externally motivating students as well. External motivators for reading may be particularly important in the case of students who struggle with reading. Once students begin reading, comprehension and appreciation of what they are reading can then serve as intermittent reinforcement that sustains their reading. However, students with reading skills deficits are likely to comprehend less as they read, thus decreasing the probability of sustained reading. Slower readers are less likely to maintain their reading because the effort required to read the material is greater when reading takes more time (Cates et al., 1999; Skinner, Neddenriep, et al., 2002). Students with reading skills deficits may be more likely to stop reading, which obviously hinders comprehension. However, procedures that enhance students' comprehension as they read are likely to increase the probability that students will sustain their reading.

During silent reading, at any moment students may choose to stop reading and do other things (e.g., talk to a peer, play with their pencil). During time allotted for reading, educators and parents should make every effort to limit distractions that may cue children to stop reading. Educators should avoid reinforcing any alternative behaviors during this time by redirecting them in a neutral but firm manner back to the text (Myerson & Hale, 1984).

Another general procedure that appears to help students sustain their silent reading behaviors is modeling. When students are engaged in independent seatwork, teachers often use this time to grade papers or finish other professional tasks. However, Methe and Hintze (2003) found that more students appeared to engage in sustained silent reading when the teacher was also engaged in sustained silent reading. Parents can have a similar effect at home by modeling sustained silent reading.

Intervening with Feedback and Reinforcement

First, reinforcement should be immediate and contingent upon correct performance. Initially, when teaching students specific pre-, during-, and postreading strategies, reinforcement should be delivered contingent upon correct use of the strategies themselves. Clear feedback should be given to correct any procedural errors and students should immediately be given the opportunity to practice the steps correctly after this feedback. As students begin to use these procedures correctly, reinforcement should also be given contingent upon their performance on comprehension assessment results. This reinforcement should include labeled praise that links the strategy to their success on comprehension assessment (e.g., "Wow! You completed the entire strategic note-taking assignment and did great on your test!"). Finally, reinforcement for following steps correctly should be faded while reinforcement for comprehending (e.g., grade on an exam) is kept in place or even strengthened in order to maintain comprehension. Eventually, this reinforcement can then be faded. Table 8.6 provides a list of these central ingredients of reinforcing successful student reading behavior.

While providing additional reinforcement for reading comprehension may be necessary, it is essential that the criterion for earning reinforcement not be too difficult or too easy. One procedure is to use very loose or randomly selected criteria (Popkin & Skinner, 2003). For example, Sharp and Skinner (2004) worked with a second-grade teacher to enhance students' reading comprehension during sustained silent reading. The class had the Accelerated Reader (Renaissance Learning, 2002) program. Students were encouraged to select material at their grade level, provided time for sustained silent reading, and were then given additional rewards (grade enhancement and teacher praise) for passing computer-delivered exams on their text after they finished reading. Although students were allowed to choose books written at their grade level, few students were passing comprehension exams or even taking the exams. Additionally, the teacher reported that many students did not appear to be reading during sustained silent reading time. Thus, the teacher and researchers wanted to develop a procedure that would encourage all students to read for comprehension. Comprehension exams were used to assess comprehension. *AR*

The primary concern was with how to set a criterion that would not be too high for some students (thereby causing some to give up), or too low for others (causing some not to perform their best). To solve this problem a contingency was used in which the teacher randomly selected a criterion (e.g., 1–13) at the end of each week. If the class as a whole passed that number of exams, the students would receive a group reward (e.g., watch a movie). Thus, each student was encouraged to do his or her best in order to increase the probability of the group earning their reward.

In addition to all the above, the group was told that they would all earn an ice cream party if everyone passed an exam in 6 weeks. The teacher and researchers, however, were concerned that some of the students would require additional instruction or assistance to pass exams. Thus, the program began with students working in pairs. During sustained silent reading time (now called quiet reading time), pairs took turns reading aloud from the same book and discussing what was happening as they read. Peers were paired so that the two students were at the same reading level, with one exception; a poor reader was paired with a strong reader. This pair took turns reading from stories written at the weaker students' reading level. After both members of the pair passed an exam, they were allowed to read on their own. Approximately half chose to continue reading in pairs and half chose to read alone.

TABLE 8.6. Reinforcing Successful Reading Behaviors

- Immediate reinforcement after correct responses.
- Explicit, consistent, immediate error correction.
- Opportunities to practice for correction.
- Labeled praise.

Results showed that whereas the class had averaged 0.7 quizzes passed per week prior to the intervention plan it increased to 7.5 quizzes passed per week during the intervention stage. Strong readers passed many more quizzes and weaker readers continued to read and attempt to pass quizzes. Because an interdependent group reward system was in place, the probability of earning the reward was increased when each student did his or her best and peers also did their best. Thus, students encouraged one another to do their best and did not pester or disrupt their peers' reading.

While the specific strategy used by Sharp and Skinner (2004) was successful, in many cases reinforcement for reading can be delivered in a less systematic manner. When students are allowed to choose what they read, a powerful and natural reinforcer is to allow students to discuss what they have read. During these discussions, parents or teachers can ask questions about the material, but they should avoid any negative evaluation. Instead, they should encourage students' enthusiasm. Literacy circles or groups where students with common interests discuss readings and provide one another with insights can provide an excellent mechanism for peer reinforcement of reading and comprehending. Additionally, by being exposed to peers' insights and interpretation of literature, participants' comprehension skills and appreciation of literature may be enhanced (Leal, 1993; Parker, Quigely, & Reilly, 1999).

Intensifying and Pacing Instruction

Students with reading skill deficits may require more time to read and comprehend material than their peers. After scanning material, they may become discouraged with long reading assignments. This section focuses on ways to intensify instruction for students who are not benefiting from existing instruction. One strategy that may help reduce frustration and allow students success is to break material down into smaller units (Wallace, Cox, & Skinner, 2003). Many content-area texts (e.g., science and social studies) and reading curricula often break large sections down to smaller units with comprehension questions, exercises, or some other activities separating these units. With other materials, educators may have to break material into smaller units. When breaking long assignments into smaller tasks by interspersing activities, the activities should be designed to enhance comprehension.

Research on academic engagement, productivity, self-management, and self-directed learning suggests that breaking down large tasks into smaller tasks can also help students maintain their academic behaviors (McCurdy, Skinner, Grantham, Watson, & Hindman, 2001; Wallace et al., 2003). Skinner (2002) found evidence suggesting that completing a discrete academic task is reinforcing. By interspersing activities throughout text, educators can construct many discrete tasks or assignments out of one long reading assignment. Thus, a 40-page chapter could be broken down into four discrete tasks by interspersing activities every 10 pages. The completion of each activity may serve as reinforcement. Such procedures can increase more frequent and sustained reading and allow students to successfully complete more academic tasks, thereby increasing the quality and rate of reinforcement associated with reading (Skinner, Hurst, Teeple, & Meadows, 2002; Teeple & Skinner, in press). Of course, the tasks must be in meaningful units and not cut up the material in arbitrary ways. The question then becomes how to break long reading tasks down into smaller, discrete tasks so that there is a clear signal or cue that students have completed each task. Without this signal or cue such procedures are unlikely to be effective (Martin, Skinner, & Neddenriep, 2001).

A general recommendation is that with less skilled readers reading comprehension activities should be interspersed more frequently (e.g., every page as opposed to every 10 pages). By providing less information to process before completing these activities, less skilled readers may have more success responding accurately and these frequent opportunities to actively consolidate information may enhance comprehension.

It is not clear which activities are superior to others. Student perceptions of these various during-reading activities may also need to be assessed. Some students may find such activities disruptive to their reading. For example, a student who is really enjoying reading a Civil War story may not want to interrupt his or her reading to perform these other requirements. However, for other students, these disruptions may be welcome and completing these activities may be rewarding (Skinner, 2002). Students' perceptions are critical because the goal of most of these activities is for students to implement them independently, without additional assistance or support. Students who find these activities tiresome are unlikely to *independently* follow the correct steps.

ASSESSMENT

At the core of a multi-tiered framework of instruction are effective assessment procedures. Student performance on many of the *reading* and *postreading* activities described earlier can be used to assess comprehension. Additionally, those who recommend using CBM probes to collect fluency data (i.e., on words correct per minute; see Chapter 6) also recommend complementing these data with comprehension assessment data collected after the student has finished reading (e.g., Good, Kaminski, & Smith, 2002; Shapiro, 1996a). These activities include retell procedures and answering specific questions along with probes.

Oral Retell Measures of Comprehension

Story Retell

Shapiro (1996b) describes a procedure for assessing comprehension after students are finished reading stories aloud. First a story is selected that contains 150–200 words (below third grade) or 250–300 words (third grade and above). The student reads aloud and CBM assessment procedures are used to collect data on words correct and errors per minute (see Chapter 6). While the assessor ceases to record errors after 1 minute the student continues to read aloud.

After the student has finished reading, the examiner asks the student to retell the story in his or her own words. Shapiro (1996b) recommends taping the student's responses so that scoring can be completed later. While listening and relistening to the tape recording, the examiner uses a scoring sheet to record each of the following story elements mentioned by the student: (1) main idea, (2) problem, (3) goal, (4) title, (5) setting, (6) main character(s), (7) initiating event, (8) climax, (9) sequence of events, (10) solution to problem, and (11) end of story.

Shapiro (1996b) notes several variations of this assessment procedure. Specifically, students can be asked to retell the story with or without being allowed to refer back to the printed story. Additionally, the examiner can provide verbal prompts during the retell process, which are recorded on a scoring sheet. Finally, rather than asking the student to read aloud, the student could be asked to read the passage silently. The student receives 1 point for each story element, with the exception of problem solution and end of story, which are worth 0.5 points. Prompted responses are noted with an asterisk, but no points are provided.

While the story retell procedure does provide a direct measure of reading comprehension, there are several limitations associated with such procedures. First, it may be difficult to find stories that are both brief and contain a comprehensive plot. While students could be asked to read longer stories, it makes this type of assessment much more time consuming (Shapiro, 1996b). Additionally, because only comprehensive stories (i.e., those with each of the story elements) can be used, the number of curricular stories available for assessment at each grade level may be reduced. Thus, procedural limitations may both increase the amount of time required to administer this form of comprehension assessment and reduce the number of available passages for assessment.

Retell Fluency Measure

Good et al. (2002) developed the Retell Fluency Measure (RFM) for use with students reading from mid-first-grade to the end of third-grade levels. Like the story retell procedure, this is administered after the student has finished a CBM probe designed to assess words correct and errors per minute. However, with this procedure students are stopped after reading aloud for 1 minute. If a student reads 10 or more words correct per minute, he or she is prompted to tell the examiner all about what he or she just read. As the student is speaking, the examiner records the number of words the student says. If the student pauses for 3 seconds, the student is prompted again to "Try to tell me everything you can." This prompt is given only once. The next time the student fails to talk about the passage (e.g., says nothing or talks about something else) for 5 seconds, the examiner stops the session. Otherwise the session lasts 1 minute.

Good et al. (2002) provide scoring procedures for the RFM. As long as the student appears to be retelling the current passage and not talking about something else, each word is scored, including words that are part of inaccurate and irrelevant statements. While minor repetitions or redundancies are counted, rote repetitions and recitations are not counted in the score. When the student pauses for 3 seconds and a prompt is delivered, if he or she repeats what he or she said prior to the prompt, these words are not counted.

Unlike the story retell procedure, retell fluency does not require the student to complete an entire story that contains all the typical components of a story (e.g., characters, conflict, problem resolution). Thus, many brief probes can be constructed across various forms of written material. Additionally, the assessment is timed (1 minute maximum), thus it may yield a more sensitive measure to changes in student performance over time and following instructional modifications. However, the measure (words spoken) is an indirect measure of reading comprehension and the time required to read the material is not factored into the assessment. Additionally, while standardized administration and scoring guidelines are provided, scoring requires many rapid judgments, making it difficult to reliably score responding.

Good et al. (2002) report a correlation of .59 between words retold and CBM words correct per minute. Because words correct per minute correlates with comprehension, this finding provides some support for this measure. However, additional research is needed that compares (correlates) the story retell results (words told) with performance on direct measures of reading comprehension that have strong psychometric properties (e.g., standardized measures of reading comprehension). Regardless, this procedure is promising, as it (1) can be used across curricula (stories and expository text), (2) is brief, and (3) may be more sensitive than other measures of comprehension.

Examiner-Written Comprehension Questions

A third procedure for assessing comprehension is to construct comprehension questions based on the passage the student just read. Shapiro (1996a) recommends that examiners develop five to eight comprehension questions for CBM probes. These should include factual and inferential questions. After the student has finished reading the passage aloud, questions are administered to assess her or his comprehension. The percent of questions answered correctly can then be used as a measure of comprehension.

There are several limitations associated with these assessment procedures when compared with the CBM reading fluency assessments. Having students read 1-minute probes from their actual reading curriculum is an efficient procedure that produces a sensitive measure of general reading skills. Additionally, because multiple forms can be developed, student performance can be sampled repeatedly over time, making CBM useful for a variety of educational decisions (e.g., where to place the student in the curriculum, when to move the student to another curricular level, and whether to continue with a specific intervention or try another intervention).

While people have recommended writing comprehension questions for each CBM probe, doing so will not yield the same quality of data as words correct per minute. Students typically do not read enough material in 1 minute to allow for the creation of a sufficient number of questions to adequately assess comprehension. Thus, the assessment can yield inaccurate or invalid data. A related concern is with the sensitivity of the comprehension measures. When only a few questions are asked, the measure is relatively insensitive to changes in student performance (as a function of instruction). Even if 10 questions could be generated for each brief probe, the range of scores is limited (i.e., students can only score between 0 and 100% correct). Thus, only large increments (e.g., 10%) of improvement can be measured. Additionally, a ceiling effect prevents students from scoring higher than 100% accurate.

Another limitation associated with requiring students to answer specific examiner-constructed questions is that it is extremely difficult to write questions of equal difficulty level. Thus, a student may score low on a comprehension assessment one week, but higher the next week as a function of question difficulty, as opposed to improved reading comprehension skills. Without equivalent forms, it is difficult to develop accurate and sensitive measures of comprehension that can be used to make educational decisions.

Another limitation is related to prior knowledge. While curricular passages can be carefully constructed so that they become progressively more difficult, each student's prior knowledge is likely to influence his or her performance on comprehension questions (Pearson & Johnson, 1978). Because there is no way to measure what portion of a student's success in answering comprehension questions is based on his or her prior knowledge, it is impossible to measure the amount of comprehension that was caused by his or her reading alone.

A final limitation is that most comprehension measures do not include a measure of fluency. One of the biggest advantages of using words correct per minute is that more than mere accuracy it also includes the rate of accurate responding. Skinner, Neddenriep, et al. (2002) provide the following rationale for why *rate of comprehension* can be a useful measure of comprehension. For instance, imagine two students who both read the same passage and score 80% correct on comprehension questions. Also imagine one student takes 10 minutes to read the passage and the other requires 30 minutes. If rate (time spent reading) is not incorporated into the measure of comprehension, one might erroneously conclude that they both have similar reading comprehension skills. However, the student who can read quickly and understands the same amount of material has stronger skills, is more likely to choose to read, and can understand much more material in the same amount of time.

Rate of Comprehension

Recently, researchers have begun to evaluate interventions using a reading comprehension rate measure (Freeland, Skinner, Jackson, McDaniel, & Smith, 2000; Jackson, Freeland, & Skinner, 2000; McDaniel et al., 2001). These researchers had students read from Spargo's (1989) *Time Readings* series. This series contains passages from fourth grade to beyond high school. For each grade level, there are fifty 400-word passages, followed by 10 multiple-choice comprehension questions (five factual and five inferential).

These passages have been used to measure comprehension rate in several studies. The procedure is the following. First, the student orally reads a passage and the examiner records the time in minutes and seconds required to complete the passage. Next, the student answers the five factual and five inference questions without referring back to the passage. The percentage of accurate answers is calculated by dividing the number of corrects by the total number of questions (i.e., 10), which provides a measure of comprehension accuracy. Then, percentage of accurate answers is converted to a rate measure by dividing the percentage of questions answered correctly by the number of seconds required to read the passage and multiplying the result by 60 seconds, thus yielding a measure of comprehension rate (i.e., the percentage of passage understood for each minute spent reading).

To illustrate the uniqueness of this measure, consider two students, Freddy and Sara, who read the same passage and both answered 80% of the comprehension questions correctly. One could say they have equal comprehension levels. However, assume Freddy only needed 2 minutes to read the passage, while Sara needed 8 minutes. In this instance, Freddy's comprehension per minute score would be 40% per minute, indicating that he understood 40% of the passage for each minute spent reading. However, Sara's comprehension per minute would only be 10%.

Converting comprehension accuracy to a rate measure based on time required to read the material may provide a more sensitive, direct, and educationally valid measure of comprehension skill development than merely measuring accuracy on comprehension questions (Skinner, Neddenriep, et al., 2002). However, there are important limitations associated with this method. As with comprehension accuracy, rate of comprehension is still influenced by a student's prior knowledge and question difficulty. Additionally, this method requires the student to read text of the same length and difficulty level (i.e., same number of words, written at the same reading level). Thus, in most instances such procedures cannot be used with the students' reading curricula unless oral reading results are first converted to words correct per minute. Furthermore, it is not yet clear whether students should read aloud or silently during these assessments. Finally, as with other measures of comprehension, additional research is needed to establish the sensitivity, validity, and reliability of measures of reading comprehension rate (Skinner, Neddenriep, et al., 2002).

Cautious Decision Making Based on Comprehension Assessment

Although words correct per minute correlates with reading comprehension, researchers who recommend using CBM probes almost always also recommend performing some sort of comprehension assessment procedure. There are several reasons for this. First, although group studies show a strong correlation with words correct per minute and reading comprehension measures, in some students this correlation may be weak. One concern is with *word callers*, students who can read rapidly, but fail to comprehend (Shapiro, 1996a). A second concern is with face validity. Regardless of the strong support for words correct per minute, many educators are not comfortable with using an indirect measure of reading comprehension (Good et al., 2002). A final concern is that correlations between words correct per minute and standardized measures of reading tend to become weaker as students progress beyond the third-grade reading level (Skinner, Neddenriep, et al., 2002). Thus, words correct per minute may not provide a very sensitive, reliable, or valid measure of reading skills in more advanced readers.

Another concern is that repeated measurement of oral reading fluency may encourage and measure undesirable reading. For example, one of the authors used the CBM procedure to assess a high school student's progress. Each week the student received a probe. Additionally, the student was provided feedback with respect to words correct per minute; his progress was shown to him on a graph. After a few weeks the student changed his behavior during the probes. Specifically, as the examiner was reading instructions the student was taking a deep breath. As the stopwatch was started and the student was told to begin reading, he would begin spewing out the passage, reading very rapidly, disregarding punctuation or inflection. It is likely that the CBM procedure encouraged this type of reading, and words correct per minute on these probes had little relation to the student's reading skill development, especially reading comprehension.

The comprehension assessment activities described above can be used as a broad gauge of students' comprehension of the specific material that they had just read. Additionally, researchers are beginning to collect data on how these data may aid in decision making. For example, Good et al. (2002) report that student retell scores are typically 50% of their words correct per minute score. They suggest that a rough rule of thumb is that when a student's retell score is 25% or lower, their words correct per minute may not provide an accurate measure of overall reading skills.

While we encourage assessment of reading comprehension, we agree with Good et al. (2002) and Shapiro (1996a) that these data should be used with caution. Specifically, while results provide some general indication of comprehension skills, much more research is needed before any important educational decisions (e.g., where to place a student in the curriculum, whether to alter reading interventions) can be based solely on these assessment probes. Instead, such procedure may be used for screening or to supplement procedures that have been shown to be valid, reliable, and sensitive (e.g., words correct per minute, standardized reading comprehension scores). Having said this, we are encouraged by the efforts researchers are making with respect to the development and evaluation of reading comprehension measures. We recommend that interested readers keep up with such procedures via the website *https://dibels.uoregon.edu*. This website describes assessment procedures and summarizes the cutting-edge research being conducted by Roland Good, his colleagues, and students at the University of Oregon.

CONCLUSIONS

Researchers have described processes and variables that cause strong readers to become better readers and weak readers to fall farther and farther behind their peers (Skinner, 1999; Stanovich, 1986; Wong, 1986). While these variables and processes differ with respect to theoretical models, one thing they all have in common is that reading skills improve when students read. Thus, as students progress to the stage where comprehension is the primary reading target, it is critical that all involved do all they can to encourage student reading. This is especially true for students with reading skill deficits who need more time and effort to read and comprehend and thus may require the kinds of intensified instruction and pacing described in this chapter. Across all tiers of a multi-tiered framework, comprehension instruction should include providing reasons for students to read; time for students to read; materials for students to read; encouraging reading behavior through modeling, teaching procedures, and strategies for enhancing comprehension; and reinforcing students for reading and comprehension.

TELLS Worksheet

WHAT IS THIS STORY ABOUT?

Title What is the title of this story? Does it give a clue as to what the story is about? What do you think it is about?

_____

_____

_____

Examine Look at each page of the story to find clues about the story. What did you find?

_____

_____

_____

_____

Look Look for and write down important words, such as ones that are bold or used frequently. What do they mean?

_____

_____

_____

_____

Look Look again through the story for hard words—words you do not know. Write them down. What do they mean?

_____

_____

_____

_____

Setting Write down clues about the setting, such as the place, date, and time period. (Hint: These clues are often found in the beginning of the story.)

_____

_____

_____

_____

FACT or FICTION? Is this a true story (fact)? Or is this a pretend story (fiction)?

_____

_____

_____

_____

_____

Preparing a Semantic Analysis Chart

Topic: _____

List the key concepts and vocabulary:

_____

_____

_____

_____

_____

_____

_____

_____

Create the semantic analysis chart:

1. Find the all-inclusive idea, which becomes the title of the graph (superordinate concept).
2. Organize the concepts and vocabulary into categories (e.g., characteristics, steps, examples, functions).
3. Each main concept becomes a coordinate concept, the next step on the graph (second, third, and fourth columns).
4. Supporting concepts and vocabulary for each coordinate concept become the subordinate concepts, the final step on the graph (down first column).
5. Fill in the relationships between coordinate and subordinate concepts by marking them with an X.

Preparing a Semantic Analysis Map

Topic: _____

List the key concepts and vocabulary:

_____

_____

_____

_____

_____

_____

_____

_____

Create the semantic analysis map:

1. Identify the all-inclusive idea, which becomes the title of the map (superordinate concept; largest circle).
2. Organize the concepts and vocabulary into categories (e.g., characteristics, steps, examples, functions).
3. Each main concept becomes a coordinate concept, the next level on the map (medium circle).
4. Supporting concepts and vocabulary for each coordinate become the subordinate concepts, the final level on the map (smallest circles).
5. Fill in the relationships between coordinate and subordinate concepts by connecting them with lines.

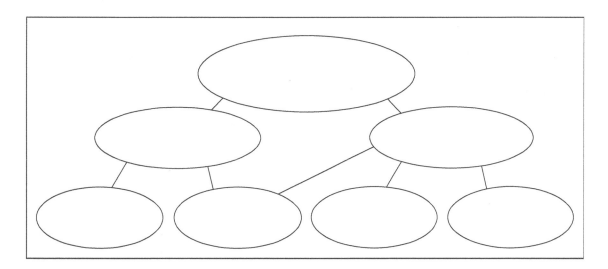

Story Grammar in Chart Form

Name: _____

Story Title: _____

↓   Characters: _____

_____

↓   Setting: _____

_____

↓   Problems: _____

_____

↓   Events: _____

_____

_____

_____

↓   Solution: _____

_____

Story Grammar in Mapping Form

Name: _____

Story Title: _____

Characters: 😐

Setting:

Problems: 🙁

Events:

Solution: 🙂

Strategic Note-Taking Form

Student Name: _____

Before reading, answer the following:

What is today's topic? Describe what you know about the topic.

_____

_____

_____

As you read, answer the following:

New Vocabulary or Terms:

_____

_____

Name three to seven main points about today's topic as they are discussed.

1. _____
2. _____
3. _____
4. _____
5. _____
6. _____
7. _____

Quickly summarize how these ideas are related.

_____

_____

New Vocabulary or Terms:

_____

_____

Name three to seven main points about today's topic as they are discussed.

1. _____
2. _____
3. _____

(continued)

Data from Boyle and Weishaar (2001).

_____

4. _____
5. _____
6. _____
7. _____

Quickly summarize how these ideas are related.

_____
_____

New Vocabulary or Terms:

_____
_____

Name three to seven main points about today's topic as they are discussed.

1. _____
2. _____
3. _____
4. _____
5. _____
6. _____
7. _____

Quickly summarize how these ideas are related.

_____
_____

At the end of reading, answer the following:

Write five main points of the lecture and describe each point.

1. _____
_____

2. _____
_____

3. _____
_____

4. _____
_____

5. _____
_____

Accountability
Are You Making a Measurable Difference?

with Ben Ditkowsky

THE MEASURE OF PROFESSIONAL PERFORMANCE

We assume that at least part of your professional motivation is to make a tangible difference in the lives of your clients by improving their reading skills. We also assume (reasonably, we think) that you have been reading this book to get new ideas about how you can have a greater impact on those you serve. You want to *see* a difference as a result of your efforts. Regardless of whether that's a correct assumption or not, we are 100% sure that you at least want or need *someone else* to see a difference. Otherwise, the client won't come back for help and you may be out of business. You will judge the value of this book according to whether it truly helps you get results. An essential part of *getting* results, however, is how you go about *finding* them. An archeologist who does an amazing restoration of an ancient site but who provides the wrong map to get to the site can't effectively share the results of his or her work, and others cannot benefit from it. You may make productive changes in reading instruction, but if you are not monitoring and evaluating the right areas (the road map for telling whether you are getting where you are going), you won't see the improvements. On the other hand, you might change what you are doing in an *un*productive way. For instance, you might put a complex intervention in place, but the intervention is no more effective than what was being done in the first place. Here, too, if you are not monitoring the

---

Ben Ditkowsky, PhD, is Director of Assessment and Program Evaluation for Barrington Community Unit School District 220 in Barrington, Illinois.

right areas, you will not see the need for other changes and will probably burden an already overloaded school system—be it a classroom, school, or district.

Our objective in this chapter is to help you create a road map for conveying the outcomes of your reading intervention services, regardless of the scope of those services (e.g., individual consulting services, multi-tier intervention program). Services that are accountable are more likely to be (1) effective and (2) sought out in the future. The fields of education and psychology increasingly recognize this simple truth. Changes in these fields are also occurring because of pressures that societal forces, such as the federal government and taxpayers, bring to bear on education. Our practices are being scrutinized more than ever. For these reasons, assessment has been a dominant theme throughout this book. Assessment information should tell you whether changes are effective; such information is especially useful when it points to the types of changes you should make to reading instruction. That is why we have concentrated on assessment methods that are direct and straightforward (i.e., don't involve leaps of inference or obscure theoretical propositions) and that facilitate ongoing monitoring of classroom or tutoring modifications. However, if you apply the model promoted in this book, you will likely accumulate a diverse collection of reading intervention cases, with data for each client in the form of repeated measures over time. Although these data may have helped you along the way with each individual case, the larger question is how effective your interventions have been across *all* of the cases you have handled. You may want to know this answer by way of evaluating your effectiveness as a consultant, or perhaps you want to evaluate a Tier 2 intervention program in your school building.

This chapter is meant to guide you in this process of evaluating outcomes beyond the individual case. Fortunately, there is not a lot of additional work, as you will be able to use the rich database that you have already generated from your individual cases to examine effectiveness more broadly. First, we review why accountability is fundamental to success and tie it to emerging educational innovations for addressing reading problems. Next, we present a model of accountability that should help you to organize the reporting of your service delivery results. Use of the model is demonstrated to get you started in documenting your effectiveness across cases. Finally, we share some concluding thoughts about putting all the pieces together.

THE IMPORTANCE OF ACCOUNTABLE PRACTICE

For many years and in many professional circles, effectiveness of psychological services was determined based on expert opinion. After all, the psychologist was the one who had the professional training in detecting and treating psychological disorders. Determination of effectiveness was reserved to "clinical judgment," which has had a hallowed status in the profession of psychology. Recently, however, society and the profession itself have woken up to the fact that expert judgments are still subjective, even if they are made by professionals. Indeed, psychologists had a material interest in being the ones who could identify pathology and in pronouncing their success at treating it. This gave them special status and legitimacy in the eyes of the public. The problem is that no amount of professional training guarantees objectivity. Cone (2001) stated, "We know, for example, that clinicians (and scientists, too, for that matter) tend to adopt a confirmatory approach to testing their understanding of a particular client. That is, they form early hypotheses about the client's problems and go about recruiting evidence to support those hypotheses" (p. 9). In other words, professionals tend to find what they are looking for in the first place, while ignoring data that fail to support, or may even contradict, preferred hypotheses (Dawes, 1995). Standard reliance on clinical judgment is often a means of guaranteeing a positive evaluation of outcomes. In this age of dwindling resources, however, our constituents are likely to be more skeptical than we are about the value of our services in light of the cost of those services. NCLB formally ushered in a new era of accountability through requirements for state accountability plans and consequences for schools based on measured student performance. Although there is considerable debate about the pros and cons of NCLB and even of its future, there is no denying that pressure for accountability in schools is here to stay in one form or another. Educators will be held responsible for outcomes, and clinical judgment alone will not be accepted as sufficient evidence of effectiveness.

Overcoming Sources of Professional Error in Practice

Making data-based judgments is a step in the right direction, but it is not a panacea if a rigorous approach is not taken. Even when judgments of intervention effectiveness are based on assessment data, there is still room for error. Although some tests are better than others, there is *always* some error in our measurements. Often, psychologists claim that through clinical judgment they can overcome that error. Their thinking goes something like the following: "Well, I'm an objective and well-trained professional. I can overcome the limitations of the assessment techniques because my finely honed clinical skills can rise above the weaknesses of the techniques I use." Unfortunately, research on professional judgment dating back to the middle of the last century does not support this view and, on the contrary, clearly indicates that professionals *cannot* improve upon the quality of assessment information through clinical judgment. Paul Meehl's groundbreaking work (Meehl, 1954; Meehl & Rosen, 1955) showing the superiority of statistical prediction over clinical prediction and Tversky and Kahneman's Nobel Prize award-winning research (Kahneman, 2003) that brought to light cognitive biases and distortions that plague clinicians spawned a prolific line of research with clear and compelling implications for professional practice.

Unpredictable environments that do not offer clear feedback on the correctness of a decision are breeding grounds for a host of cognitive distortions that impair judgment (Gilovich, Griffin, & Kahneman, 2002; Kahneman & Klein, 2009). Schools and classrooms are anything but predictable; they are highly complex environments in which a multitude of difficult-to-identify factors impact student performance, and outcomes are never guaranteed, making the circumstances ripe for decision errors. In a review of the research in this area, Dawes (1994) pointed out that professionals are only as accurate as the techniques they use, and that professional experience does not increase accuracy at all. Therefore, the decisions made based on assessment information are only as good as the quality of the assessment information itself. This conclusion is humbling for those of us who like to think that our professional experience somehow makes us more qualified than the average layperson to determine effectiveness. Frankly, it represents wrong thinking. Our job should be to *show* the layperson how we are effective (*when* we are effective) through high-quality data and to *modify* our activities when we are not effective. We haven't fulfilled our responsibility to society, the community, and our clients if (1) we can't objectively show what's working, and (2) we are unresponsive or defensive and territorial about an ineffective intervention plan. In this chapter, we intend to show you how to do this for reading interventions.

The Need for Local Validation of Outcomes for Professional Services

Changes in professional attitudes about the importance of choosing evidence-based treatments reflect this trend toward accountable practice. A couple of developments are noteworthy in this respect. Two divisions of the American Psychological Association—Divisions 12 and 16—have developed coding manuals for identifying effective interventions that have appeared in the research literature (Division 16's coding manual can be accessed online at *www.indiana.edu/~ebi/EBI-Manual.pdf*). Making use of these coding manuals will help the respective fields of clinical and school psychology to identify and disseminate interventions that are likely to be effective. In the field of education, the U.S. Department of Education's Institute of Education Sciences (IES) has created the What Works Clearinghouse (*http://ies.ed.gov/ncee/wwc*) to provide an independent and objective database for effective educational interventions in areas such as beginning reading instruction, effective math instruction, adult literacy, and a host of other topics. All of these examples point to the fact that standards for the quality of interventions expected by the public in the areas of education and mental health are increasing; interventions are expected to be scientifically sound. These developments are very exciting and have potential for improving literacy, as practitioners and clients become more knowledgeable about evidence-based and scientifically sound interventions.

There is a caveat to the use of widely disseminated knowledge bases for selecting empirically valid interventions. Just because an intervention has been shown to be effective in research studies does not guarantee that it will work for your students. If you choose a scientifically sound intervention, the chances are perhaps greater that the reading intervention will work. However, it is your professional responsibility to *show* that it works. In other words, you choose a valid intervention, and then you must validate it for the client: Can you prove that the intervention worked for this student? As noted earlier, experts could not be more wrong when they assume that their many hours of experience ensure the effectiveness of their services. *Effective* experts monitor their performance and take a more skeptical and objective attitude about the quality of their services prior to intervention and validation of outcome. Also, they regularly monitor effectiveness during intervention and adjust practices according to the data after intervention. This concept also applies to the range of services you deliver when you consider all the students that you or your program serve(s). Can you prove that your services are effective across students? The evaluation model described in this chapter is applicable to questions about effectiveness for individuals as well as questions about effectiveness for groups. The model intersects well with whatever organizational level and scope you wish to target, all the way from the "Lone Ranger" who is fearlessly helping to solve reading problems on a case-by-case basis to those implementing district-level, multi-tier intervention programs.

It Starts with the Individual

Although schools address the educational needs of a local group of students, the point of education is to ensure that *each and every* student is learning, regardless of whatever grouping decisions are made. Accountable practice, therefore, begins with checking the reading performance of individuals. Is the student learning what he or she must learn? Is he or she on an appropriate instructional level? Is he or she making adequate progress? These questions must be answered for every student in the school relative to the five areas of reading instruction (phonic awareness, phonics, reading fluency, comprehension, and vocabulary). Fortunately, for the vast majority of students, intensive, individualized assessments are not necessary. However, for students who are already experiencing learning problems or who are at risk for learning problems, one must take a closer look. Progress monitoring on sensitive indicators of performance permits a more fine-grained analysis of student performance so that instructional adjustments can be made more rapidly. The assessment tools described in previous chapters will allow you to achieve this objective. Proper instructional adjustments based on assessment results tailored to the skill(s) being taught to the student will improve a student's rate of progress. The best method for validating instruction for a particular student is to measure performance on vital skills that readily change with instruction. Measurements can be more infrequent when a mere "check-up" is needed to verify that the student is doing well. Measurements should be more frequent when there is concern about a student's proficiency level and rate of progress. A solid multi-tiered intervention model establishes an assessment plan that samples all students' performance in relevant skills, from the student who is making adequate progress to the student whose level and rate of progress are below what is expected. The difference across students is the frequency of assessment, with the latter student receiving more frequent, repeated assessments of the skills most critical to the student now in his or her growth toward independent reading and comprehension.

Visual Analysis of Data for Instructional Decision Making

Data from frequent, repeated assessments are best displayed and analyzed graphically. Graphs prompt more frequent instructional decisions, which has been shown to lead to greater improvements in student achievement (Fuchs, Deno, & Mirkin, 1984; Fuchs & Fuchs, 1986; Fuchs, Fuchs, & Stecker, 1989; Wesson et al., 1988; Wesson, Skiba, Sevcik, King, & Deno, 1984). Graphed data are analyzed visually within a planned evaluation design. The simplest evaluation design for practice is the single-case A/B design. In the single-case A/B design, an initial baseline (the "A" phase) is established and then followed by an instructional or intervention phase (the "B" phase). Repeated measures throughout both phases provide the data for interpretation of instructional effectiveness. The baseline reveals the current level of performance prior to a change of some type (e.g., a new or more intense form of instruction). The intervention phase establishes whether performance improved relative to baseline. Results are inspected within each phase and then compared across phases to guide decision making about whether the intervention was effective. Example graphs that include both baseline and intervention phase are displayed in Figure 9.1.

A graph is a complex visual display that communicates a lot of information. On the one hand, every session's results can be inspected individually, while on the other hand, patterns in the data can be detected based on relationships between the data points. As data are collected over time, a picture of the student's responsiveness to instruction unfolds. The decision that needs to be made, however, is a simple summary judgment of effectiveness, which means that the interpreter has to reduce the complexity of the data to a binary judgment (effective or not effective?). To do so, the interpreter has to pay attention to the most critical features in the data that contribute to the decision. Level, trend, and variability are the primary characteristics that guide interpretation of graphed data. They are considered first within phases (e.g., baseline and intervention) and then across phases. Level refers to a central area within a phase around which the data points cluster. In Figure 9.1 (top graph), the baseline data range in value from 37 (second session) to 53 (first and fifth sessions). To interpret level, one ignores the variability in the data and imagines—or even draws—a horizontal line to reflect some measure of central location. For example, a mean line (the dotted line) has been added to the baseline and intervention phases in Figure 9.1, making it easier to see differences in performance level across phases. The mean line is simply a straight line at the mean value of the vertical axis for the phase. Because they simplify interpretation, it is tempting to routinely add mean lines. However, there are important forms of variability that can be overlooked if one relies too much on interpreting level with mean lines. So, it is important to examine the other characteristics of the data in conjunction with an analysis of level. The mean line was added in this case to distinguish level from variability.

Trend refers to whether the data systematically increase or decrease over time. Trend is a form of variability that is distinct from the "noise" one often sees in data. In other words, a trend is a systematic increase or decrease over time that rises above variability that might be due to measurement error and less relevant variables that nonetheless affected performance (e.g., the child had a nagging cough on the assessment day). For reading, an increasing trend is desired, of course; it means that the student's reading skills are improving. The middle graph in Figure 9.1 displays data that have a decreasing trend in baseline and an increasing trend during the intervention phase. A trendline has been added to the data for each phase to illustrate systematic deceleration (baseline) and systematic acceleration (intervention) that differs from noisy variability. The variability around the trendlines is common, and represents variability that cannot be accounted for. Variability, or the degree to which results change from one assessment occasion to another, is both a good thing and a bad thing. Variability is a good thing when data points change because the instruction or intervention improves the level or trend of responding. Variability is not such a good thing when it is due to random error or uncontrolled factors. In the bottom graph of Figure 9.1, there is a large degree of variability in both the baseline and intervention phases. A mean

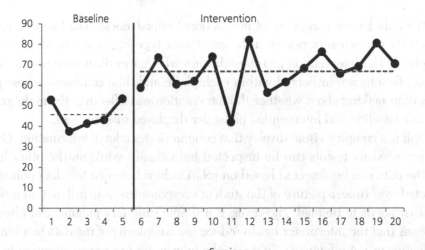

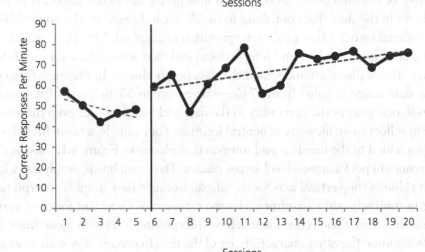

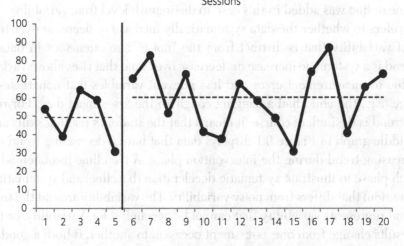

FIGURE 9.1. Examples of single-case A/B graphs of reading intervention data.

line has been added to make the variability more apparent. One can see that there is a difference in level between baseline and intervention. However, the variability in the data masks a possible intervention effect. Extreme variability within phases means that either there is error during the assessments or the intervention effects are not consistent. The best thing to do in this case is to investigate why there is so much variability before proceeding, correct the problem, and measure results within the phase until they stabilize.

Judging level, trend, and variability within phases is merely the first step of interpretation. The next step is to compare results across phases to arrive at an interpretation of effectiveness. Ideally for reading instruction, there would be a stable level of responding (i.e., little variability and no trend) in baseline followed by an increasing trend during the instruction/intervention phase. One wouldn't normally expect an immediate change in level for a skilled behavior like reading because proficiency grows over time. Therefore, a positive trend is sought. Results like those that appear in the middle graph of Figure 9.1 would lead one to conclude that the intervention is probably effective.

The amount and type of variability in baseline will affect interpretation. In general, the less the variability in baseline, the easier it will be for intervention data points in the second phase to exceed whatever level or trend is established in baseline. Greater variability in baseline will make it more difficult to "see" an intervention effect, unless the intervention has an immediate and strong effect on the results. This point is illustrated in Figure 9.2. It will be easier to see an intervention effect in the top graph where variability is minimal than in the other two graphs where data are highly variable (middle graph) or moderately variable (bottom graph). Therefore, minimal variability in baseline (e.g., the top graph in Figure 9.2) creates the ideal conditions for interpretation. In reality, however, modest and high levels of variability are more typical in school settings where a multitude of factors may affect performance on a given day. Variability may result from the materials used for progress monitoring (Christ & Ardoin, 2009), when and where assessments are conducted (e.g., in a noisy room or hallway as compared with a quiet setting), changes in who conducts the assessment, and motivational factors (e.g., the student may perceive that harder work will be given if he or she reads faster and therefore reads less fluently). When variability is high, the assessor should make every effort to standardize the conditions if possible before beginning the intervention. Sometimes, variability is reduced over time as the child gets used to the standardized assessment procedures. Therefore, although educators are often eager to change instruction as soon as a problem is detected, taking additional time and making efforts to standardize assessment conditions to stabilize the results during baseline may have a bigger payoff in terms of providing a more accurate picture of intervention effects. It lengthens the baseline phase, but will provide greater clarity when it comes time to make a decision about intervention effectiveness. When there is a high degree of variability in baseline (e.g., Figure 9.2, middle graph), some systematic factor may be influencing the results. It is worthwhile examining what is different on days when performance is high (e.g., Sessions 1 and 3) from days when performance is low (e.g., Days 2 and 5). What is occurring before or during the assessment that is affecting the results?

Intervention effectiveness is determined based on differing patterns of level, trend, and variability across phases—baseline and intervention. The logic of visual analysis for a

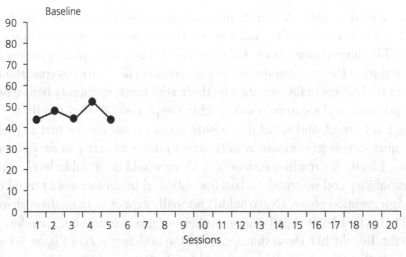

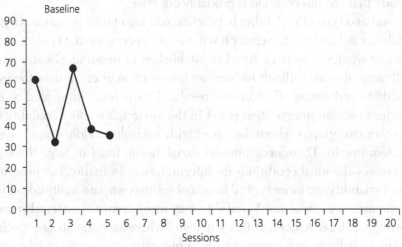

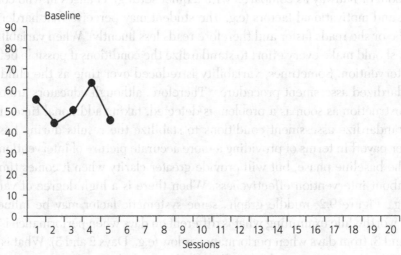

FIGURE 9.2. Differing amounts of variability in baseline: small (top), large (middle), and moderate (bottom).

skilled behavior like reading (where growth is expected) dictates that the level and/or trend of intervention data points should exceed the level, trend, and variability established in baseline. Furthermore, the degree to which data overlap between phases also influences judgments of effectiveness. Fewer data overlap between phases strengthens the case for intervention effectiveness, and more data overlap between phases weakens it. For example, in Figure 9.1 there are fewer data overlap between phases in the top graph than in the bottom graph, making it easier to infer an intervention effect in the top graph than in the bottom graph. In the middle graph, there is some data overlap early in the intervention phase, but the increasing trend over time leads to very little data overlap between baseline and intervention by the end of the phase, suggesting that the intervention is effective.

We have described the most basic accountability design (the A/B design) here because it is the one that is used most often in practice. There is, however, a world of other types of individual designs that allow one to isolate instructional factors. Those designs are built upon the foundation of the A/B design, but are beyond the scope of the current discussion. For readers who are interested in more advanced applications, we recommend that you consult Riley-Tillman and Burns (2009) who describe a range of options in addressing more complex questions regarding reading interventions.

Tools for Individual Decision Making

The previous section discussed basic principles of visual interpretation for graphic displays of progress monitoring data. Fortunately, there are a number of useful tools that can help you generate excellent graphs for decision making. You can access the methods discussed below on the Internet (the URLs are given below). In all cases, you simply need to input your data (baseline and intervention) and read the results. The complicated analyses are done for you; you simply need to know how to interpret the results. In the remainder of this section, we describe these tools and how to use them for deciding whether an intervention is effective.

Structured Criteria for Improving Visual Inspection

Fisher, Kelley, and Lomas (2003) devised a method for structuring visual inspection of graphed results for A/B designs in an objective manner. The conservative dual-criteria (CDC) method standardizes interpretation of results in a way that minimizes decision errors, including decisions that an intervention is effective when it is not and decisions that an intervention is not effective when it is. Indeed, in a Monte Carlo simulation study, the CDC method outperformed a number of statistical methods for analyzing graphed data, showing good decision accuracy and power for detecting intervention effects when they exist. Directions and a Microsoft Excel file are available at *MeasuredEffects.com*. (Click the Files and Templates tab.) One enters the data into the Microsoft Excel file by putting baseline data in one column and intervention data in another column (as specified in the directions), which automatically produces both a graph and a table of results for interpretation.

In the discussion of visual analysis in the previous section, we presented mean- and trendlines to facilitate interpretation of the results. The CDC method takes the use of these judgment aids a step further. The CDC method projects the mean- and trendline from the baseline phase *into* the intervention phase to make it easier to see just how much actual data overlap there is and if the intervention phase is merely continuing a trend started in baseline. Therefore, the mean- and trendlines are superimposed on the intervention phase. The CDC method adjusts the mean- and trendlines by adding one-fourth of the baseline standard deviation to the mean and slope (for trend). Fisher et al. (2003) found that this more conservative approach led to fewer decision errors. An example of a graph with CDC lines can be found in Figure 9.3. The horizontal line represents the adjusted baseline mean line and the rising line represents the adjusted baseline trendline. Again, these lines are

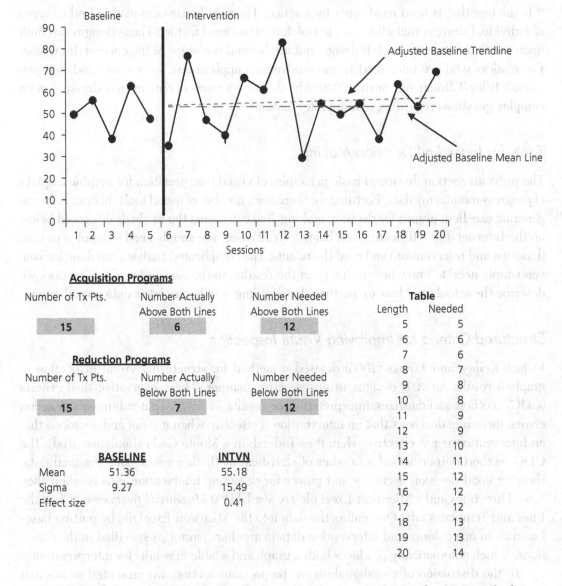

FIGURE 9.3. An example of an ineffective intervention according to the CDC method.

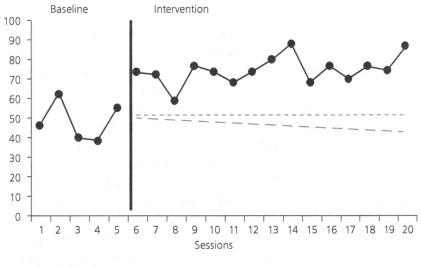

Acquisition Programs

Number of Tx Pts.	Number Actually Above Both Lines	Number Needed Above Both Lines
15	15	12

Reduction Programs

Number of Tx Pts.	Number Actually Below Both Lines	Number Needed Below Both Lines
15	0	12

	BASELINE	INTVN
Mean	48.77	74.11
Sigma	10.00	7.17
Effect size		2.53

Table

Length	Needed
5	5
6	6
7	6
8	7
9	8
10	8
11	9
12	9
13	10
14	11
15	12
16	12
17	12
18	13
19	13
20	14

FIGURE 9.4. An example of an effective intervention according to the CDC method.

projected from the baseline data, making it easier to determine just how much data overlap there is between baseline and intervention phases. One can see that the majority of intervention data points appear below both lines in Figure 9.3. Another example is presented in Figure 9.4. In this graph, all of the intervention data points fall above the adjusted mean- and trendlines, indicating that the intervention is effective.

The CDC method also provides further statistical analysis of the results by examining whether a significant number of data points exceed both the baseline mean- and trendlines to justify a decision supporting treatment effectiveness. This analysis is based on the assumption that if the intervention is effective, a significantly greater number of data points should be above both lines (in the case of a reading intervention) than below both lines. Significance is determined based on what would be expected by "chance." The CDC method uses the binomial distribution (a distribution for determining probability based on two outcomes, "sufficient number of data points above both lines" or "not a sufficient number of data points above both lines" in the present case) to indicate whether the effect is significant. The results are displayed in a table much like the ones presented at the bottom of Figures 9.3 and 9.4. For example, in Figure 9.3, the results in the table indicate that for an acquisition program at least 12 data points must exceed the mean- and trendlines to be significant. The table indicates that only 6 data points exceed both lines, meaning that the effect is not significant. In Figure 9.4, the results in the table indicate that for an acquisition program at least 12 data points must exceed the baseline mean- and trendlines. In this case, all 15 intervention points fell above both lines. Thus, the intervention is judged to be effective. The Microsoft Excel file is easy to use (input is limited to putting data in the appropriate cells) and interpret (both a graph and simple table are produced based on data input). The CDC method adds objectivity and can be useful for prompting ongoing (formative) decisions about instructional effectiveness and summative decisions about case effectiveness.

Measured Effects Resources

Measuredeffects.com is another useful resource for graphing solutions. One of us (BD) created this website to put easy-to-use graphing and decision tools into the hands of educators. The tools actually rely on very sophisticated methods of statistical analysis. But, BD has made understanding and using them very simple for those of us lacking knowledge about proper use of measurement formulas. The theme of the website is using measures of student performance to arrive at valid decisions that improve their academic skills. *Measuredeffects.com* has a number of tools for both individual decision making and group decision making, all organized under a multi-tiered intervention model. The tools themselves are mostly Microsoft Excel files in which you can plot your data and watch the results appear in colorful graphs that instruct you in what to do next. If you want to check them out, go to *Measuredeffects.com* and click the link titled "Files and Templates." We give a brief explanation of the individual progress monitoring tool here, which can be very useful to you if you track reading intervention effects in the ways described in the previous chapters. You will find much more information (including technical explanations of how it all works) on the website.

Individual progress monitoring is at the heart of accountability, as we noted earlier. *Measuredeffects.com* has a Microsoft Excel file called "Progress Monitor with Confidence" (PMWC) under the Tier 3 Tools link. (It is called "DBG_SL_free_V4.8.10.xls.") Although both tools prompt decisions about intervention efficacy, this tool accomplishes different things from the structured criteria method described above. PMWC allows you to compare the student's actual improvement with a goal and desired rate of improvement through the use of a goal, an aim line, a trendline, and confidence intervals that surround the data. It even gives cues and instructions for what to do next with each data point that you plot. It is very simple to use and interpretation is straightforward, once you understand what appears in the Microsoft Excel file. First, download the file and read the instructions that appear on the first worksheet. You will see that your student's data are entered on the second worksheet. When you enter data, the results magically appear on a graph under the tab titled "Dashboard."

An example appears in Figure 9.5. A sample worksheet for entering data appears at the top, and the control panel and graph that appear on the Dashboard worksheet appear at the bottom. The actual files are much more colorful, making it easier to see cues more readily. (Alas, color was not in our budget!) The data entry sheet allows you to enter the name of the teacher, student, the behavior to increase (oral reading fluency, in this example), the expected goal level, and the number of weeks in which the student is expected to meet the goal. In addition, there is space provided for the week number and individual data collected for each student. Data for baseline (weeks labeled "0" in the first row) and intervention (Weeks 1 through 5) are displayed at the top of Figure 9.5. You can keep multiple students' data in a single Microsoft Excel file by entering additional students in the following rows. In the example, data for two students (Sally and Pete, who are both in Mrs. Jones's class) appear.

The DASHBOARD tab displays a control panel and the graph for one student. The settings for the chart are chosen in the control panel, which is set up to allow you to select the student and whether you want the graph to display the trend, goal, and confidence intervals. In the example, the evaluator selected Sally from a dropdown button that appears in the control panel of the Microsoft Excel file. You also see entries that say "true" and "false." These entries reflect the selections you make in the Excel spreadsheet through drop-down buttons. You can turn features on and off by setting them to true or false. In the case of Sally, the evaluator chose to display the trend for all data and projected the graph 42 days into the future. The evaluator also chose to display the goal value and date (which are automatically

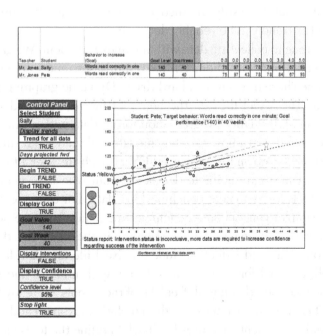

FIGURE 9.5. An example from PMWC.

filled in from the data entry page when true is chosen), a 95% confidence interval for the trendline, and the stoplight, but did not choose to display interventions (set to "false").

Pete's results (the second student) appear in the graph next to the control panel in Figure 9.5. In the graph, in addition to individual data points, there is a line to distinguish baseline and intervention, a trendline that reflects the actual trend in the data (the solid line becomes a dotted line after there are no more data points), an aim line that represents the rate of improvement the student should achieve to meet his or her goal (appearing as the dashed line with a star at the end), and a confidence interval for the trend (the lines enveloping the data points). You can also choose to set a beginning trend and an ending trend for the data (not done in the example). The graph and various lines (aim, trend, and confidence intervals) allow you to compare the student's actual progress (as indicated by the data points, trendline, and confidence intervals) to the student's expected rate of progress (as indicated by the aim line and the eventual goal represented as the star on the graph) to help you decide whether to continue the intervention or to change it. A neat feature of PMWC is the stoplight. As you enter data, the Excel file compares the confidence interval range with the aim line. The stoplight prompts you for what to do next. A green light indicates that there is a sufficient number of data points and that the intervention is having the intended effect. You can see it visibly on a graph when the trendline and confidence intervals match or exceed the aim line. In this case, you should proceed on course, or, if the student has met the goal, consider removing the intervention. A yellow light indicates a nonconclusive result, which occurs when there are too few data points to accurately compare the trend with the aim line. A red light indicates that there is a sufficient number of data points to conclude that the intervention is ineffective and needs to be changed. In this case, the trendline and confidence intervals will fall below the aim line. In our example, the light in the center of the stoplight indicates that the results are inconclusive to date and that further data need to be gathered before the trend can be reliably determined.

Educators are prone to collecting data without analyzing them. We gather gobs of data, but often do not do anything with them. All too often, assessments are conducted and the data sit in a pile somewhere or even on a hard drive. Dynamic graphing tools like PMWC can change all that. The Excel files do the heavy lifting for you, and you can enjoy all the benefits of having high-quality progress monitoring data without having to set up the graphs. You simply need to learn how to enter the data and read the results. PMWC is only one of many tools you will find on the Measured Effects website. Tier 1 tools like the Simple Chutes and Ladders Chart can facilitate decisions about who is in need of intervention. There are multiple tools for analyzing benchmarking data. For example, with the Triangle Charts 1 tool, you can plot your school's benchmarking data to analyze percentages of students at all three tiers to analyze your core curriculum in the way it was discussed in Chapter 3. Tier 2 tools on Measured Effects include an Excel file template for tracking groups of students, as well as a tool for progress monitoring with middle- and secondary school students. And did we mention that it is all free! All of these tools are ready for download and immediate use. BD is even courageous enough to include his e-mail address so you can ask him questions or make comments. He uses feedback to refine the tools and the website and is very responsive to questions.

The Changing Context for Meeting the Needs of Students with Reading Problems

Before we move on to a description of the components and use of the model, we want to point out one more reason why accountability is so important and explore its implications for the current context of reading assessment and intervention. Until recently, psychologists who conducted assessments were largely concerned with the psychometric properties of the tests they administered. The psychometric properties basically boiled down to how well the test correlated with itself under various conditions (reliability) and how well it correlated with other known measures of the same factor (validity). The various types of correlation and other forms of test data analysis relate to the empirical reliability and validity of the tests. Although these concerns were important, the perspective remained incomplete until Messick (1995) helped the field to understand the critical need for examination of the *social consequences* of testing and assessment. Whenever educators and psychologists conduct assessments, there are potential social consequences for the students. Obviously, if the social consequences are not positive, then the whole enterprise is questionable. If the consequences are neutral (i.e., there are no real positive or negative consequences for students), then districts and taxpayers have wasted money on unnecessary testing (and the ultimate outcome is not really so neutral). If the consequences are bad, then they not only wasted money, but they also harmed the very students they are serving! This is why it is so essential to consider issues such as testing bias and minority overrepresentation in special education programs. Barnett and Macmann (1992) reduced both of these issues to two questions:

1. What can be said with confidence (i.e., the psychometric properties)?
2. What can be said that might be helpful (i.e., the social consequences)?

These questions set the standard according to which services should be judged; they should be applied to every database that is used for any decision we make about our clients (Barnett, Lentz, & Macmann, 2000).

Recent, radical changes in practices for identifying reading disabilities demonstrate that these are not just theoretical issues of limited practical significance. The very reasons why traditional psychodiagnostic approaches to identifying learning disabilities are being replaced by RTI service-delivery models is because of concerns about unreliability, questionable validity on various grounds (e.g., an inability to discriminate between experiential and cognitive bases of disability), and questionable treatment outcomes for students once they are identified (Kavale & Forness, 1999; Macmann & Barnett, 1999; Vellutino, Scanlon, & Tanzman, 1998). This is a case where a widespread assessment and diagnostic practice (1) could not inspire confidence in its own results, and (2) had not proven helpful to the students to whom the model was being applied.

RTI represents an attempt to redress the problem of poor outcomes for students labeled by the categorical, discrepancy-based learning disabilities model through a multi-tiered *treatment-based approach* to identifying disabilities (Fuchs & Fuchs, 1998; Fuchs, Fuchs, & Speece, 2002; Gresham, 2001; Vaughn et al., 2003; Vellutino et al., 1998). By successively implementing a series of carefully monitored interventions, practitioners can directly determine (1) whether they have confidence in the results, and (2) whether their services are actually helpful by conducting ongoing evaluation, validation, and adjustment in response to results achieved with each intervention. Even when a child is ultimately classified as learning disabled, this model of validation should still apply (and with all the more reason). This shift in approach illustrates how the field responded to a call to take responsibility for outcomes by directly monitoring students' responsiveness to intervention.

ROUNDING OUT YOUR READING INTERVENTION-BASED SERVICES WITH AN ACCOUNTABILITY COMPONENT

An Explicit Model of Service Delivery

When students are referred to you or your reading program, what can stakeholders (i.e., parents, teachers) expect of you? What exactly will you do? What common factors, issues, or characteristics span your cases, despite the different circumstances that lead up to each referral? How can you justify your professional preferences, choices, and actions relative to other methods you could be employing to address the problems? How do you respond to legal, ethical, and professional mandates for best practice? How can you demonstrate all the reasons for your choices to those you serve as well as to your colleagues? These questions point to the importance of having an explicit and justifiable model of service delivery. Inadequate answers to any of these questions mean that the services provided (1) are not standard across clients (which will lead to varying outcomes across clients), (2) cannot be justified to constituents and other professionals, and (3) may not be an efficient and productive use of anyone's time.

An Explicit Model of Accountability

The first step to demonstrating your accountability is establishing the validity of the model you apply to reading referrals. This means that you need to describe those procedures that you follow for each and every case (i.e., standard services). Going through this process forces you to think through why these procedures are necessary and how they relate to the overall objectives of your program and the priorities of the setting in which you work. This kind of planning is likely to improve your efficacy. Furthermore, each case comes with ethical and legal obligations that you must fulfill. You had better be prepared to describe what you do and explain how your procedures help you to meet your ethical and legal responsibilities when questions come up (and they will!).

The next step in demonstrating accountability involves careful documentation of the specifics of each case. Who was served? Why? How long? By whom? What exactly was done? These questions relate to the implementation of services. The final broad area of accountability is that of client outcomes. Since you probably have multiple clients, you need to be able to summarize results across those cases to show the broad impact of the standard services you provide (beyond the individual child findings). You need methods for quantifying those outcomes for when people say "Show me!" These three areas of accountability are summarized in Table 9.1.

The first item in Table 9.1 refers to a procedural checklist, which is the operational definition of your service delivery model. Such a checklist outlines the steps that you take with each and every case (despite peculiarities and differences across cases) and serves as a communication tool for explaining how you serve clients; it holds those responsible for the services accountable for key aspects of the model in every case (Barnett et al., 1999). A sample 10-item procedural checklist can be found in Worksheet 9.1 at the end of the chapter. The circumstances of your service delivery (e.g., individual consultant vs. a member of a problem-solving team) will create slightly different priorities. The example in Worksheet 9.1 describes the minimal procedural steps necessary for conducting adequate problem solving. A checklist that addresses all your legal, ethical, organizational, and professional requirements should be developed prior to services. In cases where a team approach is used, this step can serve as a very useful collaborative exercise for achieving agreement among members about exactly what assessments and interventions will be administered with each case. The checklist should be filled out for each case and filed with other data on an ongoing basis. The results will tell you whether the minimal, standard steps are being followed for each case. If all the steps are followed routinely but outcomes are disappointing, then you know that your model needs to be changed in some way. If the steps are not followed routinely, then you know that there is inconsistency in service delivery.

The procedural checklist constitutes one source of data that indicates whether the overall model is being implemented consistently, as planned. For individual cases, the percentage of steps completed can be calculated by dividing the number of steps completed (e.g., nine steps) by the total number of steps on the checklist (10 in the example; producing a score of 90%). Descriptive statistics such as mean, median, range, and standard deviation can be reported to give an indication of how consistently the model is implemented. This source of data ("procedural integrity") is one of the multiple data sources cited in Table 9.2. When summarized with other types of data, and when the results are consistently high across data sources, you have converging, supportive evidence that indicates the impact of your services on clients.

Data Summarization Methods

Repeated assessments conducted across time for each case—the basic model for reading assessment that has been presented in this book—creates the database needed for evaluat-

---

TABLE 9.1. An Evaluation Model for Data-Based Consultation and Intervention Services

- Requires an explicit model for service delivery that is described in a procedural checklist.
- Requires documentation of the services implemented.
- Produces a quantitative synthesis across sources of information (data).

**TABLE 9.2. Means of Synthesizing
Various Sources of Data**

- Effect size
- Percentage of nonoverlapping data
- Percentage of successful interventions using
  the conservative dual-criteria method
- Goal-attainment scaling
- Treatment integrity
- Treatment acceptability

ing results across cases. Child outcomes can be summarized and synthesized via the techniques that appear in Table 9.2. Each of the data summary methods has advantages and disadvantages, and no single method is sufficient, in itself, to evaluate service quality. Combined, however, they can give an overall indication of consultant or program effectiveness. Each is discussed in turn.

Effect Size

Although this sounds like a complicated and intimidating statistic, effect sizes are computationally simple and not particularly difficult to interpret. Indeed, they have become so important that the American Psychological Association requires that they be reported in its journals (American Psychological Association, 2010). Effect sizes can be calculated for studies and for individual cases that have repeated measures of baseline and intervention phases. A collection of cases with each case having one or more effect size can be summarized by reporting the descriptive statistics (i.e., means, medians, ranges, and standard deviations). First, let's start with what an effect size means (no pun intended). For individual cases, the effect size describes where the average intervention data point stands in the distribution of baseline data. Imagine that you didn't do anything for the client; you just measured his or her performance repeatedly over a brief period of time (before new learning could occur). You would get some variability in the results because of error and irrelevant differences from one assessment to the next. However, with a good measure, the results should cluster around an average in somewhat of a normally distributed manner (like the bell curve you see in statistics books).

Now, fast-forward to when you have actually intervened and have enough data points (e.g., 7–10) to evaluate the treatment. You would expect those data points in the baseline (no intervention) distribution to be higher than most of the baseline data points. Right? An effect size tells you where the average intervention data point stands in the distribution of baseline data points. For an academic skill such as reading, you would expect the difference between the intervention mean and the baseline mean to be a positive number (i.e., intervention mean – baseline mean > 0). An effect size merely describes that difference in standard deviation units. The standard deviation expresses the average amount of variability in the distribution of scores. This figure is important because different types of scores will produce larger or smaller differences, making it impossible to compare across scores without some means of standardizing results. Because the effect size is described in standard deviation units, it standardizes *all* reporting of effect sizes. This way, you can compare effect sizes across completely different measures. The larger the effect size, the stronger the treatment. Cohen's (1988) guidelines for effect sizes are often cited to assist with interpretation: An effect size of 0.20 is considered *small*, an effect size of 0.50 is considered *moderate*, and an effect size of 0.80 or greater is considered *large*. An effect size of +1.0 means that the average intervention data point stands 1 standard deviation above the baseline mean (this is good for skilled behaviors such as reading); an effect size of –1.0 means that the average intervention data point stands 1 standard deviation below the baseline mean (this is bad for skilled behaviors such as reading—it means that things are getting worse rather than better). Kratochwill, Elliott, and Busse (1995) argue that an effect size of +1.0 or greater represents a clinical and practical change of significant magnitude. Effect sizes have been calculated for the data displayed in Figures 9.3 and 9.4. They appear in the tables below the graphs. The effect size in Figure 9.3 is 0.41, and the effect size in Figure 9.4 is 2.53, moderate and large, respectively. If you compare them with the graphs, you can see visually the difference in treatment effects. The intervention in Figure 9.4 is clearly more effective than the intervention that was used in Figure 9.3.

Although there are a number of different computational formulas for calculating effect sizes, and statisticians debate the virtues of each method, a simple approach that makes no assumptions about underlying distributions of scores and is appropriate for individual casework data is described here (Busk & Serlin, 1992). The formula and an example appear in Figure 9.6. You can see the corresponding graph of the data. As noted earlier, the mean of the baseline data is subtracted from the mean of the intervention data, and the result is

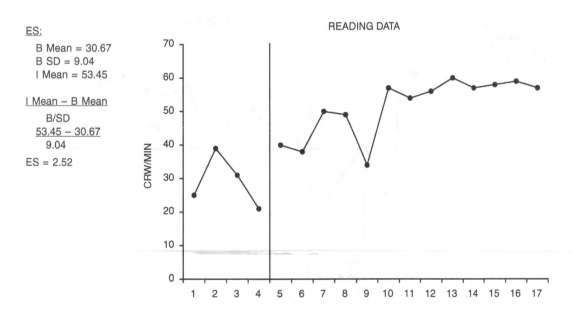

FIGURE 9.6. An example of calculating an effect size.

divided by the baseline standard deviation. In the example in Figure 9.6, the effect size is quite large relative to conventional standards. This large effect size corresponds with the clear, visible increase in trend during the intervention phase. If you are already sweating about the calculations, we now share some information that will make it much easier for you: There is a website that will do all the computational work for you. At *www.interventioncentral.org*, the "Chart Dog Graphmaker" tool (under Tools to the right) will plot your data on a graph (sweet, huh!), and you can ask it to calculate an effect size for each chart that you make by clicking the Data Analysis tab below the graph.

Percentage of Nonoverlapping Data

Here's another statistic with an intimidating name that betrays a deceptively simple idea. One way to figure out whether there has been a difference between baseline and intervention is to calculate the percentage of data points that are higher than the highest baseline data point. Although not as elegant or as robust as the effect size, the percentage of nonoverlapping data (PND) is a simple summary statistic that is easy to calculate. You will find an example in Figure 9.7 for the same graph that was used in the effect size example in Figure 9.6. In all, there are 12 intervention data points, and 11 of those data points are higher than 38 (the highest baseline data point). Therefore, the statistic is computed, in this case, as 11/12, or 92%. PND is especially useful when you cannot calculate effect sizes; you won't be able to calculate effect sizes when you have a standard deviation of 0 (i.e., undefined; a rare occurrence) or when you have fewer than 2 baseline data points (because you won't be able to calculate a standard deviation). We suggest that you use PND as a backup for the few cases where you can't calculate effect sizes. The Chart Dog Graphmaker feature at

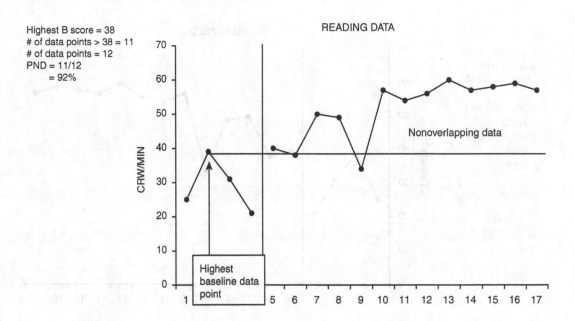

FIGURE 9.7. An example of calculating the percentage of nonoverlapping data.

www.interventioncentral.org will also calculate PND for you. (Isn't this getting easier all the time?)

Percentage of Successful Interventions Using the Conservative Dual-Criteria Method

The success of an intervention for individual cases can be determined on the basis of the CDC method described earlier. This information can be compiled across cases to measure the percentage of successful cases. For example, in an evaluation of school-based consultation cases, Andersen et al. (2010) found that 77% of the measured target behaviors revealed significant effects following intervention according to the CDC. In our experience, the CDC yields a conservative estimate of effect, which sets a higher bar for intervention effect than the more liberal effect size measure described earlier.

Goal-Attainment Scaling

Goal-attainment scaling is a method for quantifying judgments of overall treatment effectiveness. After considering the circumstances of the case, the outcome data, and the degree to which the client achieved (or failed to achieve) goals, you assign a number to the case. A higher number means that greater goal attainment was achieved, a 0 means that no progress was made toward the goal, and a negative number means that things got worse rather than better for the client. The larger the negative number, the worse things got after treatment.

Goal-attainment scaling is commonly used in consultation research. For instance, Kratochwill et al. (1995) used goal-attainment scaling when they reported the effects of training 17 school psychology graduate students in behavioral consultation. The trainees engaged in case-centered consultation that involved problem solving, continuous progress monitoring, and data-based decision making (much like the model presented in this book). The trainees served as consultants on multiple cases. Cases were rated based on reports, effect sizes, and graphs on a scale from +2 to –2. Definitions for ratings appear in Table 9.3. In all, there were 44 cases. Several cases were terminated early for various reasons, so goal-attainment scaling ratings were made in 37 cases. The researchers found that the behavioral goal was fully met (score of +2) for 30% of the cases ($n = 11$) and partially met (score of +1) for 51% of the cases ($n = 19$). For 16% of the cases ($n = 6$), there was no progress toward the goal (score of 0), and for one case (3%) the behavior was somewhat worse.

TABLE 9.3. Goal-Attainment Scaling Definitions for Ratings

- +2 = behavioral goal fully met
- +1 = behavioral goal somewhat met
- 0 = no progress toward goal
- –1 = behavior somewhat worse
- –2 = behavior significantly worse

In a similar evaluation of consultant training outcomes, Barnett et al. (1999) used a goal-attainment scale from +2 to –2. The median goal-attainment scaling rating was +1 (range, –1 to +2). The results indicated that 42% of the cases fully met their goal (+2), 42% partially met their goal (+1), 14% did not make progress toward the goal (0), and one case (2%) was somewhat worse after services (rated as –1). These reports are instructive for two reasons. First, the results for goal-attainment scaling and the other measures they used (e.g., effect sizes, PND, procedural checklists) clearly indicate that services were effective in most cases. Therefore, those pursuing data-based consultation service delivery should be encouraged. Additionally, the researchers demonstrate how to summarize results across cases when the cases are individualized (to meet clients' needs) and target very different factors. Essentially, each case is a kind of mini-experiment in itself, in which the same flexible model is applied.

If you follow the model presented in this book, you will have the database to generate goal-attainment scaling ratings. We suggest a five-step procedure (see Table 9.4). First, look for objective, independent, but knowledgeable professionals who can serve as raters for your cases. After you have collected a number of cases (e.g., at the end of the year), tell the raters that you will take them out to lunch if they will read your case summaries and rate them. Second, we suggest that you have multiple raters evaluate cases at one time. This procedure is most efficient and will allow you to get multiple ratings for each case at the same time. Schedule a time for the work and *then* feed them lunch. Third, assure them that their ratings will be anonymous. We suggest that you arrange a pile of cases for them to pick from (taking, for example, from the top and working down).

What kind of information will you need to compile for the raters? At a minimum, you will need a graph of the data (including a goal line that displays the time frame in which the student should have met the goal) and a description of the intervention procedures that were used with the case. If you have any other summary statistics, such as effect sizes or PND, they can be helpful too and should be added to the case file. Case reports that include these items will do nicely.

Fourth, explain to the raters that you want their best judgment according to the criteria in Table 9.3. Finally, we suggest that you arrange for at least two ratings for each case. Two ratings will allow you to examine whether raters tended to agree (Were most ratings within ±1 point of each other?). Furthermore, we suggest that you take the *lower* of the two rat-

---

TABLE 9.4. Steps for Obtaining Goal-Attainment Scaling Ratings

1. Identify independent raters.

2. Gather raters at a single meeting time.

3. Explain that ratings will be done anonymously so that you won't know how any individual rater scored a case (more raters make this easier).

4. Present the range of scores (+2 to –2) and ask raters to consider all the case information before making a judgment and assigning a score.

5. Obtain at least two ratings for each case (on independent score sheets) and take the lower of the two ratings as the score.

ings as the actual score. The lower rating is a more conservative (and probably less prone to error) rating of the case. Be sure to make a coding sheet for yourself that identifies the cases for you when the raters are finished. Confidentiality is important. Therefore, assign cases identification numbers that don't mean anything to the raters. The point is to be able to match up the ratings with the cases when the raters are dismissed. *Be very careful to protect client rights to confidentiality by eliminating any information that could potentially identify clients.*

Goal-attainment scaling is the least objective of the measures described in this chapter, so we don't recommend that you rely exclusively on it. However, when it is included as one additional piece of evidence with other evidence such as effect sizes, it can give an indication of the clinical significance of your outcomes across cases from the perspective of respected but independent colleagues or other stakeholders. It may be the most direct measure of *perceived* clinical significance of your services.

Treatment Integrity

An essential part of evaluating outcomes is determining whether the plan was implemented in the way it was intended in the first place. If the results of an intervention are poor, there are at least two possibilities. Either the intervention was not the right choice for this case or the intervention was not done as planned. This issue is so important that we advise against deciding that a child failed to respond to an intervention until you have firmly documented that the plan was implemented properly and as frequently as intended. In short, the first step in evaluating any intervention is to assess the consistency and frequency with which it was applied—otherwise known as *treatment integrity* or *treatment fidelity.*

Assessing treatment integrity is relatively straightforward if intervention plans are organized as protocols, as are the ones found in Chapters 5 through 8. With such protocols in place, an intervention session can be observed directly by an independent person, who checks whether or not each step was followed. At the end of an intervention session, you can divide the number of steps correctly completed by the total number of steps that were supposed to be followed to determine the percentage of steps correctly completed. If seven steps of an eight-step protocol were followed, the percentage of steps correctly completed is 87.5% for that session. When treatment integrity data are collected for multiple sessions (which is highly advisable), the results can be summarized, like the other data summarization techniques, with descriptive statistics (i.e., mean, median, range, and standard deviation). A high mean and median suggest that the intervention was done mostly correctly (when it *was* done). You can report the percentage of sessions sampled by dividing the number of sessions observed by the total number of intervention sessions administered. For example, if a reading intervention was to be carried out 4 days a week for 8 weeks, there should be 32 intervention sessions in all. If treatment integrity ratings were obtained for eight sessions, the percentage of sessions sampled was 25%.

Low treatment integrity can tell you when there is a problem. The person responsible for doing the intervention may not have sufficient knowledge of the procedures. In this case, you will probably need to teach the individual how to do the intervention by coaching and modeling the procedures, observing and prompting the trainee when steps are not fol-lowed, and giving feedback (praise for correct implementation and corrective feedback for steps missed or done incorrectly). On the other hand, the person may be knowledgeable but unmotivated. Either the individual doesn't care about changing the situation or other things are competing for his or her time. In some cases, a successful intervention could undermine the objectives of an intervention agent. For example, a teacher who wants a child out of his or her classroom may want to see the intervention fail. (These issues are discussed in greater depth in Chapter 2.) Our point here is to emphasize how you can still take a data-based approach even in this nebulous area of procedural consistency. Summarizing percentage of steps completed over sessions for a particular case gives you some objective numbers to work with when things are not being done so that the issue does not become one of contra-dictory opinions ("Did too . . . Did not . . . Did too . . . Did not . . . .").

There is another positive side to investigating treatment integrity. Good treatment integrity results for a case or a collection of cases suggests that the intervention plans were "doable" (i.e., the persons responsible actually followed through with the procedures in spite of other things that were probably competing for their time) and were probably even acceptable to the person(s) administering them. Why would he or she bother, unless the procedures seemed acceptable and promising? Of course, a person could implement a plan he or she hates. (However, this will be an unlikely explanation in most cases.) Assess-ing whether the plan was implemented is one part of determining its overall acceptability (Gresham & Lopez, 1996). Gathering systematic treatment integrity data nets one more source of converging evidence about the overall implementation and effectiveness of the intervention plan. Individual case summary statistics (means and medians) can be collated across cases to provide summary statistics (means and medians of individual means and medians) for the program model.

Treatment Acceptability

You can have a case that shows great results on your graph but still be deemed unsuccessful in the eyes of your constituents. If they don't *value* the areas on which you are working or see enough progress, then they probably won't have a very high opinion of the services; for clients and other stakeholders, the treatment and outcomes have low acceptability. Their opinions constitute yet another important source of information for summarizing your over-all impact. Of course, from a consultative perspective, you should be working closely with key stakeholders from the very beginning to secure agreement on what you are trying to change and how you will try to elicit that change. Along the way, you should check on acceptability by exploring their preferences, explaining the various ways things can be done and offering choices, and asking for their opinions as unforeseen problems arise. This input is very important information for the case; it is hard, however, to catalogue and organize these unstandardized statements and interactions across cases. The easiest solution is to conduct a survey. If you use a standard survey across cases, you can summarize the results across cases.

There are a number of different acceptability surveys available (Eckert & Hintze, 2000), each with advantages and disadvantages. We have included a simple five-item intervention acceptability survey that has proven very useful in clinical work in Worksheet 9.2 at the end of the chapter. This form can be used flexibly across different types of interventions and can be filled out by teachers, parents, or other key stakeholders. The items are drawn from the Intervention Rating Profile (Martens, Witt, Elliott, & Darveaux, 1985) and represent the five strongest items that assessed overall acceptability. You can give this survey to key stakeholders (e.g., parents) when there are sufficient data to evaluate a treatment plan. Because the items are standard across cases (regardless of the nature of the referral or the intervention), descriptive statistics such as means, medians, range, and standard deviation can be calculated for all cases being reviewed.

Pulling the Data Together and Reporting Results

Now that you know a little something about data summarization methods, you will need to organize your database to facilitate reporting across cases. Like anything else in life, keeping up with this task is half the battle. From a practical standpoint, if you have a plan before you even start taking cases, you can routinely apply certain measures while you are collecting individual case data; doing so will make "pulling it all together" easier in the end. From an evaluation standpoint, it is far better to have a plan for evaluating outcomes before you begin your program than to make it up after the relevant information and data have been collected. We now walk you through the process of planning, maintaining, organizing, and reporting the results (summarized in Table 9.5).

First, you want to start with a database. We recommend creating a file using a spreadsheet program such as Microsoft Excel or an equivalent program. A sample worksheet can be found in Table 9.6. In this example, there are 13 columns for entering data. The first five columns list relevant identifying information. In most cases, except for the child ID number (which allows you to cancel identifying information, for example, when you have others do goal-attainment scale ratings), this information is confidential and only a limited number of people should be allowed to have access to it. The next two columns identify

---

TABLE 9.5. Steps for Collating and Summarizing Data

1. Plan to keep a database and summarize cases as you complete them.

2. Summarize nonquantitative outcomes in terms of
   - Clients served
   - Settings
   - Target behaviors
   - Interventions and their components
   - Intervention agents (who they were)

3. Calculate descriptive statistics (means, medians, range, standard deviation) for each quantitative outcome category and evaluate outcomes.

TABLE 9.6. A Sample Database

Child ID	Name	Grade	Sex	Age	Target Behavior(s)	Intervention(s)	Proc. Int.	ES	PND	GAS	TI	Acceptability
0401	Wilkinson	5	F	11	Reading Fluency	RR with peer, self-monitor, reward	100%	2.52		+1	94%	5.4
0402	Stewert	1	M	6	Phon Segmenting	Self-monitoring	87%	1.53		+1	67%	5.6
0403	Newell	2	F	7	Reading Fluency	Peer tutoring (LPP/RR/EC)	92%	1.97		+2	100%	5.2
0404	Michelson	4	M	9	Reading Fluency	Small group (LPP/RR/EC)	100%	0.58		+1	96%	4.6
0405	Coughlin	6	M	12	Comprehension	Preview questions (RR)	100%		57%	+1	100%	4.8

Note. Proc. Int., procedural integrity; ES, effect size; PND, percentage of nonoverlapping data; GAS, goal-attainment scaling; TI, treatment integrity; Acceptability, mean of five items on the Intervention Acceptability Scale; RR, repeated readings; LPP, listening passage preview; EC, error correction.

the "target behavior" (i.e., the area in need of change) and a brief description or name of intervention components. The remaining columns list procedural integrity (i.e., percentage of procedural checklist steps completed), effect sizes, PND, goal-attainment scaling scores, treatment integrity, and acceptability ratings. You will note that there is only one data point in the PND column. In this hypothetical example, PND was calculated only when it was not possible to calculate an effect size. The comprehension intervention for Coughlin presumably had only two baseline data points that were equal (e.g., 60% and 60% correct), leaving the standard deviation undefined. Once again, it is not possible to calculate an effect size with an undefined standard deviation. So PND was calculated in this case.

Most of the information can be entered in the database as the cases unfold. For example, as soon as there is a referral, identifying information can be entered. Target behaviors and interventions are identified early in the process and can be entered then. At the end of the intervention period, procedural integrity, effect size, PND, and treatment integrity can be calculated. Additionally, the Intervention Acceptability Questionnaire (see Worksheet 9.2) can be given at this time to parents, teachers, or other key stakeholders. The mean of all five items can serve as the individual case score in the database. Goal-attainment scaling scores can be obtained at one time with a group of raters, as noted above. These data can be entered later, as cases are coming to an end.

Following these steps will allow you to develop a broad, descriptive database such as those reported in the literature for consultative, intervention-based services (e.g., Barnett et al., 1999; Kratochwill et al., 1995). In Table 9.6, you can see that a range of ages/grades was served across the three primary areas of reading proficiency. A variety of intervention procedures and formats (e.g., peer tutoring, self-monitoring) was used. The quantitative data can be summarized as means, medians, ranges, and standard deviations. Most spreadsheet programs will calculate the summary statistics for you. In the example, the mean procedural integrity was 96%, the median was 100%, the standard deviation was 6.02%, and the range was 87–100%. For effect sizes, the mean was 1.65, the median was 1.75, the standard deviation was 0.82, and the range was 0.58–2.52. In the one case where an effect size was not calculable, 57% of the data points were above the highest baseline data point.

For goal-attainment scaling, the mean was 1.2, the median was 1, the standard deviation was 0.45, and the range was 1–2. For treatment integrity, the mean was 91%, the median was 96%, the standard deviation was 13.89%, and the range was 67–100%. For acceptability, the mean was 5.12, the median was 5.2, the standard deviation was 0.41, and the range was 4.2–5.8. Eighty percent of the cases obtained goal-attainment scaling scores of +1, and the remaining case obtained a goal-attainment scaling score of +2. Therefore, the results were uniformly positive for all cases. These data in this hypothetical example would serve as a convincing demonstration of the efficacy of the model, in part, because of the variety of sources of information (adherence to the model, student outcomes, high treatment integrity, and high acceptability) that speak to the overall impact of (1) how well the model was carried out, (2) its effects on students, (3) its effects on those responsible for interventions, and (4) the perceptions of key stakeholders. Since developing it with a colleague a few years ago (see Barnett et al., 1999, for a report of the first year of data), one of us (EJD) has routinely used it when supervising graduate students implementing intervention-based services in schools.

Gauging Your Outcomes: Establishing a Basis for Comparison

We anticipate that some readers will be unfamiliar with at least some of the data synthesis methods just reviewed. When a measure is new to you (e.g., effect sizes), it is hard to gauge exactly what the results mean until you develop a basis for comparison. To that end, Table 9.7 reports the results of a small sample of recent and relevant evaluation studies that use many (and then some) of the measures discussed earlier. Three of the studies are pertinent (Daly & Barnett, 2000; Kratochwill et al., 1995; McDougal, Clonan, & Martens, 2000) because they report outcomes of intervention-based consultation cases along a number of different dimensions. The first two of these studies (Daly & Barnett, 2000; Kratochwill et al., 1995) document the actual effects of training graduate students in an innovative pilot program of problem-solving intervention-based consultation on real cases. Students were being prepared for these roles, and actual cases provided an opportunity to examine the effectiveness of their training. We found similar, positive outcomes for the training, meaning that even with trainees, the intervention process led to good social consequences for clients in most cases. The McDougal et al. (2000) study examined the same area, but with professionals already working in schools.

The other two studies (Torgesen et al., 2001; Vaughn et al., 2003) report the results of reading interventions that were conducted with groups of students. These studies had more of an instructional focus; they examined various instructional approaches that can be used with students who have reading problems. Nonetheless, you will see that they gathered some of the same types of data to evaluate outcomes. Torgesen et al. (2001) were primarily interested in effects that could be achieved with a very strong and intense intervention. From the perspective of the children served, their efforts certainly "paid off." The Vaughn et al. (2003) study is unique because it operationalized reading problems from an RTI perspective. The study should allow schools to estimate the degree of success they might expect within and across students if they use a similar model for identifying and treating reading problems *before* classifying the students as learning disabled.

Not all of the data have been reported for each of the studies. Only data germane to our purposes are used to illustrate how some of these different data analysis methods of reporting results to others might be summarized. How will your data compare with the data reported in these studies? You can use the findings from these studies as a benchmark for gauging your success. There are two outcomes reported in these studies that are not discussed above but which might be an important source of information to you. For example, McDougal et al. (2000) synthesized building and district referral rates for special education evaluations. Their data suggest that (1) there were clear reductions in the number of referrals to special education in buildings where school-based intervention teams (SBITs) operated, (2) referrals remained stable in comparable school buildings without the SBIT process,

TABLE 9.7. Reported Outcomes in the Professional Research Literature (a Sample of Behavioral Consultation and Reading Intervention Evaluation Studies)

Study	Clients	Overall purpose and outcomes
Daly & Barnett (2000)	133 children, ages 3–19 years, preschool through high school (some special education), 67% male, 33% female, 76% white, 20% African American, 4% other	(see below)

Purpose

Evaluated the outcomes of intervention-based, client-centered services provided by school psychologists in training. Thirty-six consultants in their second year of graduate training provided consultative services for 1 year over a 3-year span on 133 cases in a variety of settings (a Head Start preschool program, public and parochial elementary, middle, and high schools, in both urban and suburban locations). A total of 158 academic and social behaviors were treated through 200 intervention plans that included instructional changes, changes to the classroom environment, reward plans, self-management, classwide interventions, and peer tutoring. Three years of data are reported (the first year is reported by Barnett et al., 1999).

Outcomes

Procedural checklist (based on a 20-item checklist that described each step that would be followed by the consultant during case management)
    Year 1: Mean = 97% (SD = 5.4), median = 100%, range = 78–100%
    Year 2: Mean = 96% (SD = 0.08), median = 100%, range = 60–100%
    Year 3: Mean = 98% (SD = 3.39), median = 100%, range = 90–100%

Effect sizes
    Year 1: Mean = 2.86, median = 1.97, range = –.33 to 16.55
    Year 2: Mean = 1.81, median = 1.25, range = –.99 to 13.1
    Year 3: Mean = 3.21, median = 1.32, range = –.42 to 49.5

Percentage of nonoverlapping data (PND)
    Year 1: Mean = 77%, median = 100%, range = 30–100%
    Year 2: Mean = 76%, median = 100%, range = 0–100%
    Year 3: Mean = 94%, median = 100%, range = 50–100%

Goal-attainment scaling
    Year 1: Mean = 1.25 (SD = 0.76), median = 1, range = –1 to +2
    Year 2: Mean = 1.23 (SD = 0.67), median = 1, range = –1 to +2
    Year 3: Mean = 1.49 (SD = 0.81), median = 1, range = –1 to +2

Treatment integrity (reported as percentage of steps completed on predetermined intervention plans written in protocol form; each plan was individualized for each case)
    Year 1: Mean = 86%, median = 97%, range = 0–100%
    Year 2: Mean = 87%, median = 93%, range = 0–100%
    Year 3: Mean = 83%, median = 91%, range = 15–100%

Acceptability (on a scale from 1 to 6, with 6 indicating the highest degree of acceptability—"Strongly Agree")
    Year 1: Mean = 5.37 (SD = 0.61), median = 5, range = 4–6
    Year 2: Mean = 5.03 (SD = 1.03), median = 5.2, range = 2–6
    Year 3: Mean = 5.50 (SD = 0.61), median = 5.85, range = 3.9–6

(continued)

TABLE 9.7. *(continued)*

Study	Clients	Overall purpose and outcomes
Kratochwill, Elliott, & Busse (1995)	169 children, ages 3–11 years, in elementary and preschool grades	**Purpose** Evaluated the effects of training in behavioral consultation for 17 preservice school psychologists over a 5-year period. (Although there was a variety of consultant outcomes, only the degree to which consultants met procedural objectives and client outcomes are reported here.) Consultants were in their first and second year of graduate training. They were grouped by training years (subgroups 1–4). Consultations addressed a variety of behavioral and academic problems. There were whole-classroom interventions, small groups, and individual case consultations.

Outcomes
Procedural integrity (reported as average percentage of *interview* objectives met by the consultant during actual problem-solving interviews)
    Subgroup 1: 84%; subgroup 2: 90%; subgroup 3: 86%; subgroup 4: 94%

Effect sizes
    Overall mean effect size for 23 cases = .95, range = −.55 to 2.90

Goal-attainment scaling
    Overall mean GAS score = 1.11, median = 1, range = 0 to +2

Acceptability (on a 15-item acceptability survey, with items ranging from 1 to 6, with 6 indicating the highest degree of acceptability; when scores were summed across items, 90 was the highest possible score)
    Overall mean score for 29 cases = 80.3 (*SD* = 6.9)

Study	Clients	Overall purpose and outcomes
McDougal, Clonan, & Martens (2000)	47 students in grades K–6 referred for academic and behavioral problems	**Purpose** Examined 2 years of outcome data for a school-based intervention team program that was implemented in four urban public elementary schools. Elements of the intervention team process were derived largely from the behavioral consultation literature and implemented in four elementary schools. Careful attention was paid to organizational change processes to increase the chances that the program would become institutionalized in the school district. At the time of the report, the program was in its fourth year.

Outcomes
Procedural integrity (based on 10 objectives of the intervention process that were to be met during multidisciplinary team meetings; ratings were made during unannounced visits by independent observers who rated each objective as either 1 [*met*], 2 [*partially met*], or 3 [*unmet*]; thus, lower ratings are desirable in this case.)
    Overall mean rating for all items = 1.5 (*SD* = 2.9)
    The authors report that "on average . . . . the 10 consultative objectives were
        either met or partially met during 90.5% of observed team meetings"
        (p. 165).

Acceptability (teacher ratings on a scale from 1 to 6, with 6 being most acceptable; ratings were gathered immediately following team meetings—preintervention— and several weeks after implementing the intervention in the classroom— postintervention.)

(continued)

TABLE 9.7. *(continued)*

Study	Clients	Overall purpose and outcomes		
			Preint. Mean (*SD*)	Postint. Mean (*SD*)
		Comfortable/collaborative atmosphere	5.6 (.83)	—
		Helpfulness of intervention team process	5.1 (1.2)	5.1 (1.3)
		How the teacher liked the procedures	4.9 (1.1)	4.7 (1.1)
		The intervention was a good way to handle the problem	4.7 (.96)	4.6 (1.1)
		How beneficial the intervention was for the child	4.7 (1.2)	4.4 (1.6)
		There were sufficient resources to implement the intervention	5.0 (.97)	4.8 (1.2)
		Overall severity of the problem	5.1 (.91)	4.5 (1.3)

(Follow-up analyses indicate a significant reduction in perceived severity of the problem.)

Referral rates (comparing referral rates for special education evaluations for the 2 years prior to implementation and the first 2 years of implementation; also, four comparable schools were chosen that were not using the school-based intervention team program.)

Year 1: Initial referrals to special education decreased by 22% when compared with the 2 years prior to the project; in contrast, referrals for matched-comparison schools increased by 18%, and overall district referrals increased by 19% during that same year.

Year 2: Initial referrals to special education decreased by an additional 15% (yielding an overall reduction of 36% in referrals from preimplementation of the intervention process). Matched schools showed a 3% decrease, whereas the district showed a 4% overall increase in special education referrals.

Study	Clients	Overall purpose and outcomes
Torgesen et al. (2001)	60 students with severe reading disabilities between the ages of 8 and 10; participants were classified as learning disabled in the state of Florida	**Purpose** The authors delivered two very intense interventions to students to determine whether it would be possible to (1) bring the skills of students with severe reading disabilities to average levels of performance; (2) determine whether there were significant differences between treatments, and (3) examine whether either method would be differentially effective for children with different cognitive, linguistic, and demographic profiles. Outcomes were measured in the areas of phonemic decoding, word identification, and passage comprehension. (Refer to the original study for a detailed description of outcomes in each of these areas. Only effect sizes and outcomes relative to continuation in special education placement are reported here.) Students received 67.5 hours of one-on-one instruction in two 50-minute sessions per day for 8 weeks in either an Auditory Discrimination in Depth program or an Embedded Phonics program.

Outcomes

Effect sizes (comparing growth during intervention with the participants' growth during the previous 16 months in learning disabilities resource rooms)

Auditory Discrimination in Depth: 4.4

Embedded Phonics: 3.9

Exited from special education

The authors report that "approximately 40% of the children were judged to be no longer in need of special education services and were returned full-time to the general education classroom within the first year following the end of the intervention" (p. 50).

(continued)

TABLE 9.7. *(continued)*

Study	Clients	Overall purpose and outcomes
Vaughn, Linan-Thompson, & Hickman (2003)	45 second-grade students at risk for reading problems who were not already receiving supplemental reading instruction and who had failed the second-grade Texas Primary Reading Inventory screening; 35 students were Hispanic, 6 were white, and 4 were African American	(see below)

Purpose

This study was intended to examine (1) the number of students who would meet predetermined exit criteria, following daily supplemental reading instruction; (2) the degree to which students who improved during supplemental instruction and met exit criteria would be successful in general education when supplemental instruction was terminated; and (3) "the feasibility of using a response-to-treatment model to identify students with LD by a school or district" (p. 384). Exit criteria included (1) a passing score on the Texas Primary Reading Inventory: Screening (i.e., five or more words, out of eight, read correctly); (2) reading at least 55 correct read words per minute on a second-grade-level passage of the Test of Oral Reading Fluency; and (3) reading at least 50 correct read words per minute, for at least 3 consecutive weeks, in second-grade fluency progress monitoring sessions. Supplemental instruction focused on phonemic awareness, phonics (especially sound–letter relationships and word families), word and text reading fluency, instructional-level reading and comprehension, and spelling; delivered daily for 35 minutes in small groups. Four tutors provided supplemental instruction.

Outcomes

Outcomes are reported by students' category of when they met exit criteria: after 10 weeks, 20 weeks, 30 weeks, or never.

Number of students who met exit criteria at different intervals

Met after 10 weeks:	10
Met after 20 weeks:	14
Met after 30 weeks:	10
Never met exit criteria:	11

Effect sizes

	During intervention	At 30-week follow-up
Met after 10 weeks:	2.74	1.72
Met after 20 weeks:	3.23	0.97
Met after 30 weeks:	6.06	6.06
Never met exit criteria:	2.66	2.66

Intervention validity checklist (a treatment integrity checklist on which features of instruction were recorded; quality of instruction was judged by independent observers for activities and materials as well as instructional time on a scale from 0 (*not observed*) to 3 (*observed most of the time*); results are reported for each area of instruction.)

Fluency: Mean rating = 2.53 (*SD* = 0.15), median = 2.5
Phonological awareness: Mean rating = 2.5 (*SD* = 0.39), median = 2.55
Instructional reading: Mean rating = 2.6 (*SD* = 0.48), median = 2.8
Word analysis: Mean rating = 2.55 (SD = 0.37), median = 2.5

and (3) referrals districtwide increased. Torgesen et al. (2001) tackled severe reading problems and were able to report an amazing percentage of students who were discharged from special education classes. This type of information is very persuasive with other professionals and constituents because it contains the types of data that school districts are routinely gathering in the first place. They just need to be "mined" by people who have the vision to ascertain how their reading intervention program compares with similar programs in other schools, and how their program affects the educational placements of participating students. Each of these reports contains an impressive amount of information, and we advise the interested reader to obtain the original publications. They are a good read—and they will help you to further refine your evaluation plan.

Sharing Your Results with Others

Sharing your results may be as important a task as all your intervention and data-collection efforts, if continuation of your program or funding for your program hinges on convincing others of its positive impact on students. Whether it be through a written report or an oral presentation to a group, you want to have a crisp, clear, and professional format for presenting your results—and then you can let the data speak for "themselves." Graphs efficiently display a lot of information and require only simple explanations for people to grasp what they mean. They are also satisfying for consumers once they understand what the results mean, because then they can judge for themselves whether or not the results are convincing.

We strongly encourage you to create one or more graphs of quantitative outcomes in any reporting you do. You will find sample graphs in Figures 9.8 and 9.9. Effect sizes, goal-attainment scaling, and intervention acceptability means are displayed in a bar graph format, using data reported by Daly and Barnett (2000). Three years of data are reported in each graph. As noted previously, you can create the same reporting format over time by using simple charting tools contained in spreadsheet programs such as Microsoft Excel or the "Chart Dog" feature at *interventioncentral.org*. Such graphs allow reviewers to see the range of outcomes obtained, where the results cluster, and, when there are data for multiple years, whether the results are consistent over time.

Tables may be helpful for displaying more descriptive statistics than just the mean. For instance, Table 9.8 contains information on number of cases per year, means, medians, and range of procedural checklist outcomes (reported as a percentage of steps completed; data from Daly & Barnett, 2000). Once again, data displays such as this one are packed with useful information. As the presenter, you can draw the attention of those reviewing the data to different features in the results, such as overall patterns, how much variability there is in the results, and whether there were changes over years or according to types of cases (if you break down the data in this way). It is helpful to try plotting your data in various ways to determine which method (1) communicates the most information and (2) highlights the key findings.

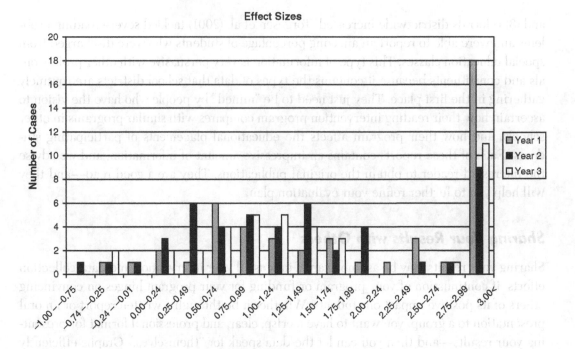

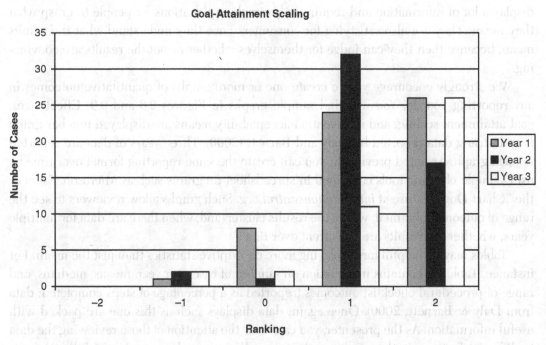

FIGURE 9.8. Summary graphs of effect sizes and goal-attainment scaling. From Daly and Barnett (2000). Reprinted by permission of the authors.

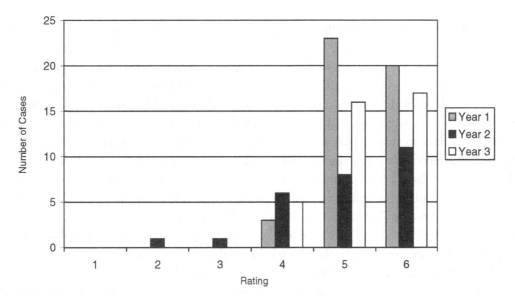

FIGURE 9.9. Summary graph of intervention acceptability data. From Daly and Barnett (2000). Reprinted by permission of the authors.

WRAPPING UP

This book presents a simple, direct approach to reading intervention that emphasizes the fundamental importance of maximizing student responding. Everything is oriented toward helping the student get the right answer, whether it is sounding out a word, reading it in a text, explaining the meaning of a term, or answering a question about something that happened in the story. A critical part of this enterprise is detecting whether the student *can* get the right answer. Thus, observation and assessment are just as important as the intervention strategies themselves. The student's response (or lack thereof) when given a reading task tells us something about his or her level of proficiency with the task (and therefore its appropriateness) and whether the student is making progress in response to instruction. Progress monitoring data are vital to establishing the kind of feedback loop teachers need to make necessary adjustments to instruction. For this very reason, the book has emphasized simple, valid, direct assessments of the critical skills identified by the research as most necessary to becoming literate.

TABLE 9.8. Procedural Checklist Outcomes

Year	No. reported	Mean (*SD*)	Median	Range
1	70	97% (5.4)	100	78–100%
2	36	96% (0.08)	100	60–100%
3	37	98% (3.39)	100	90–100%

Note. From Daly and Barnett (2000). Reprinted with permission from the authors.

Linking assessment data to the interventions themselves requires conceptual tools for understanding what to do based on a student's current level of responding. Here too, we have tried to show that simpler is better. Therefore, we encouraged you to consider whether the student has the prerequisite skills necessary to benefit from instruction. The instructional hierarchy was also presented, as it is particularly helpful for cueing us as to what to look for: Effective instruction will lead to a smooth progression from improved accuracy to fluent responding to generalization to new tasks. A breakdown at any point (e.g., a student hampered by high error rates) signals that instruction is not matched to the student's needs. Chapter 4 described a host of important considerations for interventions with ELs. Paying attention to all of these factors and adjusting instruction accordingly is what we refer to early in the book as "responsive instruction." The teacher is responding to the student just as the student is responding to the teacher. Again, this is where reliable, valid progress monitoring data are essential for the student in need of intervention.

The area of reading interventions has progressed significantly since the last edition of this book, not so much in terms of the interventions themselves—after all, students still learn the same ways and there are only so many ways you can organize instructional time; rather, improvements have been in the area of implementing multi-tiered intervention programs that apply to large groups of students (e.g., an entire elementary school). As RTI swept the country, schools began providing a continuum of instruction and intervention for every student in the school. A core component of RTI is routine data collection for instructional decision making. Schools doing RTI are using the progress-monitoring measures described earlier, albeit with varying levels of frequency for students—less often for students making adequate progress and more often for students making inadequate progress. Therefore, the database we recommend for individual decision making is directly relevant to multi-tiered intervention models as well. The reading interventions in this book can be used on a larger scale within an RTI program to strengthen existing instruction (Tier 1) and interventions (Tiers 2 and 3) based on what the data say for both individuals and groups (Chapter 3).

If you are engaging in all these assessment and intervention activities, we have one final task for you. The current chapter demonstrated how establishing continuity in the database across students as one does with multi-tiered intervention models and expanding it a bit can help you in yet another important task—evaluating *your* effectiveness. How well are you serving your students? Wouldn't you like to know whether your intervention efforts are having an impact? To this end, we presented a framework within which you start by defining your intervention model and operationalizing it as a set of steps to be followed with every case. Documenting these results will tell you whether you are following the model consistently or not. Next, you need to use the data analytic tools presented in this chapter. They will provide you with a rich database for summarizing how effective your interventions are. The results can be useful to you for evaluating your intervention program and adjusting as needed. They can also be useful for broadcasting your results to your constituents. In this day of shrinking resources and increased accountability, these data may be the difference between whether your program survives or not. Being strategic in this way will ultimately broaden your impact on students.

Procedural steps	Date completed

1. Obtain parent permission and discuss the problem and available resources with parent, teacher(s), and other stakeholders (SPECIFY: _____)   _____

2. Establish a baseline (minimum of 3 data points with standardized procedures for assessing early literacy, reading fluency, and/or reading comprehension) and display the results on a graph.   _____

3. Establish a data-based goal that describes the learner, conditions of ongoing assessment (time and materials for responding), how many corrects and incorrects are expected (expected performance), and a goal date. Draw the goal on the graph.   _____

4. An intervention plan is established that describes what will be done, where, when, how many times a week, how long (per session), by whom, and with what resources. The plan is written out and shared with the parents and other team members.   _____

5. A plan evaluation date and time are set for no more than 8 weeks after the first plan is established. (SPECIFY DATE AND TIME: _____)   _____

6. Arrangements are made for an independent person to directly observe whether the plan is being done during scheduled sessions. A recording plan is established for determining how many steps were correctly followed during scheduled intervention sessions.   _____

7. At least 8–10 data points are gathered during the intervention period. (SPECIFY BY WHOM: _____)   _____

8. The plan is evaluated according to:
   (a) whether the plan was carried out as intended and as frequently as intended; and
   (b) whether the student is progressing toward meeting the goal.   _____

9. Agreement is achieved on the decision to:
   - Continue the plan unmodified.
   - Modify the plan.
   - Terminate the plan.

   (Check the appropriate box and explain the decision and next steps at the end of the checklist.)   _____

10. The acceptability of the plan, process, and results were assessed with the acceptability questionnaire by the parent, the child, and the teacher.   _____

Intervention Acceptability Scale

Child's Name: _____

Name of rater and relationship with child: _____

Date: _____

Intervention: _____

Please rate the intervention procedures using the following scale:

1 = Strongly Disagree
2 = Disagree
3 = Slightly Disagree
4 = Slightly Agree
5 = Agree
6 = Strongly Agree

1. I like the procedures used in this intervention.	1	2	3	4	5	6
2. This intervention is a good way to handle this problem.	1	2	3	4	5	6
3. Overall, this intervention is beneficial for the student.	1	2	3	4	5	6
4. This intervention is reasonable for the problem.	1	2	3	4	5	6
5. I would be willing to use this intervention in the classroom setting in the future.	1	2	3	4	5	6

Please make any comments below. Use the back if necessary.

References

Abedi, J. (2004). The No Child Left Behind Act and English language learners: Assessment and accountability issues. *Educational Researcher, 33*(1), 4–14.

Adams, M. J. (1990). *Beginning to read: Thinking and learning about print.* Cambridge, MA: MIT Press.

Adams, M. J., Foorman, B., Lundberg, I., & Beeler, T. (1998). *Phonemic awareness in young children.* Baltimore: Brookes.

Adelman, H. S. (1982). Identifying learning problems at an early age: A critical appraisal. *Journal of Clinical Child Psychology, 11,* 255–261.

Adelman, H. S., & Taylor, L. (1998). Reframing mental health in schools and expanding school reform. *Educational Psychologist, 33,* 135–152.

Adelman, H. S., & Taylor, L. (1999). Mental health in schools and system restructuring. *Clinical Psychology Review, 19,* 137–163.

Al Otaiba, S., Petscher, Y., Pappamihiel, N., Williams, R. S., Dyrlund, A. K., & Connor, C. (2009). Modeling oral reading fluency development in Latino students: A longitudinal study across second and third grade. *Journal of Educational Psychology, 101*(2), 315–329.

Alesandri, K. L. (1982). Imagery-eliciting strategy and meaningful learning. *Journal of Mental Imagery, 6,* 125–141.

American Educational Research Association. (1999). *The standards for educational and psychological testing.* Washington, DC: Author.

American Psychological Association. (2010). *Publication manual of the American Psychological Association* (6th ed.). Washington, DC: Author.

Anderman, R. C., & Williams, J. M. (1986, April). *Teaching test-taking and note-taking skills to learning disabled high school students.* Paper presented at the annual convention of the Council for Exceptional Children, New Orleans, LA. (ERIC Document Reproduction Service No. ED268772)

Andersen, M. N., Hofstadter, K. L., Kupzyk, S., Daly, E. J., III, Bleck, A. A., Collaro, A. L., et al. (2010). A guiding framework for integrating the consultation process and behavior analytic practice in schools: The treatment validation consultation model. *Journal of Behavioral Assessment and Intervention in Children, 1*(1), 53–84.

Anderson, R. C., & Freebody, P. (1981). Vocabulary knowledge. In J. T. Guthrie (Ed.), *Comprehension and teaching: Research reviews* (pp. 77–117). Newark, DE: International Reading Association.

Anderson, R. C., & Nagy, W. E. (1992). The vocabulary conundrum. *American Educator, 16,* 14–18, 44–47.

Anthony, L. (2008). *Developing handwriting-based*

intelligent tutors to enhance mathematics learning. Unpublished doctoral dissertation, Carnegie Mellon University, Pittsburgh, PA.

Aud, S., Hussar, W., Kena, G., Bianco, K., Frohlich, L., Kemp, J., et al. (2011). *The Condition of Education 2011* (NCES 2011-033). Washington, DC: U.S. Government Printing Office.

August, D., & Hakuta, K. (Eds.). (1997). *Improving schooling for language minority children: A research agenda.* Washington, DC: National Academy Press.

August, D., Kenyon, D., Malabonga, V., Carglarcan, S., Louguit, M., Francis, D., et al. (2001). *Test of Phonological Processing in Spanish.* Washington, DC: Center for Applied Linguistics.

August, D., & Shanahan, T. (2006). *Developing literacy in second language learners. Report of the National Literacy Panel on Language-Minority Children and Youth.* Mahwah, NJ: Erlbaum.

August, D., & Siegel, L. (2006). Literacy instruction for language-minority children in special education settings. In D. August & T. Shanahan (Eds.), *Developing literacy in second-language learners: Report of the National Literacy Panel on Language-Minority Children and Youth* (pp. 523–553). Mahwah, NJ: Erlbaum.

Bailey, A. L. (Ed.). (2007). *The language demands of school: Putting academic English to the test.* New Haven, CT: Yale University Press.

Baker, S. K., & Good, R. (1995). Curriculum-based measurement for English reading with bilingual Hispanic students: A validation study with second-grade students. *School Psychology Review, 24,* 561–578.

Ball, E. W., & Blachman, B. A. (1991). Does phoneme awareness training in kindergarten make a difference in early word recognition and developmental spelling? *Reading Research Quarterly, 26,* 49–66.

Barnett, D. W., Daly, E. J., III, Hampshire, E. M., Hines, N. R., Maples, K. A., Ostrom, J. K., et al. (1999). Meeting performance-based training demands: Accountability in an intervention-based practicum. *School Psychology Quarterly, 14,* 357–379.

Barnett, D. W., Lentz, F. E., Jr., & Macmann, G. (2000). Psychometric qualities of professional practice. In E. S. Shapiro & T. R. Kratochwill (Eds.), *Behavioral assessment in schools: Theory, research, and clinical foundations* (2nd ed., pp. 355–386). New York: Guilford Press.

Barnett, D. W., & Macmann, G. M. (1992). Aptitude–achievement discrepancy scores: Accuracy in analysis misdirected. *School Psychology Review, 21,* 494–508.

Batsche, G., Elliott, J., Graden, J. L., Grimes, J.,

Kovaleski, J. F., Prasse, D., et al. (2006). *Response to intervention: Policy considerations and implementation.* Alexandria, VA: National Association of State Directors of Special Education.

Baumann, J. F., Kame'enui, E. J., & Ash, G. E. (2003). Research on vocabulary instruction: Voltaire redux. In D. C. Simmons & E. J. Kame'enui (Eds.), *What reading research tells us about diverse children's needs* (pp. 183–218). Mahwah, NJ: Erlbaum.

Baumann, J. F., Seifert-Kessel, N., & Jones, L. A. (1992). Effect of think-aloud instruction on elementary students' comprehension monitoring abilities. *Journal of Reading Behavior, 24,* 143–172.

Beck, I., & McKeown, M. G. (2001). Text talk: Capturing the benefits of read-aloud experiences for young children. *The Reading Teacher, 55*(1), 10–20.

Beck, I. L. (1997, October/November). Response to "overselling phonics." *Reading Today,* 17.

Beck, I. L., & McKeown, M. G. (2003). Taking advantage of read alouds to help children make sense of decontextualized language. In A. van Kleeck, S. A. Stahl, & E. B. Bauer (Eds.), *Storybook reading* (pp. 159–176). Mahwah, NJ: Erlbaum.

Beck, I. L., McKeown, M. G., & Kucan, L. (2013). *Bringing words to life: Robust vocabulary instruction* (2nd ed.). New York: Guilford Press.

Belfiore, P. J., Skinner, C. H., & Ferkis, M. A. (1995). Effects of response repetition in sight-word training for students with learning disabilities. *Journal of Applied Behavior Analysis, 28,* 347–348.

Bergan, J. R., & Kratochwill, T. R. (1990). *Behavioral consultation and therapy.* New York: Plenum Press.

Bialystok, E., & Herman, J. (1999). Does bilingualism matter for early literacy? *Bilingualism: Language and Cognition, 2*(1), 35–44.

Biancarosa, G., & Snow, C. E. (2004). *Reading next: A vision for action and research in middle and high school literacy: A report from the Carnegie Corporation of New York.* Washington, DC: Alliance for Excellent Education.

Biemiller, A. (2001). Teaching vocabulary: Early, direct, and sequential. *American Educator, 25,* 25–28.

Biemiller, A., & Slonim, N. (2001). Estimating root word vocabulary growth in normative and advantaged populations: Evidence for a common sequence of vocabulary acquisition. *Journal of Educational Psychology, 93*(3), 498–520.

Binder, C. (1996). Behavioral fluency: Evolution of a new paradigm. *The Behavior Analyst, 19,* 163–197.

Blachman, B. A. (1994). Early literacy acquisition: The role of phonological awareness. In G. P. Wallach & K. G. Butler (Eds.), *Language learning dis-*

abilities in school-aged children and adolescents (pp. 253–274). New York: Merrill.

Blachman, B. A., Ball, E. W., Black, R. S., & Tangel, D. M. (2000). *Road to the code: A phonological awareness program for young children.* Baltimore: Brookes.

Black, M. P., Forbes, B. E., Yaw, J. S., & Skinner, C. H. (2013, February). *A comparison of sight-word learning rates across three computer-based interventions.* Paper presented at the annual meeting of the National Association of School Psychologists, Seattle, WA.

Bliss, S., Skinner, C. H., & Adams, R. (2006). Enhancing sight-word reading with a time delay taped-words intervention with an English language learning fifth-grade student. *School Psychology Review, 35,* 663–670.

Blum, I. H., & Koskinen, P. S. (1991). Repeated reading: A strategy to enhance fluency and foster expertise. *Theory into Practice, 30,* 195–200.

Bos, C. S., & Anders, P. L. (1990). Interactive practice for teaching content and strategic knowledge. In T. E. Scruggs & B. Y. L. Wong (Eds.), *Intervention research in learning disabilities* (pp. 116–185). New York: Springer-Verlag.

Bos, C. S., Anders, P. L., Filip, D., & Jaffe, L. E. (1989). The effects of an interactive instructional strategy for enhancing reading comprehension and content area learning for students with learning disabilities. *Journal of Learning Disabilities, 22,* 384–390.

Boyle, J. R., & Weishaar, M. (2001). The effects of a strategic note-taking technique on the comprehension and long term recall of lecture information for high school students with LD. *LD Research and Practice, 16*(3), 125–133.

Brandoff-Matter, E. (1989). Visualize to improve comprehension. *The Reading Teacher, 42,* 338.

Browder, D. M., & Xin, Y. P. (1998). A meta-analysis and review of sight word research and its implication for teaching functional reading to individuals with moderate to severe disabilities. *Journal of Special Education, 32,* 130–153.

Brown, R., Pressley, M., Van Meter, P., & Schuder, T. (1996). A quasi-experimental validation of transactional strategies instruction with previously low-achieving second-grade readers. *Journal of Educational Psychology, 88,* 18–37.

Buehl, D. (2011). *Developing readers in the academic disciplines.* Newark: DE: International Reading Association.

Burns, M. K. (2004). Empirical analysis of drill ratio research: Refining the instructional level for drill tasks. *Remedial and Special Education, 25,* 167–175.

Burns, M. K., Riley-Tillman, T. C., & VanDerHeyden, A. M. (2012). *RTI applications, Volume 1: Academic and behavioral interventions.* NY: Guilford Press.

Burns, M. K., Zaslofsky, A. F., Kanive, R., & Parker, D. C. (2012). Meta-analysis of incremental rehearsal using phi coefficients to compare single-case and group designs. *Journal of Behavioral Education, 21,* 185–202.

Busk, P. L., & Serlin, R. C. (1992). Meta-analysis for single-case research. In T. R. Kratochwill & J. R. Levin (Eds.), *Single-case research design and analysis: Applications in psychology and education* (pp. 187–212). Hillsdale, NJ: Erlbaum.

Carnine, D., & Kinder, B. D. (1985). Teaching low-performing students to apply generative and schema strategies to narrative and expository material. *Remedial and Special Education, 6,* 20–30.

Carnine, D., Silbert, J., Kame'enui, E., & Tarver, S. G. (2010). *Direct instruction reading* (5th ed.). Upper Saddle River, NJ: Pearson.

Carnine, D. W. (1976). Effects of two teacher presentation rates of off-task behavior, answering correctly, and participation. *Journal of Applied Behavior Analysis, 9,* 199–206.

Cates, G. L., Skinner, C. H., Watkins, C. E., Rhymer, K. N., McNeill, B. S., & McCurdy, M. (1999). Effects of interspersing additional brief math problems on student performance and perception of math assignments: Getting students to prefer to do more work. *Journal of Behavioral Education, 9,* 177–193.

Catts, H. W. (1995). *Language basics of reading disabilities: Implications for early identification and remediation.* Paper presented at the annual conference of the Speech, Language and Hearing Association of Alberta, Canada.

Cazzell, S. S., Browarnik, B. L., Skinner, A. L., Cihak, D. F., Skinner, C. H., & Forbes, B. (in press). Extending research on a computer-based flashcard reading intervention to adults with disabilities. *Research in Developmental Disabilities.*

Chafouleas, S. M., Lewandowski, L. J., Smith, C. R., & Blachman, B. A. (1997). Phonological awareness skills in children: Examining performance across tasks and ages. *Journal of Psychoeducational Assessment, 15,* 334–347.

Chafouleas, S. M., VanAuken, T., & Dunham, K. (2001). Not all phonemes are created equal: The effects of linguistic manipulations on phonological awareness tasks. *Journal of Psychoeducational Assessment, 19,* 216–226.

Chall, J. S. (1996). *Stages of reading development* (2nd ed.). New York: Harcourt Brace. (Original work published 1983)

Chan, L. K. S., Cole, P. G., & Barfett, S. (1987). Comprehension monitoring: Detection and identification of text inconsistencies by learning disabled and normal students. *Learning Disability Quarterly, 10,* 114–124.

Chan, L. K. S., Cole, P. G., & Morris, J. N. (1990). Effect of instruction in the use of visual-imagery strategy on the reading-comprehension competence of disabled and average readers. *Learning Disability Quarterly, 13,* 1–11.

Chard, D. J., Vaughn, S., & Tyler, B. J. (2002). A synthesis of research on effective interventions for building reading fluency with elementary students with learning disabilities. *Journal of Learning Disabilities, 35,* 386–406.

Chiappe, P., Siegel, L. S., & Gottardo, A. (2002). Reading-related skills of kindergarteners from diverse linguistic backgrounds. *Applied Psycholinguistics, 23,* 95–116.

Christ, T. J. (2006). Short-term estimates of growth using curriculum-based measurement of oral reading fluency: Estimating standard error of the slope to construct confidence intervals. *School Psychology Review, 35,* 128–133.

Christ, T. J., & Ardoin, S. P. (2009). Curriculum-based measurement of oral reading: Passage equivalence and probe-set development. *Journal of School Psychology, 47,* 55–75.

Christ, T. J., & Silberglitt, B. (2007). Estimates of the standard error of measurements for curriculum-based measures of oral reading fluency. *School Psychology Review, 36,* 130–146.

Christ, T. J., Zopluoglu, C., Long, J. D., & Monaghen, B. D. (2012). Curriculum-based measurement of oral reading: Quality of progress monitoring outcomes. *Exceptional Children, 78,* 356–373.

Christ, T. J., Zopluoglu, C., Monaghen, B. D., & Van Norman, E. R. (2013). Curriculum-based measurement of oral reading: Multi-study evaluation of schedule, duration, and dataset quality on progress monitoring outcomes. *Journal of School Psychology, 51,* 19–57.

Ciancio, D., Strait, A. D., Schall, M., McCullough, K., Skinner, C. H., Wilhoit, B. E., et al. (2013, August). *MAZE and oral reading fluency measures: Variance in broad reading accounted for by reading speed.* Paper presented at the annual convention of the American Psychological Association, Honolulu, HI.

Coady, J. (1993). Research on ESL/EFL vocabulary acquisition: Putting it in context. In T. Huckin, M. Haynes, & J. Coady (Eds.), *Second language reading and vocabulary learning* (pp. 3–23). Norwood, NJ: Ablex.

Cohen, J. (1988). *Statistical power analysis for the behavioral sciences.* Hillsdale, NJ: Erlbaum.

Collier, C. (2010). *RTI for diverse learners: More than 200 instructional interventions.* Thousand Oaks, CA: Corwin.

Colón, E. P., & Kranzler, J. H. (2006). Effects of instruction on curriculum-based measurement of reading. *Journal of Psychoeducational Assessment, 24,* 318–328.

Cone, J. D. (2001). *Evaluating outcomes: Empirical tools for effective practice.* Washington, DC: American Psychological Association.

Cosden, M., Gannon, C., & Haring, T. (1995). Teacher-control versus student-control over choice of task and reinforcement for students with severe behavior problems. *Journal of Behavioral Education, 5,* 11–27.

Coxhead, A. (2000). A new academic word list. *Teachers of English to Speakers of Other Languages, Inc. (TESOL), 34*(2), 213–238.

Coyne, M. D., McCoach, B., & Kapp, S. (2007). Vocabulary intervention for kindergarten students: Comparing extended instruction to embedded instruction and incidental exposure. *Learning Disability Quarterly, 30,* 74–88.

Coyne, M. D., Simmons, D. C., Kame'enui, E. J., & Stoolmiller, M. (2004). Teaching vocabulary during shared storybook readings: An examination of differential effects. *Exceptionality, 12,* 145–162.

Crawford, J. (2004). *Educating English learners: Language diversity in the classroom* (5th ed.). Los Angeles: Bilingual Educational Services.

Cummins, J. (1984). *Bilingual education and special education: Issues in assessment and pedagogy.* San Diego, CA: College Hill.

Cummins, J. (1991). Interdependence of first- and second-language proficiency to academic achievement among bilingual students. In C. Rivera (Ed.), *Language proficiency and academic achievement* (pp. 2–19). Clevedon, UK: Multilingual Matters.

Cummins, J. (2000). *Language, power and pedgogy: Bilingual children in the crossfire.* Clevedon, UK: Multilingual Matters.

Cunningham, A. E., & Stanovich, K. E. (1997). Early reading acquisition and its relation to reading experience and ability 10 years later. *Developmental Psychology, 33*(6), 934–945.

Cunningham, A. E., & Stanovich, K. E. (1998). What reading does for the mind. *American Educator, 22*(1–2), 8–15.

D'Alessio, J. A. (1996). *Retelling in the improvement of reading comprehension scores of urban, lower socio-economic fourth graders.* Master's Project, Kean College of New Jersey. (ERIC Document Reproduction No. ED 394135)

Daly, E. J., Chafouleas, S. M., Persampieri, M., Bonfiglio, C. M., & Lafleur, K. (2004). Teaching phoneme segmenting and blending as critical early literacy skills: An experimental analysis of minimal textual repertoires. *Journal of Behavioral Education, 13,* 165–178.

Daly, E. J., Wright, J. A., Kelly, S. Q., & Martens, B. K. (1997). Measures of early academic skills: Reliability and validity with a first-grade sample. *School Psychology Quarterly, 12,* 268–280.

Daly, E. J., III, & Barnett, D. W. (2000). *Meeting performance-based demands for practicum training: Three years of data.* Paper presented at the annual convention of the National Association of School Psychologists, New Orleans, LA.

Daly, E. J., III, Garbacz, S. A., Olson, S. C., Persampieri, M., & Ni, H. (2006). Improving oral reading fluency by influencing students' choice of instructional procedures: An experimental analysis with two students with behavioral disorders. *Behavioral Interventions, 21,* 13–30.

Daly, E. J., III, Lentz, F. E., & Boyer, J. (1996). The instructional hierarchy: A conceptual model for understanding the effective components of reading interventions. *School Psychology Quarterly, 11,* 369–386.

Daly, E. J., III, & Martens, B. K. (1994). A comparison of three interventions for increasing oral reading performance: Application of the instructional hierarchy. *Journal of Applied Behavior Analysis, 27,* 459–469.

Daly, E. J., III, Martens, B. K., Barnett, D., Witt, J. C., & Olson, S. C. (2007). Varying intervention delivery in response-to-intervention: Confronting and resolving challenges with measurement, instruction, and intensity. *School Psychology Review, 36,* 562–581.

Daly, E. J., III, Martens, B. K., Dool, E. J., & Hintze, J. M. (1998). Using brief functional analysis to select interventions for oral reading. *Journal of Behavioral Education, 8,* 203–218.

Daly, E. J., III, Martens, B. K., Kilmer, A., & Massie, D. (1996). The effects of instructional match and content overlap on generalized reading performance. *Journal of Applied Behavior Analysis, 29,* 507–518.

Daly, E. J., III, & Murdoch, A. (2000). Direct observation in the assessment of academic skill problems. In E. S. Shapiro & T. R. Kratochwill (Eds.), *Behavioral assessment in schools: Theory, research, and clinical foundations* (2nd ed., pp. 46–77). New York: Guilford Press.

Daly, E. J., III, O'Connor, M. A., & Young, N. D. (2014). Best practices in oral reading fluency interventions. In A. Thomas & P. Harrison (Eds.), *Best practices in school psychology VI* (pp. 115–128).

Washington, DC: National Association of School Psychologists.

Daneman, M., & Carpenter, P. A. (1980). Individual differences in working memory and reading. *Journal of Verbal Learning and Verbal Behavior, 19,* 450–466.

Dawes, R. M. (1994). *House of cards: Psychology and psychotherapy built on myth.* New York: Free Press.

Dawes, R. M. (1995). Standards of practice. In S. C. Hayes, V. M. Follette, R. M. Dawes, & K. E. Grady (Eds.), *Scientific standards of psychological practice: Issues and recommendations* (pp. 49–66). Reno, NV: Context Press.

Deno, S. L., Fuchs, L. S., Marston, D., & Shin, J. (2001). Using curriculum-based measurement to establish growth standards for students with learning disabilities. *School Psychology Review, 30,* 507–524.

Denton, C., Anthony, J., Parker, R., & Hasbrouck, J. (2004). Effects of two tutoring programs on the English reading development of Spanish–English bilingual students. *Elementary School Journal, 104,* 289–305.

Derr-Minneci, T. F., & Shapiro, E. S. (1992). Validating curriculum-based measurement in reading from a behavioral perspective. *School Psychology Quarterly, 7,* 2–16.

Dowhower, S. L. (1989). Repeated readings: Research into practice. *The Reading Teacher, 42,* 502–507.

Duke, N. K., & Pearson, P. D. (2002). Effective practices for developing reading comprehension. In A. E. Farstrup & S. J. Samuels (Eds.), *What research has to say about reading instruction* (pp. 205–242). Newark, DE: International Reading Association.

Dunlap, G., DePerzcel, M., Clark, S., Wilson, D., Wright, S., & Gomez, A. (1994). Choice making to promote adaptive behavior for students with emotional and behavioral challenges. *Journal of Applied Behavior Analysis, 27,* 505–518.

Dunlap, G., Kern-Dunlap, L., Clarke, S., & Robbins, F. (1991). Functional assessment, curricular revision, and severe behavior problems. *Journal of Applied Behavior Analysis, 24,* 387–397.

Dunn, L. M., & Dunn, D. M. (2007). *Peabody Picture Vocabulary Test—Fourth Edition (PPVT-4).* Minneapolis, MN: Pearson Assessments.

Dyer, K., Dunlap, G., & Winterling, V. (1990). Effects of choice making on the serious problem behaviors of students with severe handicaps. *Journal of Applied Behavior Analysis, 23,* 515–524.

Echevarria, J., & Vogt, M. (2011). *Response to intervention (RTI) and English learners. Making it happen.* Boston: Pearson Education.

Eckert, T. L., Ardoin, S. P., Daly, E. J., III, & Martens, B. K. (2002). Improving oral reading fluency: An examination of the efficacy of combining skill-based and performance-based interventions. *Journal of Applied Behavior Analysis, 35,* 271–281.

Eckert, T. L., & Hintze, J. M. (2000). Behavioral conceptions and applications of acceptability: Issues related to service delivery and research methodology. *School Psychology Quarterly, 15,* 123–148.

Edmonds, M., & Briggs, K. L. (2003). The instructional content emphasis instrument: Observations of reading instruction. In S. Vaughn & K. L. Briggs (Eds.), *Reading in the classroom: Systems for the observation of teaching and learning* (pp. 31–52). Baltimore: Brookes.

Elley, W. B. (1989). Vocabulary acquisition from listening to stories. *Reading Research Quarterly, 24,* 174–187.

Engelmann, S., Granzin, A., & Severson, H. (1979). Diagnosing instruction. *Journal of Special Education, 13,* 355–363.

Englert, C. S., & Mariage, T. V. (1991). Making students partners in the comprehension process: Organizing the reading "POSSE." *Learning Disability Quarterly, 14,* 123–138.

Erchul, W. P., & Martens, B. K. (2010). *School consultation: Conceptual and empirical bases of practice* (3rd ed.). New York: Springer.

Fahmy, J. J., & Bilton, L. (1990, April). *Lecture comprehension and note-taking for L2 students.* Paper presented at the World Congress of Applied Linguistics, Thessalonica, Greece. (ERIC Document Reproduction Service No. ED323785)

Ferkis, M. A., Belfiore, P. J., & Skinner, C. H. (1997). The effects of response repetitions on sight word acquisition for students with mild disabilities. *Journal of Behavioral Education, 7,* 307–324.

Fien, H., Smith, J. L. M., Baker, S. K., Chaparro, E., Baker, D. L., & Preciado, J. A. (2011). Including English learners in a multitiered approach to early reading instruction and intervention. *Assessment for Effective Intervention, 36,* 143–157.

Fisher, D., Frey, N., & Rothenberg, C. (2011). Implementing RTI with English learners. Bloomington, IN: Solution Tree.

Fisher, W. W., Kelley, M. E., & Lomas, J. E. (2003). Visual aids and structured criteria for improving visual inspection and interpretation of single-case designs. *Journal of Applied Behavior Analysis, 36,* 387–406.

Fletcher, J. M., Lyon, G. R., Fuchs, L. S., & Barnes, M. A. (2007). *Learning disabilities: From identification to intervention.* New York: Guilford Press.

Forbes, B. E., Maurer, K. M., Taylor, E. P., & Skinner, C. H. (2013, February). *The effect of task instructions on reading fluency measures.* Paper presented at the annual meeting of the National Association of School Psychologists, Seattle, WA.

Fox, B., & Routh, D. K. (1975). Analyzing spoken language into words, syllables, and phonemes: A developmental study. *Journal of Psycholinguistic Research, 4,* 331–342.

Francis, D., Rivera, M., Lesaux, N., Kieffer, M., & Rivera, H. (2006). *Practical guidelines for the education of English language learners: Research-based recommendations for instruction and academic interventions.* Portsmouth, NH: RMC Research Corporation, Center on Instruction.

Francis, D. J., Santi, K. L., Barr, C., Fletcher, J. M., Varisco, A., & Foorman, B. R. (2008). Form effects on the estimation of students' oral reading fluency using DIBELS. *Journal of School Psychology, 46,* 315–342.

Freeland, J. T., Skinner, C. H., Jackson, B., McDaniel, C. E., & Smith, S. (2000). Measuring and increasing silent reading comprehension rates via repeated readings. *Psychology in the Schools, 37,* 415–429.

Freeman, T. J., & McLaughlin, T. F. (1984). Effects of a taped-words treatment procedure on learning disabled students' sight-word reading. *Learning Disability Quarterly, 7,* 49–54.

Friman, P. C., & Poling, A. (1995). Making life easier with effort: Basic findings and applied research on response effort. *Journal of Applied Behavior Analysis, 28,* 583–590.

Fuchs, D., Fuchs, L. S., & Vaughn, S. (Eds.). (2008). *Response to intervention: A framework for reading educators.* Newark, DE: International Reading Association.

Fuchs, L. S., & Deno, S. L. (1982). *Developing goals and objectives for educational programs* (Teaching guide). Minneapolis: Institute for Research in Learning Disabilities, University of Minnesota.

Fuchs, L. S., Deno, S. L., & Mirkin, P. K. (1984). The effects of frequent curriculum-based measurement and evaluation on pedagogy, student achievement, and student awareness of learning. *American Educational Research Journal, 21,* 449–460.

Fuchs, L. S., & Fuchs, D. (1986). Effects of systematic formative evaluation: A meta-analysis. *Exceptional Children, 53,* 199–208.

Fuchs, L. S., & Fuchs, D. (1998). Treatment validity: A unifying concept for reconceptualizing the identification of learning disabilities. *Learning Disabilities Research and Practice, 13,* 204–219.

Fuchs, L. S., Fuchs, D., Hamlett, C. L., Walz, L., & Germann, G. (1993). Formative evaluation of academic progress: How much growth can we expect? *School Psychology Review, 22,* 27–48.

Fuchs, L. S., Fuchs, D., Hosp, M. K., & Jenkins, J. R. (2001). Oral reading fluency as an indicator of reading competence: A theoretical, empirical, and historical analysis. *Scientific Studies of Reading, 5,* 239–256.

Fuchs, L. S., Fuchs, D., Mathes, P. G., & Simmons, D. C. (1997). Peer-assisted learning strategies: Making classrooms more responsive to academic diversity. *American Educational Research Journal, 34,* 174–206.

Fuchs, L. S., Fuchs, D., & Speece, D. L. (2002). Treatment validity as a unifying construct for identifying learning disabilities. *Learning Disabilities Quarterly, 25,* 33–45.

Fuchs, L. S., Fuchs, D., & Stecker, P. M. (1989). Effects of curriculum-based measurement on teachers' instructional planning. *Journal of Learning Disabilities, 22,* 51–59.

Gándara, P., Rumberger, R. W., Maxwell-Jolly, J., & Callahan, R. M. (2003). English learners in California schools: Unequal resources, unequal outcomes. *Education Policy Analysis Archives, 11.* Retrieved from *http://epaa.asu.edu/epaa/v11n36.*

Garner, R., Brown, R., Sanders, S., & Menke, D. (1992). "Seductive details" and learning from text. In K. A. Renninger, S. Hidi, & A. Krapp (Eds.), *The role of interest in learning and development* (pp. 239–254). Hillsdale, NJ: Erlbaum.

Gersten, R., Baker, S. K., Shanahan, T., Linan-Thompson, S., Collins, P., & Scarcella, R. (2007). *Effective literacy and English language instruction for English learners in the elementary grades: A practice guide* (NCEE 2007-4011). Washington, DC: National Center for Education Evaluation and Regional Assistance, Institute of Education Sciences, U.S. Department of Education.

Gersten, R., Compton, D., Connor, C. M., Dimino, J., Santoro, L., Linan-Thompson, S., & Tilly, W. D. (2008). *Assisting students struggling with reading: Response to intervention and multi-tier intervention for reading in the primary grades. A practice guide* (NCEE 2009-4045). Washington, DC: National Center for Education Evaluation and Regional Assistance, Institute of Education Sciences, U.S. Department of Education. Retrieved from *http://ies.ed.gov/ncee/wwc/publications/practice-guides.*

Gettinger, M. (1995). Increasing academic learning time. In A. Thomas & J. Grimes (Eds.), *Best practices in school psychology III* (pp. 943–954). Washington, DC: National Association of School Psychologists.

Geva, E. (2000). Issues in the assessment of reading disabilities in L2 children. *Dyslexia, 6,* 13–28.

Geva, E., Yaghoub-Zadeh, Z., & Schuster, B. (2000). Understanding individual differences in word recognition skills of ESL children. *Annals of Dyslexia, 50,* 121–154.

Gickling, E. E., & Rosenfield, S. (1995). Best practices in curriculum-based assessment. In A. Thomas & J. Grimes (Eds.), *Best practices in school psychology III* (pp. 587–596). Washington, DC: National Association of School Psychologists.

Giesen, C., & Peeck, J. (1984). The effect of imagery instruction on reading and retaining of literary text. *Journal of Mental Imagery, 8*(2), 79–90.

Gilger, J. W., Pennington, B. F., & DeFries, J. C. (1991). Risk for reading disability as a function of family history in three family studies. *Reading and Writing: An Interdisciplinary Journal, 3,* 205–217.

Gilovich, T., Griffin, D., & Kahneman, D. (Eds.). (2002). *Heuristics and biases: The psychology of intuitive judgment.* New York: Cambridge University Press.

Good, R. H., & Kaminski, R. A. (Eds.). (2001). *Dynamic indicators of basic early literacy skills* (5th ed.). Eugene, OR: Institute for the Development of Educational Achievement. Available at *http://dibels.uoregon.edu.*

Good, R. H., Kaminski, R. A., & Smith, S. (2002). Word use fluency. In R. H. Good & R. A. Kaminski (Eds.), *Dynamic indicators of basic early literacy skills* (6th ed.). Eugene, OR: Institute for the Development of Educational Achievement. Available at *http://dibels.uoregon.edu.*

Good, R. H., III, & Shinn, M. R. (1990). Forecasting accuracy of slope estimates for reading curriculum-based measurement: Empirical evidence. *Behavioral Assessment, 12,* 179–193.

Graham, L., & Wong, B. Y. L. (1993). Comparing two modes of teaching a question–answering strategy for enhancing reading comprehension: Didactic and self-instructional training. *Journal of Learning Disabilities, 26,* 270–279.

Granowsky, A. (2000). Dinosaur fossils. In SRA/McGraw-Hill, *Open court reading book 1 grade 2.* Columbus, OH: McGraw-Hill.

Graves, M. F. (1986). Vocabulary learning and instruction. In E. Z. Rothkopf & L. C. Ehri (Eds.), *Review of research in education* (Vol. 13, pp. 49–89). Washington, DC: American Educational Research Association.

Gravois, T. A., & Gickling, E. E. (2002). Best practices in curriculum-based assessment. In A. Thomas & J. Grimes (Eds.), *Best practices in school psychology* (4th ed., pp. 885–898). Bethesda, MD: National Association of School Psychologists.

Greenwood, C. R. (1991a). Classwide peer tutoring: Longitudinal effects on the reading, language, and mathematics achievement of at-risk students. *Reading, Writing, and Learning Disabilities, 7,* 105–123.

Greenwood, C. R. (1991b). Longitudinal analysis of time, engagement, and achievement in at-risk versus non-risk students. *Exceptional Children, 57,* 521–535.

Greenwood, C. R., Delquadri, J. C., & Carta, J. J. (1997). *Together we can!: Classwide peer tutoring to improve basic academic skills.* Longmont, CO: Sopris West.

Greenwood, C. R., Delquadri, J., & Hall, R. V. (1984). Opportunity to respond and student academic performance. In W. L. Heward, T. E. Heron, J. Trap-Porter, & D. S. Hill (Eds.), *Focus on behavior analysis in education* (pp. 58–88). Columbus, OH: Merrill.

Greenwood, C. R., Terry, B., Marquis, J., & Walker, D. (1994). Confirming a performance-based instructional model. *School Psychology Review, 23,* 652–668.

Gresham, F. M. (2001). *Responsiveness to intervention: An alternative approach to the identification of learning disabilities.* Paper prepared for the OSEP Learning Disabilities Initiative, Office of Special Education Program, U.S. Department of Education, Washington, DC.

Gresham, F. M., & Lopez, M. F. (1996). Social validation: A unifying concept for school-based consultation research and practice. *School Psychology Quarterly, 11,* 204–227.

Grossen, B., & Carnine, D. (1991). Strategies for maximizing reading success in the regular classroom. In G. Stoner, M. R. Shinn, & H. M. Walker (Eds.), *Interventions for achievement and behavior problems* (pp. 333–356). Silver Spring, MD: National Association of School Psychologists.

Gunn, B. K., Simmons, D. C., & Kame'enui, E. J. (1995). *Emergent literacy: Synthesis of the research.* Retrieved from *http://idea.uoregon.edu/~ncite/documents/techrep/tech19.html.*

Guthrie, J. T., Wigfield, A., & Perencevich, K. C. (2004). *Motivating reading comprehension: Concept-oriented reading instruction.* Mahwah, NJ: Erlbaum.

Hale, A. D., Skinner, C. H., Wilhoit, B., Ciancio, D., & Morrow, J. A. (2012, November). Variance in broad reading accounted for by measures of reading speed embedded within MAZE and comprehension rate measures. *Journal of Psycho-Educational Assessment, 30,* 539–554.

Hale, A. D., Skinner, C. H., Winn, B. D., Oliver, R., Allin, J. D., & Molloy, C. C. M. (2005). An investigation of listening and listening-while-reading accommodations on reading comprehension levels and rates in students with emotional disorders. *Psychology in the Schools, 42,* 39–52.

Hansen, J. (1981). The effects of inference training and practice on young children's comprehension. *Reading Research Quarterly, 16,* 391–417.

Hargis, C. H. (1995). *Curriculum-based assessment: A primer* (2nd ed.). Springfield, IL: Charles C Thomas.

Haring, N. G., Lovitt, T. C., Eaton, M. D., & Hansen, C. L. (1978). *The fourth R: Research in the classroom.* Columbus, OH: Merrill.

Harper, G. L., Maheady, L., Mallette, B., & Karnes, M. (1999). Peer tutoring and the minority child with disabilities. *Preventing School Failure, 43,* 45–51.

Hart, B., & Risley, T. R. (1995). *Meaningful differences in the everyday experience of young American children.* Baltimore: Brookes.

Hasbrouck, J. E., & Tindal, G. (1992). Curriculum-based oral reading fluency norms for students in grades 2 through 5. *Teaching Exceptional Children, 24,* 41–44.

Hawkins, J., Skinner, C. H., & Oliver, R. (2005). The effects of task demands and additive interspersal ratios on fifth-grade students' mathematics accuracy. *School Psychology Review, 34,* 543–555.

Hayes, D. P., & Ahrens, M. G. (1988). Vocabulary simplifications for children: A special case of "motherese"? *Journal of Child Language, 15,* 395–410.

Hiebert, E. H. (2005). The effects of text difficulty on second graders' fluency development. *Reading Psychology, 26,* 183–209.

Hiebert, E. H., & Fisher, C. W. (2005). A review of the National Reading Panel's studies on fluency: On the role of text. *Elementary School Journal, 105,* 443–460.

Hilton-Mounger, A. N., Hopkins, M. B., Skinner, C. H., & McCane-Bowling, S. (2011). Enhancing sight-word reading in second-grade students using a computer-based sight-word reading system. *Journal of Evidence-Based Practices in the Schools, 12,* 205–218.

Hintze, J. M., Callahan, J. E., III, Matthews, W. J., Williams, S. A. S., & Tobin, K. G. (2002). Oral reading fluency and prediction of reading comprehension in African American and Caucasian elementary school children. *School Psychology Review, 31,* 540–553.

Hintze, J. M., & Silberglitt, B. (2005). A longitudinal examination of the diagnostic accuracy and predictive validity of R-CBM and high-stakes testing. *School Psychology Review, 34,* 372–386.

Hopkins, M. B., Hilton, A. N., & Skinner, C. H. (2011). Implementation guidelines: How to design a computer-based sight-word reading system using

Microsoft PowerPoint. *Journal of Evidence-Based Practices in the Schools, 12*, 219–222.

Hoskisson, K., & Krohm, B. (1974). Reading by immersion: Assisted reading. *Elementary English, 51*, 832–836.

Howell, K. W., & Kelly, B. (2002). Curriculum clarification, lesson design, and delivery. In K. L. Lane, F. M. Gresham, & T. E. O'Shaughnessy (Eds.), *Interventions for children with or at risk for emotional and behavioral disorders* (pp. 57–73). Boston: Allyn & Bacon.

Howell, K. W., & Nolet, V. (2000). *Curriculum-based evaluation: Teaching and decision making* (3rd ed.). Belmont, CA: Wadsworth.

Idol-Maestas, L. (1985). Getting ready to read: Guided probing for poor comprehenders. *Learning Disability Quarterly, 8*, 243–254.

Individuals with Disabilities Education Improvement Act of 2004, P.L. 108–446, 20 U.S.C. § 1400 et seq.

Jackson, B. J., Freeland, J. T., & Skinner, C. H. (2000, November). *Using reading previewing to improve reading comprehension rates for secondary students with reading deficits.* Paper presented at the annual meeting of the Mid-South Educational Research Association, Bowling Green, KY.

Jacob, S., Decker, D. D., & Hartshorne, T. (2011). *Ethics and law for school psychologists* (6th ed.). New York: Wiley.

Joseph, L., Eveleigh, E., Konrad, M., Neef, N., & Volpe, R. (2012). Comparison of the efficiency of two flashcard drill methods on children's reading performance. *Journal of Applied School Psychology, 28*, 317–337.

Joseph, L. M., & Nist, L. M. (2006). Comparing the effects of unknown–known ratios on word reading learning versus learning rates. *Journal of Behavioral Education, 15*, 69–79.

Joshi, R. M., & Aaron, P. G. (2011). Assessment of reading problems among ELLs based on the component model. In A. Durgunoglu & C. Goldenberg (Eds.), *Language and literacy development in bilingual settings* (pp. 304–331). New York: Guilford Press.

Juel, C. (1991). Beginning reading. In R. Barr, M. L. Kamil, P. B. Mosenthal, & P. D. Pearson (Eds.), *Handbook of reading research* (pp. 759–788). New York: Longman.

Kahneman, D. (2003). A perspective on judgment and choice: Mapping bounded reality. *American Psychologist, 58*, 697–720.

Kahneman, D., & Klein, G. (2009). Conditions for intuitive expertise: A failure to disagree. *American Psychologist, 64*, 515–526.

Kame'enui, E. J., & Simmons, D. C. (2001). Introduc-

tion to this special issue: The DNA of reading fluency. *Scientific Studies of Reading, 5*, 203–210.

Kaminski, R. A., & Good, R. H. (1996). Toward a technology for assessing basic early literacy skills. *School Psychology Review, 25*, 215–227.

Kamps, D. M., Barbetta, P. M., Leonard, B. R., & Delquadri, J. (1994). Classwide peer tutoring: An integration strategy to improve reading skills and promote peer interactions among students with autism and general education peers. *Journal of Applied Behavior Analysis, 27*, 49–61.

Kavale, A. K., & Forness, S. R. (1999). Effectiveness of special education. In C. R. Reynolds & T. B. Gutkin (Eds.), *The handbook of school psychology* (3rd ed., pp. 984–1024). New York: Wiley.

Kinder, D., & Carnine, D. (1991). Direct instruction: What it is and what it is becoming. *Journal of Behavioral Education, 1*, 193–213.

Kodak, T., Fisher, W. W., Clements, A., & Bouxsein, K. J. (2011). Effects of computer-assisted instruction on correct responding and procedural integrity during early intensive behavioral intervention. *Research in Autism Spectrum Disorders, 5*, 640–647.

Kranzler, J. H., Brownell, M. T., & Miller, M. D. (1998). The construct validity of curriculum-based measurement of reading: An empirical test of a plausible rival hypothesis. *Journal of School Psychology, 36*, 399–415.

Kratochwill, T. R., & Bergan, J. R. (1990). *Behavioral consultation in applied settings: An individual guide.* New York: Plenum Press.

Kratochwill, T. R., Elliott, S. N., & Busse, R. T. (1995). Behavior consultation: A five-year evaluation of consultant and client outcomes. *School Psychology Quarterly, 10*, 87–117.

Kucan, L. (2012). What is most important to know about vocabulary? *The Reading Teacher, 65*(6), 360–366.

Kupzyk, S., Daly, E. J., III, & Andersen, M. N. (2011). A comparison of two flashcard methods for improving sight-word reading. *Journal of Applied Behavior Analysis, 44*, 781–792.

Kupzyk, S., Daly, E. J., III, Ihlo, T., & Young, N. D. (2012). Modifying instruction within tiers in multitiered intervention programs. *Psychology in the Schools, 49*, 219–230.

LaBerge, D., & Samuels, S. J. (1974). Toward a theory of automatic information processing in reading. *Cognitive Psychology, 6*, 293–323.

Lane, K. L., Gresham, F. M., & O'Shaughnessy T. E. (Eds.). (2002). *Interventions for children with or at risk for emotional and behavioral disorders.* Boston: Allyn & Bacon.

Lawrence, J. F., White, C., & Snow, C. (2010). The

words students need. *Educational Leadership, 68*(2), 23–26.

Leal, D. (1993). The power of literacy peer-group discussions. How children collaboratively negotiate meaning. *The Reading Teacher, 47,* 114–121.

Lentz, F. E., Allen, S. J., & Ehrhardt, K. E. (1996). The conceptual elements of strong interventions in school settings. *School Psychology Quarterly, 11,* 118–136.

Lesaux, N., & Geva, E. (2006). Synthesis: Development of literacy in language-minority students. In D. August & T. Shanahan (Eds.), *Developing literacy in second-language learners: Report of the national literacy panel on language-minority children and youth.* Mahwah, NJ: Erlbaum.

Lesaux, N. K., Kieffer, M. J., & Faller, S. E. (2010). The effectiveness and ease of implementation of an academic vocabulary intervention for linguistically diverse students in urban middle schools. *Reading Research Quarterly, 45*(2), 196–228.

Lesaux, N. K., & Siegel, L. S. (2003). The development of reading in children who speak English as a second language (ESL). *Developmental Psychology, 39*(6), 1005–1019.

Lesgold, A. M., & Perfetti, C. A. (1978). Interactive processes in reading comprehension. *Discourse Processes, 1,* 323–336.

Lesgold, A. M., & Resnick, L. (1982). How reading difficulties develop: Perspectives from a longitudinal study. In J. Das, R. Mulcahy, & A. Wall (Eds.), *Theory and research in learning disabilities* (pp. 155–187). New York: Plenum Press.

Lewis, T. J., & Sugai, G. (1999). Effective behavior support: A systems approach to proactive school-wide management. *Effective School Practices, 17,* 47–53.

Liberman, I. Y., Shankweiler, D., Fischer, F. W., & Carter, B. (1974). Explicit syllable and phoneme segmentation in the young child. *Journal of Experimental Child Psychology, 18,* 201–212.

Limbos, M. M., & Geva, E. (2001). Accuracy of teacher assessments of second-language students at risk for reading disability. *Journal of Learning Disabilities, 34,* 136–151.

Linan-Thompson, S., & Vaughn, S. (2010). Evidence-based reading instruction: Developing and implementing reading programs at the core, supplemental, and intervention levels. In G. G. Peacock, R. A. Ervin, E. J. Daly, III, & K. W. Merrell (Eds.), *Practical handbook of school psychology: Effective practices for the 21st century* (pp. 274–286). New York: Guilford Press.

Lindamood, P., & Lindamood, P. (1998). *The Lindamood phoneme sequencing program for reading, spelling, and speech.* Austin, TX: PRO-ED.

Lovitt, T., Rudsit, J., Jenkins, J., Pious, C., & Benedetti, D. (1986). Adapting science materials for regular and learning disabled seventh graders. *Remedial and Special Education, 7*(1), 31–39.

Lyon, G. R. (1995). Toward a definition of dyslexia. *Annals of Dyslexia, 45,* 3–27.

Mace, F. C., Neef, N. A., Shade, D., & Mauro, B. C. (1996). Effects of problem difficulty and reinforcer quality on time allocated to concurrent arithmetic problems. *Journal of Applied Behavior Analysis, 29,* 11–24.

Macmann, G. M., & Barnett, D. W. (1999). Diagnostic decision making in school psychology: Understanding and coping with uncertainty. In C. R. Reynolds & T. Gutkin (Eds.), *The handbook of school psychology* (3rd ed., pp. 519–548). New York: Wiley.

Macon, L. (Ed.). (1991). *Learning disabilities in the high school: A methods booklet for secondary special subject teachers.* Pittsburgh: Learning Disabilities Association of America.

Mandell, N., & Malone, B. (2007). Thinking like a historian: Rethinking history instruction. Madison: Wisconsin Historical Society Press.

Marinak, B., & Gambrell, L. B. (2010). Reading motivation: Exploring the elementary gender gap. *Literacy Research and Instruction, 49,* 129–141.

Marshall, J. (1972). *George and Martha.* Boston: Houghton Mifflin.

Marston, D., & Tindal, G. (1995). Performance monitoring. In A. Thomas & J. Grimes (Eds.), *Best practices in school psychology III* (pp. 597–608). Washington, DC: National Association of School Psychologists.

Marston, D. B. (1989). A curriculum-based measurement approach to assessing academic performance: What it is and why do it. In M. R. Shinn (Ed.), *Curriculum-based measurement: Assessing special children* (pp. 18–78). New York: Guilford Press.

Marston, D. B., & Magnusson, D. (1988). Curriculum-based measurement: District level implementation. In J. L. Graden, J. E. Zins, & M. J. Curtis (Eds.), *Alternative educational delivery systems: Enhancing options for all students* (pp. 137–172). Washington, DC: National Association of School Psychologists.

Martens, B. K., Witt, J. C., Elliott, S. N., & Darveaux, D. (1985). Teacher judgments concerning the acceptability of school-based interventions. *Professional Psychology: Research and Practice, 16,* 191–198.

Martin, J. J., Skinner, C. H., & Neddenriep, C. E. (2001). Extending research on the interspersal procedure to perceptions of continuous reading assignments: Applied and theoretical implications of a failure to replicate. *Psychology in the Schools, 38*, 391–400.

Martiniello, M. (2008). Language and the performance of English-language learners in math word problems. *Harvard Educational Review, 78*, 333–368.

Marulis, L. M., & Neuman, S. B. (2010). *The effects of vocabulary intervention on young children's word learning: A meta-analysis. 80*(3), 300–335.

Mastropieri, M. G., Scruggs, T. E., Hamilton, S. L., Wolfe, S., Whedon, C., & Canevaro, A. (1996). Promoting thinking skills of students with learning disabilities: Effects on recall and comprehension of expository prose. *Exceptionality, 6*, 1–11.

McBride-Chang, C. (1995). What is phonological awareness? *Journal of Educational Psychology, 87*, 179–192.

McCallum, E., Evans, S., Friedrich, K., & Long, K. (2011, February). *The spelling intervention: Improving spelling using taped-problems procedures.* Participant Information Exchange (PIE) session presented at the annual meeting of the National Association of School Psychologists, San Francisco, CA.

McCallum, E., Skinner, C. H., & Hutchins, H. (2004). The taped-problems intervention: Increasing division fact fluency using a low-tech self-managed time-delay intervention. *Journal of Applied School Psychology, 20*, 129–147.

McCurdy, M., Skinner, C. H., Grantham, K., Watson, T. S., & Hindman, P. M. (2001). Increasing on-task behavior in an elementary student during mathematics seat-work by interspersing additional brief problems. *School Psychology Review, 30*, 23–32.

McDaniel, C. E., Watson, T. S., Freeland, J. T., Smith, S. L., Jackson, B., & Skinner, C. H. (2001, May). *Comparing silent repeated reading and teacher previewing using silent reading comprehension rate.* Paper presented at the annual convention of the Association for Applied Behavior Analysis: New Orleans, LA.

McDougal, J. L., Clonan, S. M., & Martens, B. K. (2000). Using organized change procedures to promote the acceptability of prereferral intervention services: The school-based intervention team project. *School Psychology Quarterly, 15*, 149–171.

McGlinchey, M. T., & Hixson, M. D. (2004). Using curriculum-based measurement to predict performance on state assessments in reading. *School Psychology Review, 33*, 193–203.

McKenna, M. C., Kear, D. J., & Ellsworth, R. A. (1995). Children's attitudes toward rewarding: A national survey. *Reading Research Quarterly, 30*, 934–955.

McKeown, M. (1985). The acquisition of word meaning from context by children of high and low ability. *Reading Research Quarterly, 20*, 482–496.

McLean, M., Bryant, P., & Bradley, L. (1987). Rhymes, nursery rhymes, and reading in early childhood. *Merrill-Palmer Quarterly, 33*, 255–281.

Meehl, P., & Rosen, A. (1955). Antecedent probability and the efficiency of psychometric signs, patterns, and cutting scores. *Psychological Bulletin, 52*, 194–216.

Meehl, P. E. (1954). *Clinical versus statistical prediction.* Minneapolis: University of Minnesota Press.

Messick, S. (1995). Validity of psychological assessment: Validation of inferences from persons' responses and performance as scientific inquiry into score meaning. *American Psychologist, 50*, 741–749.

Methe, S. A., & Hintze, J. M. (2003). Evaluating teacher modeling as a strategy to increase student reading behavior. *School Psychology Review, 32*, 617–623.

Miller, W. H. (1982). *Reading correction kit* (2nd ed). New York: Center of Applied Research in Education.

Moats, L. (1999). *Teaching reading is rocket science.* Washington, DC: American Federation of Teachers.

Myerson, J., & Hale, S. (1984). Practical implications of the matching law. *Journal of Applied Behavior Analysis, 17*, 367–380.

Nagy, W., & Townsend, D. (2012). Words as tools: Learning academic vocabulary as language acquisition. *Reading Research Quarterly, 47*, 91–108.

Nagy, W. E. (2007). Metalinguistic awareness and the vocabulary-comprehension connection. In R. K. Wagner, A. E. Muse, & K. R. Tannenbaum (Eds.), *Vocabulary acquisition implications for reading comprehension* (pp. 52–77). New York: Guilford Press.

Nagy, W. E., Anderson, R. C., & Herman, P. A. (1987). Learning word meanings from context during normal reading. *American Educational Research Journal, 24*, 237–270.

Nagy, W. E., & Scott, J. A. (2000). Vocabulary processes. In M. Kamil, P. B. Mosenthal, P. D. Pearson, & R. Barr (Eds.), *Handbook of reading research* (Vol. 3, pp. 269–284). Mahwah, NJ: Erlbaum.

National Center for Education Statistics. (2011). *The nation's report card: Reading 2011* (NCES 2012-457). Washington, DC: Institute of Education Sciences, U.S. Department of Education.

National Center for Education Statistics. (2013). *A first look: 2013 mathematics and reading.* Washington, DC: U.S. Department of Education. Available at *https://nces.ed.gov/pubsearch/pubsinfo. asp?pubid=2014451.*

National Reading Panel. (2000). *Teaching children to*

read: An evidence-based assessment of the scientific research literature on reading and its implications for reading instruction. Washington, DC: National Institute of Child Health and Human Development.

National Research Council. (1998). *Preventing reading difficulties in young children*. Washington, DC: National Academy Press.

Neef, N. A., Mace, F. C., Shea, M. C., & Shade, D. (1992). Effects of reinforcer rate and reinforcer quality on time allocation: Extension of matching theory to educational settings. *Journal of Applied Behavior Analysis, 25*, 691–699.

Neef, N. A., Shade, D., & Miller, M. S. (1994). Assessing influential dimensions of reinforcers on choice in students with serious emotional disturbance. *Journal of Applied Behavior Analysis, 27*, 575–583.

Nelson, J. R., Smith, D. J., & Dodd, J. M. (1992). The effects of a summary skills strategy to students identified as learning disabled on their comprehension of science text. *Education and Treatment of Children, 15*, 228–243.

Newby, R. F., Caldwell, J., & Recht, D. R. (1989). Improving the reading comprehension of children with dysphonetic and dyseidetic dyslexia using story grammar. *Journal of Learning Disabilities, 22*, 373–380.

Noell, G. H. (2008). Research examining the relationships among consultation process, treatment integrity, and outcomes. In W. P. Erchul & S. M. Sheridan (Eds.), *Handbook of research in school consultation* (pp. 323–341). Mahwah, NJ: Erlbaum.

Notari-Syverson, A., O'Connor, R. E., & Vadasy, P. F. (1998). *Ladders to literacy: A preschool activity book*. Baltimore: Brookes.

O'Connor, R. E., Notari-Syverson, A., & Vadasy, P. F. (1998). *Ladders to literacy: A kindergarten activity book*. Baltimore: Brookes.

Open Court Reading. (1995). Collections for young scholars. Chicago: SRA/McGraw-Hill.

O'Shea, L. J., Munson, S. M., & O'Shea, D. J. (1984). Error correction in oral reading: Evaluating the effectiveness of three procedures. *Education and Treatment of Children, 7*, 203–214.

Otis-Wilborn, A. K. (1984). *The evaluation of the effects of four reading instructional procedures on the achievement of hearing-impaired children*. Unpublished doctoral dissertation, University of Kansas, Lawrence.

Ouellette, G. P. (2006). What's meaning got to do with it: The role of vocabulary in word reading and reading comprehension. *Journal of Educational Psychology, 98*(3), 554–566.

Palincsar, A., & Brown, A. (1984). Reciprocal teaching of comprehension-fostering and comprehension-monitoring activities. *Cognition and Instruction, 1*, 117–175.

Paris, S. G., Cross, D. R., & Lipson, M. Y. (1984). Informed strategies for learning: A program to improve children's reading awareness and comprehension. *Journal of Educational Psychology, 76*(6), 1239–1252.

Parker, S. M., Quigely, M. C., & Reilly, J. B. (1999). *Improving student reading comprehension through the use of literacy circles*. Master's research project, Saint Xavier University, Chicago. (ERIC Document Reproduction No. ED433504)

Parrish, T. B., Merickel, A., Perez, M., Linquanti, R., Socias, M., Spain, A., et al. (2006, January). *Effects of the implementation of Proposition 227 on the education of English learners, K–12: Findings from a five-year evaluation*. Final Report for AB 56 and AB 1116. Washington, DC: American Institutes for Research and WestEd.

Pearson, P. D., Hiebert, E. H., & Kamil, M. L. (2007). Theory and research into practice: Vocabulary assessment: What we know and what we need to learn. *Reading Research Quarterly, 42*(2), 282–296.

Pearson, P. D., & Johnson, D. D. (1978). *Teaching reading comprehension*. New York: Holt, Rinehart and Winston.

Penno, J. F., Wilkinson, I. A. G., & Moore, D. W. (2002). Vocabulary acquisition from teacher explanation and repeated listening to stories: Do they overcome the Matthew Effect? *Journal of Educational Psychology, 94*(1), 23–33.

Perfetti, C. (1977). Language comprehension and fast decoding: Some psycholinguistic prerequisites for skilled reading comprehension. In J. Guthrie (Ed.), *Cognition, curriculum, and comprehension* (pp. 20–41). Newark, DE: International Reading Association.

Poncy, B. C., McCallum, E., & Skinner, C. H. (2011). Advocating for effective instruction: School psychologists as instructional leaders. In T. M. Lionetti, E. Snyder, & R. W. Christner (Eds.), *A practical guide to developing competencies in school psychology* (pp. 155–173). New York: Springer.

Poncy, B. C., Skinner, C. H., & Axtell, P. K. (2005). An investigation of the reliability and standard error of measurement of words read correctly per minute using curriculum-based measurement. *Journal of Psychoeducational Assessment, 23*, 326–338.

Popkin, J., & Skinner, C. H. (2003). Enhancing academic performance in a classroom serving students with serious emotional disturbance: Interdependent group contingencies with randomly selected components. *School Psychology Review, 32,* 282–295.

Pratt, A. C., & Brady, S. (1988). Relation of phonological awareness to reading disability in children and adults. *Journal of Educational Psychology, 80,* 319–323.

President's Commission on Excellence in Special Education. (2002). *A new era: Revitalizing special education for children and their families.* Available at *www.ed.gov/inits/commissionsboards/whspecialeducation.*

Quiroga, T., Lemos-Britton, Z., Mostafapour, E., Abbott, R. D., & Berninger, V. W. (2002). Phonological awareness and beginning reading in Spanish-speaking ESL first graders: Research into practice. *Journal of School Psychology, 40*(1), 85–111.

RAND Reading Study Group. (2002). Executive summary. In C. E. Snow (Ed.), *Toward an R&D program in reading comprehension* (pp. xi–xxi). Santa Monica, CA: RAND Corporation. Available at *www.rand.org/pubs/monograph_reports/2005/MR1465.pdf.*

Raphael, T. (1984). Teaching learners about sources of information for answering comprehension questions. *Journal of Reading, 27,* 303–311.

Raphael, T. (1986). Teaching question/answer relationship, revisited. *The Reading Teacher, 39,* 516–522.

Rashotte, C. A., & Torgesen, J. K. (1985). Repeated reading and reading fluency in learning-disabled children. *Reading Research Quarterly, 20,* 180–188.

Renaissance Learning. (2002). *Accelerated reading: Learning information system for reading and literacy systems.* Wisconsin Rapids, WI: Author.

Reschly, A. L., Busch, T. W., Betts, J., Deno, S. L., & Long, J. D. (2009). Curriculum-based measurement oral reading as an indicator of reading achievement: A meta-analysis of the correlational evidence. *Journal of School Psychology, 47,* 427–469.

Reschly, D. J., & Bergstrom, M. K. (2009). Response to intervention. In T. B. Gutkin & C. R. Reynolds (Eds.), *Handbook of school psychology* (4th ed., pp. 434–460). New York: Wiley.

Rhodes, R. L., Ochoa, S. H., & Ortiz, S. O. (2005). *Assessing culturally and linguistically diverse students: A practical guide.* New York: Guilford Press.

Riley-Tillman, T. C., & Burns, M. K. (2009). *Evaluating educational interventions: Single-case design for measuring response to intervention.* New York: Guilford Press.

Robbins, C., & Ehri, L. C. (1994). Reading storybooks to kindergartners helps them learn new vocabulary words. *Journal of Educational Psychology, 86,* 54–64.

Robinson, D. H., & Skinner, C. H. (1996). Why graphic organizers facilitate search processes: Fewer words of efficient indexing? *Contemporary Educational Psychology, 21,* 166–180.

Robinson, F. P. (1946). *Effective study.* New York: Harper & Brothers.

Rose, T. L. (1984a). Effects of previewing on the oral reading of mainstreamed behaviorally disordered students. *Behavioral Disorders, 10,* 33–39.

Rose, T. L. (1984b). The effects of previewing on retarded learners' oral reading. *Education and Treatment of the Mentally Retarded, 19,* 49–52.

Rose, T. L. (1984c). The effects of two prepractice procedures on oral reading. *Journal of Learning Disabilities, 17,* 544–548.

Rosenshine, B. V. (1980). How time is spent in elementary classrooms. In C. Denham & A. Lieberman (Eds.), *Time to learn* (pp. 107–126). Washington, DC: U.S. Department of Education.

Rousseau, M. K., & Tam, B. K. (1991). The efficacy of previewing and discussion of key words on the oral reading proficiency of bilingual learners with speech and language impairments. *Education and Treatment of Children, 14,* 199–209.

Rumberger, R., & Anguiano, B. (2004). *Understanding and addressing the California Latino achievement gap in early elementary school* (Working paper). Retrieved from *http://lmri.ucsb.edu.*

Saenz, L. M., Fuchs, L. S., & Fuchs, D. (2005). Peer-assisted learning strategies for English language learners with learning disabilities. *Exceptional Children, 71,* 231–247.

Samuels, S. J. (1979). The method of repeated readings. *Reading Teacher, 32,* 403–408.

Samuels, S. J. (1988). Decoding and automaticity: Helping poor readers become automatic at word recognition. *The Reading Teacher, 41,* 756–760.

Scarborough, H. S. (1998). Predicting the future achievement of second graders with reading disabilities: Contributions of phonemic awareness, verbal memory, rapid naming, and IQ. *Annals of Dyslexia, 48*(1), 115–136.

Schleppegrell, M. J. (2001). Linguistic features of the language of schooling. *Linguistics and Education, 12*(4), 431–459.

Schleppegrell, M. J. (2004). *The language of schooling: A functional linguistics perspective.* Mahwah, NJ: Erlbaum.

Schumaker, J., Deshler, D., Alley, G., Warner, M., & Denton, P. (1982). Multipass: A learning strategy for improving reading comprehension. *Learning Disability Quarterly, 5,* 295–304.

Senechal, M., & Cornell, E. H. (1993). Vocabulary acquisition through shared reading experiences. *Reading Research Quarterly, 28,* 360–374.

Shanahan, T., Callison, K., Carriere, C., Duke, N. K., Pearson, P. D., Schatschneider, C., et al. (2010). Improving reading comprehension in kindergarten through 3rd grade: A practice guide (NCEE 2010–4038). Washington, DC: National Center for Education Evaluation and Regional Assistance, Institute of Education Sciences, U.S. Department of Education. Retrieved from *whatworks.ed.gov/ publications/practiceguides*.

Shapiro, E. S. (1996a). *Academic skills problems: Direct assessment and intervention* (2nd ed.). New York: Guilford Press.

Shapiro, E. S. (1996b). *Academic skills problems workbook*. New York: Guilford Press.

Shapiro, E. S. (2004). *Academic skills problems: Direct assessment and intervention* (3rd ed.). New York: Guilford Press.

Shapiro, E. S., & McCurdy, B. L. (1989). Direct and generalized effects of a taped-words treatment on reading proficiency. *Exceptional Children, 55,* 321–325.

Sharp, S., & Skinner, C. H. (2004). Using interdependent group contingencies with randomly selected criteria and paired reading to enhance class-wide reading performance. *Journal of Applied School Psychology, 20,* 29–45.

Shaywitz, S. (2003). *Overcoming dyslexia: A new and complete science-based program for reading problems at any level*. New York: Knopf.

Shefelbine, J. (1990). Student factors related to variability in learning word meanings from context. *Journal of Reading Behavior, 22,* 71–97.

Shinn, M. R. (Ed.). (1989). *Curriculum-based measurement: Assessing special children*. New York: Guilford Press.

Shinn, M. R., Good, R. H., III, Knutson, N., Tilly, W. D., III, & Collins, V. L. (1992). Curriculum-based measurement of oral reading fluency: A confirmatory analysis of its relation to reading. *School Psychology Review, 21,* 459–479.

Shinn, M. R., & Hubbard, D. (1992). Curriculum-based measurement and problem-solving assessment: Basic procedures and outcomes. *Focus on Exceptional Children, 24,* 1–20.

Short, D., & Fitzsimmons, S. (2007). *Double the work: Challenges and solutions to acquiring language and academic literacy for adolescent English language learners—a report to Carnegie Corporation of New York*. Washington, DC: Alliance for Excellent Education.

Sindelar, P. T., Monda, L. E., & O'Shea, L. J. (1990). Effects of repeated readings on instructional- and masterly-level readers. *Journal of Educational Research, 83,* 220–226.

Skinner, C. H. (1998). Preventing academic skills deficits. In T. S. Watson & F. M. Gresham (Eds.), *Handbook of child behavior therapy* (pp. 61–82). New York: Plenum Press.

Skinner, C. H. (1999). Preventing academic skills deficits. In T. S. Watson & F. Gresham (Eds.), *Handbook of child behavior therapy* (pp. 61–83). New York: Plenum.

Skinner, C. H. (2002). An empirical analysis of interspersal research: Evidence, implications, and applications of the discrete task completion hypothesis. *Journal of School Psychology, 40,* 347–368.

Skinner, C. H., Adamson, K. L., Woodward, J. R., Jackson, R. R., Atchison, L. A., & Mims, J. W. (1993). The effects of models' rates of reading on students' reading during listening previewing. *Journal of Learning Disabilities, 26,* 674–681.

Skinner, C. H., Cooper, L., & Cole, C. L. (1997). The effects of oral presentation previewing rates on reading performance. *Journal of Applied Behavior Analysis, 30,* 331–333.

Skinner, C. H., Hurst, K. L., Teeple, D. F., & Meadows, S. O. (2002). Increasing on-task behavior during mathematics independent seat-work in students with emotional disorders by interspersing additional brief problems. *Psychology in the Schools, 39,* 647–659.

Skinner, C. H., Johnson, C. W., Larkin, M. J., Lessley, D. J., & Glowacki, M. L. (1995). The influence of rate of presentation during taped-words interventions on reading performance. *Journal of Emotional and Behavioral Disorders, 3,* 214–223.

Skinner, C. H., Logan, P., Robinson, D. H., & Robinson, S. L. (1997). Myths and realities of modeling as a reading intervention: Beyond acquisition. *School Psychology Review, 26,* 437–447.

Skinner, C. H., McCleary, D. F., Poncy, B. C., Cates, G. L., & Skolits, G. J. (2013). Emerging opportunities for school psychologists to enhance our remediation procedure evidence base as we apply response to intervention. *Psychology in the Schools, 50,* 272–289.

Skinner, C. H., Neddenriep, C. E., Bradley-Klug, K. L., & Ziemann, J. M. (2002). Advances in curriculum-based measurement: Alternative rate measures for assessing reading skills in pre- and advanced readers. *Behavior Analyst Today, 3,* 270–281.

Skinner, C. H., & Shapiro, E. S. (1989). A comparison of taped-words and drill interventions on reading fluency in adolescents with behavior disorders. *Education and Treatment of Children, 12,* 123–133.

Skinner, C. H., Skinner, A. L., & Armstrong, K. (2000). Shaping leisure reading persistence in a client with chronic schizophrenia. *Psychiatric Rehabilitation Journal, 24,* 52–57.

Skinner, C. H., Skinner, A. L., & Burton, B. (2009). Applying group-oriented contingencies in classrooms. In K. A. Akin-Little, S. G. Little, M. Bray, & T. Kehle (Eds.), *Behavioral interventions in schools: Evidence-based positive strategies* (pp. 157–170). Washington, DC: American Psychological Association Press.

Skinner, C. H., Smith, E. S., & McLean, J. E. (1994). The effects of intertribal interval duration on sight-word learning rates in children with behavioral disorders. *Behavioral Disorders, 19,* 98–107.

Skinner, C. H., Wallace, M. A., & Neddenriep, C. E. (2002). Academic remediation: Educational applications of research on assignment preference and choice. *Child and Family Behavior Therapy, 24,* 51–65.

Skinner, C. H., Williams, J. L., Morrow, J. A., Hale, A. D., Neddenriep, C., & Hawkins, R. O. (2009). The validity of a reading comprehension rate: Reading speed, comprehension, and comprehension rates. *Psychology in the Schools, 46,* 1036–1047.

Skrtic, T. M. (1991). *Behind special education: A critical analysis of professional culture and school organization.* Denver, CO: Love.

Smith, S. B., Simmons, D. C., & Kame'enui, E. J. (1998). Phonological awareness: Instructional and curricular basics and implications. In D. C. Simmons & E. J. Kame'enui (Eds.), *What reading research tells us about children with diverse learning needs: Bases and basics.* Mahwah, NJ: Erlbaum.

Snow, C. (2010). Academic language and the challenge of reading for learning about science. *Science, 328*(5977), 450–452.

Snow, C., Burns, S., & Griffin, P. (1998). *Preventing reading difficulties in young children.* Washington, DC: National Research Council.

Snow, C. E. (1994). What is so hard about learning to read?: A pragmatic analysis. In J. Duchan, R. Sonnemeier, & L. Hewitt (Eds.), *Pragmatics: From theory to practice* (pp. 164–184). Englewood Cliffs, NJ: Prentice Hall.

Snow, C. E., & Kim, Y-S. (2006). Large problem spaces: The challenge of vocabulary for English language learners. In R. K. Wagner, A. Muse, & K. Tannenbaum (Eds.), *Vocabulary acquisition and its implications for reading comprehension* (pp. 123–139). New York: Guilford Press.

Snow, C. E., Porsche, M. V., Tabors, P. O., & Harris, S. R. (2007). *Is literacy enough? Pathways to academic success for adolescents.* Baltimore: Brookes.

Snow, C. E., & Uccelli, P. (2009). The challenge of academic language. In D. R. Olsen & N. Torrance (Eds.), *The Cambridge handbook of literacy* (pp. 112–133). Cambridge, UK: Cambridge University Press.

Sorrell, A. L. (1990, January). Three reading comprehension strategies: TELLS, story mapping, and QARs. *Academic Therapy, 25,* 359–368.

Spargo, E. (1989). *Time readings* (3rd ed.). Providence, RI: Jamestown.

Stahl, N. A. (2011). Building a foundation together. *The Reading Teacher, 65*(3), 179–182.

Stahl, S. A. (1986). Three principles of effective vocabulary instruction. *Journal of Reading, 29,* 662–668.

Stahl, S. A., Duffy-Hester, A. M., & Stahl, K. A. (1998). Everything you wanted to know about phonics (but were afraid to ask). *Reading Research Quarterly, 33,* 338–355.

Stahl, S. A., & Nagy, W. (2006). *Teaching word meanings.* Mahwah, NJ: Erlbaum.

Stahl, S. A., & Shiel, T. G. (1999). Teaching meaning vocabulary: Productive approaches for poor readers. In *Read all about it! Readings to inform the profession* (pp. 291–321). Sacramento: California State Board of Education.

Stallman, A. C., Pearson, P. D., Nagy, W. E., Anderson, R. C., & Garcia, G. E. (1995). *Alternative approaches to vocabulary assessment* (Tech. Rep. No. 607). Urbana–Champaign: Center for the Study of Reading, University of Illinois.

Stanovich, K. E. (1986). Matthew effects in reading: Some consequences of individual differences in the acquisition of literacy. *Reading Research Quarterly, 21,* 360–406.

Stein, M., Johnson, B., & Gutlohn, L. (1999). Analyzing beginning reading programs: The relationship between decoding instruction and text. *Remedial and Special Education, 20,* 275–287.

Sterling, H., Robinson, S. L., & Skinner, C. H. (1997). The effects of two taped-words interventions on sight-word reading in students with mental retardation. *Journal of Behavioral Education, 7,* 25–32.

Strategic Education Research Partnership. (2011). *Word generalization: Join the national conversation!* Retrieved September 7, 2012, from *http://wg.serpmedia.org.*

Suarez-Orozco, C., Suarez-Orozco, M., & Todorova, I. L. G. (2008). *Learning a new land.* Cambridge, MA: Harvard University Press.

Swain, M. (2005). The output hypothesis: Theory and research. In E. Hinkel (Ed.), *Handbook of research in second-language teaching and learning* (pp. 471–483). Mahwah, NJ: Erlbaum.

Taylor, E. A. P., Skinner, C. H., McCallum, E., Poncy,

B. C., & Orsega, M. (2013). Enhancing basic academic skills with audio-recordings. *Educational Research Quarterly, 27*, 22–60.

Teeple, D. F., & Skinner, C. H. (in press). Enhancing grammar assignment perceptions by increasing assignment demands: An extension of interspersal research. *Journal of Emotional and Behavioral Disorder.*

Torgesen, J. K., Alexander, A. W., Wagner, R. K., Rashotte, C. A., Voeller, K. S., & Conway, T. (2001). Intensive remedial instruction for children with severe reading disabilities: Immediate and long-term outcomes from two instructional approaches. *Journal of Learning Disabilities, 34*, 33–58.

Torgesen, J. K., & Bryant, B. R. (1994). *Phonological awareness training for reading.* Austin, TX: PRO-ED.

Torgesen, J. K., Wagner, R. K., & Rashotte, C. A. (1994). Longitudinal studies of phonological processing and reading. *Journal of Learning Disabilities, 27*, 276–287.

Turner, J. C. (1995). The influence of classroom contexts on young children's motivation for literacy. *Reading Research Quarterly, 30*, 410–441.

Twyman, J. S., & Sota, M. (2008). Identifying research-based practices for RTI: Scientifically-based instruction. *Journal of Evidence-Based Practices for Schools, 9*, 86–97.

U.S. Department of Education. (1999). *Reading Excellence Program Overview.*

U.S. Department of Education, Office of Elementary and Secondary Education. (2011). *Report to Congress on the Elementary and Secondary Education Act, School Year 2008–09.* Washington, DC: Author.

Vargas, J. S. (1984). What are your exercises teaching? An analysis of stimulus control in instructional materials. In W. L. Heward, T. E. Heron, D. S. Hill, & J. Trap-Porter (Eds.), *Focus on behavior analysis in education* (pp. 126–141). Columbus, OH: Merrill.

Vaughn, S., Cirino, P. T., Linan-Thompson, S., Mathes, P. G., Carlson, C. D., Cardenas-Hagan, E., et al. (2006). Effectiveness of a Spanish intervention and an English intervention for English-language learners at risk for reading problems. *American Educational Research Journal, 43*(3) 449–487.

Vaughn, S., Linan-Thompson, S., & Hickman, P. (2003). Response to instruction as a means of identifying students with reading/learning disabilities. *Exceptional Children, 69*, 391–409.

Vaughn, S., Linan-Thompson, S., Mathes, P. G., Cirino, P., Carlson, C. D., Hagan, E. C., et al. (2006). Effectiveness of a Spanish intervention and an English intervention for first-grade English language learners at risk for reading difficulties. *Journal of Learning Disabilities, 39*, 56–73.

Vellutino, F. R., Scanlon, D. M., & Tanzman, M. S. (1998). The case for early intervention in diagnosing specific reading disability. *Journal of School Psychology, 36*, 367–397.

Verhoeven, L., Van Leeuwe, J., & Vermeer, A. (2011). Vocabulary growth and reading development across the elementary school years. *Scientific Studies of Reading, 15*(1), 8–25.

Wagner, R. K., & Torgeson, J. K. (1987). The nature of phonological awareness and its causal role in the acquisition of reading skills. *Psychological Bulletin, 101*, 192–212.

Wallace, M. A., Cox, E. A., & Skinner, C. H. (2003). Increasing independent seat-work: Breaking large assignments into smaller assignments and teaching a student with retardation to recruit reinforcement. *School Psychology Review, 23*, 132–142.

Walsh, D. J., Price, G. G., & Gillingham, M. G. (1988). The critical but transitory importance of letter naming. *Reading Research Quarterly, 23*, 108–122.

Wechsler, D. (2009). *Wechsler Individual Achievement Test—Third Edition* (WIAT III). San Antonio, TX: Pearson Assessments.

Wesson, C. L., Deno, S., Mirkin, P., Maruyama, G., Skiba, R., King, R., et al. (1988). A causal analysis of the relationships among ongoing curriculum-based measurement and evaluation, the structure of instruction, and student achievement. *Journal of Special Education, 22*, 330–343.

Wesson, C. L., Skiba, R., Sevcik, B., King, R., & Deno, S. (1984). The effects of technically adequate instructional data on achievement. *Remedial and Special Education, 5*, 17–22.

Wigfield, A., & Guthrie, J. T. (1997). Relations of children's motivation for reading to the amount and breadth of their reading. *Journal of Educational Psychology, 89*, 420–432.

Wiley, H. I., & Deno, S. L. (2005). Oral reading and MAZE measures as predictors of success for English language learners on a state standards assessment. *Remedial and Special Education, 26*(4), 207–214.

Williams, J. L., Skinner, C. H., Floyd, R. G., Hale, A. D., Neddenriep, C., & Kirk, E. (2011, February). Words correct per minute: The variance in standardized reading scores accounted for by reading speed. *Psychology in the Schools, 48*, 87–101.

Williams, K. T. (2007). *Expressive Vocabulary Test, Second Edition.* Circle Pines, MN: AGS Publishing.

Wolery, M., Bailey, D. B., Jr., & Sugai, G. M. (1988).

Effective teaching: Principles and procedures of applied behavior analysis with exceptional children. Boston: Allyn & Bacon.

Wong, B. Y. L. (1986). Problems and issues in the definition of learning disabilities. In J. K. Torgesen & B. Y. L. Wong (Eds.), *Psychological and educational perspectives on learning disabilities* (pp. 1–26). New York: Academic Press.

Woodcock, R. W. (1990). *Woodcock Language Proficiency Battery–Revised.* Allen, TX: DLM Teaching Resources.

Woodcock, R. W., & Muñoz-Sandoval, A. F. (1993). *Woodcock–Muñoz Language Survey: Comprehensive manual.* Chicago: Riverside.

Woodcock, R. W., & Muñoz-Sandoval, A. F. (2001). *Woodcock–Muñoz Language Survey normative update, English form.* Itasca, IL: Riverside.

Worden, P. E., & Boettcher, W. (1990). Young children's acquisition of alphabet knowledge. *Journal of Reading Behavior, 22,* 277–295.

World-Class Instructional Design and Assessment. (2011). *WIDA.* Retrieved from *www.wida.us/index.aspx.*

Yaw, J. S. (2013). *Three studies evaluating a computer-based sight-word reading intervention system across special-needs students.* Unpublished dissertation. University of Tennessee, Knoxville, TN.

Yaw, J. S., Skinner, C. H., Orsega, M., Parkhurst, J., Chambers, K., & Booher, J. (2012). Evaluating a computer-based sight-word reading intervention in a student with intellectual disabilities. *Journal of Applied School Psychology, 28,* 354–366.

Yaw, J. S., Skinner, C. H., Parkhurst, J., Taylor, C., Booher, J., & Chambers, K. (2011). Extending research on a computer-based sight word reading intervention to a student with autism. *Journal of Behavioral Education, 20,* 44–54.

Ysseldyke, J., & Christenson, S. (1993). *The instructional environment system–II.* Longmont, CO: Sopris West.

Index

Note. The letter *f* following a page number indicates figure, the letter *t* indicates table.